WALKING THE WALK

Published under licence by Brown Dog Books and
The Self-Publishing Partnership, 7 Green Park Station, Bath BA1 1JB

www.selfpublishingpartnership.co.uk

ISBN printed book: 978-1-83952-212-3
ISBN e-book: 978-1-83952-213-0

Cover design by Becky James
Internal design by Andrew Easton

Printed and bound in the UK

This book is printed on FSC certified paper

WALKING THE WALK
(Memoirs of a mature long-distance walker)

STEVE ATHAWES

BROWN
DOG
BOOKS

Dedicated to the memory of my late parents and to my long-suffering wife, without whose support and understanding this would not have been possible.

Thanks also to Frances and the team at SPP for their valued assistance in the production of this book.

"One should always have a definite objective, in a walk as in life – it is so much more satisfying to reach a target by personal effort than to wander aimlessly. An objective is an ambition, and life without ambition is, well....... aimless wandering."

Alfred Wainwright ("AW") – author, artist and fell walker

(1907–91)

Foreword

For over 130 years, SSAFA – the Armed Forces charity, have existed to relieve need, suffering and distress amongst personnel from all branches of our Armed Forces, veterans, and their families. We are committed to ensuring that they get the best possible help and support when they need it. That support can be lifelong and take many forms, though our focus is on providing direct support to individuals in need of physical or emotional care.

Addiction, relationship breakdown, debt, homelessness, post-traumatic stress, depression and disability are all issues that can affect members of our Armed Forces community. Many of these problems only become apparent when an individual leaves the Forces to join 'Civvy Street', and SSAFA is committed to helping our brave men and women overcome these problems and rebuild their lives.

The needs of service personnel and veterans are becoming more diverse as the world and military landscape changes. What makes SSAFA unique is that, working in partnership with other military charities and specialist organisations, we work hard to make sure our services are flexible – constantly tailoring and adapting them to fit with the people we support. We do this via a volunteer network which reaches into every county in the UK and 11 countries around the world. Our work is financed, to a large degree, by generous donations from members of the public. This relies on the dedication and generosity of our supporters, without whom we would not be able to provide such comprehensive support to our Armed Forces community.

One of these supporters is Steve Athawes, who undertook a 1,200-mile, unsupported, solo walk from Land's End to John o' Groats to raise funds for SSAFA. I met Steve at a reception in London in 2018 and was very interested to hear about his journey and the challenges he faced. Steve has now written this book about his walk, which includes an account of his earlier hike across England. I hope you enjoy reading this inspirational and informative account of a journey which Steve himself described as life-enhancing.

Sir Andrew Gregory KBE, CB
Controller/Chief Executive (SSAFA)

Chapter One

It has been said that everybody has a book in them. Well, this is mine. It's not *War & Peace* and I doubt it'll win any literary prizes, but I hope you enjoy reading it as much as I enjoyed the adventures, challenges and experiences that inspired it.

I think it was December 1989 when I first had the crazy notion of walking from Land's End to John o' Groats. I'd watched a TV movie called *First and Last* about a shy man in his sixties, coincidentally also from my birth town of Carshalton, who, despite never having walked more than a dozen miles in his life, decides to fulfil a lifelong ambition and walk the length of Britain. The central character is Alan Holly, played by Joss Ackland, and the film centres around his discovery of himself, the relationship with his wife and family, who are clearly unsure of his reasons for undertaking this epic walk, and the colourful and not so colourful characters he meets on his travels. Like Alan Holly, I wanted to 'do something', to journey forth at least once on an adventure which might prove an inspiration to others. To use his words, "I thought I'd go out and look at the land I'd spent my life in. Feel it under my feet. Get the measure of it." Like him, I was never going to climb

Mount Everest or sail single-handed round the world but watching this movie I thought, *I could do that.*

For the next 25 years or so, the flame that was lit that day became more of a pilot light as family and work commitments naturally took precedence. It was reignited in 2012 and that year was to prove pivotal for several reasons. I'd been working at the BBC since 2004 and in fairness I'd let myself go a bit. I was considerably overweight with high cholesterol and high blood pressure, and I was starting to experience problems with my joints. It was fair to say I was not in the best of health.

To put it into context, on 1st January 2012 I weighed in at just short of 21 stone and at that point I realised I needed to take myself seriously in hand. 2012 was the year of the London Olympics and as the BBC was the designated 'Olympic broadcaster', much talk was of the forthcoming games and the focus was very much on all things healthy. It was also the year of my 30th wedding anniversary and having booked a surprise Aegean cruise for that summer, I had no intention of embarrassing my poor wife by resembling a whale that had been heaved up onto the deck of the ship!

Combined with sensible eating, I needed an exercise regime but something low-impact so as not to put too much pressure on the old knee joints. Walking fit the bill and seemed the perfect solution. The health benefits of walking have long been appreciated: indeed the historian G. M. Trevelyan once observed that he had 'two doctors; my left leg and my right'. I started off gently enough, a mile or two here and there, and through the wonders of internet route-finding sites I was soon able to assemble a library of circuitous routes from home, ranging from one to ten miles from which I put together a schedule of walks for each day of the week. For the next twelve months or so I dragged myself out of bed at around 4.15am and hit the streets for an hour, which equated to about four miles at a smart pace, before returning home to carry out my ablutions, take my wife her tea and biscuits and head off to work. I quite often repeated the day's route in the evening as well, clocking up around 50 miles a week. At weekends, I opted for a slightly later start and followed a 5-mile route, taking in Nonsuch Park. This 250-acre open space is the nearest worthwhile expanse of green to our house and for over thirty years has been a frequent haunt when I feel the need for the restorative power of nature. Town living has its merits, but it would be unbearable without those little moments.

By the summer of 2012 I'd managed to shed over four stone through a combination of walking and a much-improved diet. I felt healthier than I had done for years and the interesting thing was that the more I walked, the more I *wanted* to walk. This, I'm reliably informed, is down to endorphins, our own private narcotic which occurs naturally in the body triggering the 'rush' that exercise sometimes prompts.

Having got myself back into some kind of shape, I decided I was ready to push myself a bit, so, after spotting an advertisement in a local newspaper, I signed up to take part in the London 2 Brighton Challenge in May 2013. This 62-mile, 24-hour endurance trek set off from the Thames at Richmond and wound its way through some fabulous countryside, crossing both the North and South Downs, to the finish line at Brighton Racecourse. I was joined by my brother and nephew who, unfortunately, was forced to drop out at around the 17-mile mark through injury. Between us, we managed to raise almost £2,000 for our chosen charity, The Royal Marines Charitable Trust Fund.

Despite the aching limbs in the immediate aftermath of the walk, it proved to be a most elevating experience and I felt compelled to take on the Thames Path Challenge in September that same year, another 62-mile stroll between Putney Bridge and Henley-on-Thames. During the course of that walk I learned of the Isle of Wight Challenge, scheduled to take place over August bank holiday weekend 2014, and immediately signed up for that one as well. Talk about glutton for punishment!

I've always loved the Isle of Wight. As a boy we spent our family summer holidays at Nodes Point Holiday Camp near Bembridge and I was really looking forward to this 66-mile circular trek around the coastal path of the island. Being a nostalgic old so and so, I decided to kill two birds with one stone and booked a family holiday for the week immediately following the walk – once more at Nodes Point, still going strong after all these years, although with more emphasis on caravans and camping now rather than the chalets of old. My brother would be joining me on this walk once again, along with my son, himself a serving member of the British Army. We would again be raising money for forces charities, this time SSAFA - the Armed Forces charity and BLESMA, which provides support to limbless veterans.

I feel sure that the aforementioned TV movie *First and*

Last was instrumental in inspiring me and many other potential 'end-to-enders' to undertake the ultimate UK long-distance walk. To my knowledge this film has never been commercially available but I'd discovered it was a BBC production and through a colleague at work I was put in touch with an extremely helpful lady in BBC Archives who kindly produced a copy for me from the master tape. So it was that I sat down one evening to watch the DVD of a film I hadn't seen for over 25 years but had thought about so often.

Seeing this movie again, coupled with the recent successful completion of the two challenge walks, reignited the Land's End to John o' Groats spark and my objective was defined and indeed broadened; specifically to walk the length *and* breadth of Great Britain in lone, unsupported, single trips, to experience the very best that the British countryside has to offer.

The *length* part of the objective would be achieved by completion of the LEJOG (as the Land's End to John o' Groats walk is commonly known) – a 1,200-mile primarily off-road trek between the two furthest points on the UK mainland. The *breadth* element, and the first to be tackled, would be Alfred Wainwright's much-loved Coast to Coast walk.

Born on 17th January 1907, Alfred Wainwright was a celebrated fell walker, guidebook author and illustrator. He is probably best known for his seven-volume *Pictorial Guides to the Lakeland Fells,* published between 1955 and 1966, which he described as his 'love letters' to the Lakeland Fells. When he was looking for a retirement project in 1971, he devised *A Coast to Coast Walk* which was published two years later and has been a firm favourite with long-distance walkers ever since. This 192-mile expedition traverses the whole of Northern England, taking in no less than three contrasting and beautiful National Parks. Despite not having National Trail status, the walk was named as the second-best walk in the world in a 2004 survey of experts, behind only Milford Track in New Zealand. It is traditionally walked from west to east between St Bees in Cumbria, on the Irish Sea coast, and Robin Hood's Bay, in North Yorkshire, on the North Sea coast, and remarkably passes through only two major towns. The date for the start of this adventure was set for 6th June 2015 and planning commenced.

Meanwhile, our training regime for the Isle of Wight Challenge had started in earnest in May 2014. I had the bright idea that each team member would 'host' a day walk of around 15 miles in the three months leading up to the main event at the end of August. My walk was a challenging romp around the South Downs between Seaford and Eastbourne. My brother's entry was an enjoyable 18-mile ramble around Warlingham and Oxted. The pièce de résistance was my son Mike's contribution. He had recently started a two-year attachment to the 22nd Special Air Service regiment and had moved into a nice little house on the outskirts of Hereford.

Mike's walk was a 15-mile trek over the stunning Brecon Beacons – my first real experience of hillwalking – on a section known as the 'Fan Dance', which culminates in a demanding 2,907-foot ascent of Pen y Fan. This section is part of the SAS selection course. We took the best part of seven hours to complete the walk. The potential recruits are tasked to do it in four hours carrying a weighty pack. In fairness, though, they probably wouldn't have been stopping for lunch or to admire the magnificent scenery.

I must have picked up an injury on the walk because a couple of days later, I started experiencing excruciating pain in my lower back and left thigh. With the IOW Challenge only a couple of weeks away I was seriously concerned but fortunately the anti-inflammatory painkillers prescribed by the doctor had the desired effect and with 10 days to go I seemed to be well on the mend.

Saturday 23rd August dawned on a beautiful sunny day. Conditions were perfect at 5.30am as I scrambled out of bed in the Newport Travelodge on the Isle of Wight, eager for the off. We had arrived on the island the afternoon before and had registered for the event that evening to save a bit of time on Saturday morning. All that remained was to get up to Northwood House in West Cowes, grab a bit of breakfast in the event catering tent, and prepare for the start.

The team, comprising my brother Nick, son Mike and myself, bade farewell to the assembled family and set off shortly after 8.00am on what was to prove a particularly challenging and, at times, painful 66-mile walk. Painful, because at around the 10-mile mark I stepped over a stile, stumbled on an exposed root, and KO'd myself on a tree trunk. Fortunately, we were only a short distance from a rest stop where the St John Ambulance guys patched me up and sent us on our way. For the next 50-odd miles, I nursed a sore head, sporting an enormous comedic lump like something from a Tom & Jerry cartoon.

Mike was unfortunately forced to retire at the 48-mile point having sustained a leg injury. I plodded on, joining my brother at the finishing line around 6.30pm on the Sunday evening – some 34 hours after setting off. Having gratefully received our medals, quaffed our complimentary glass of bubbly, and posed for the celebratory photographs (somewhat spoiled by my bruised and battered head), I was driven back to our caravan at Nodes Point and slept soundly until the next morning. The Isle of Wight Challenge had certainly been the toughest walk I'd undertaken to that point, but it had been a great hike and as a team we raised the best part of £4,000 for our chosen charities.

Isle of Wight Challenge 2014 with son Mike (centre) and brother Nick (right)

So-called comfort eating is a terrible thing. In the early summer of 2014, I found myself at risk of redundancy from my job at the BBC. At the ripe old age of 57 and without any professional qualifications to speak of, this was a worrying situation to be in. It's fair to say that I fell off the wagon a bit on the food front, and with the inevitable excesses over the Christmas period that year, my weight had gone back up to over 18 stone. Thus it was, in January 2015, with my 'Coast to Coast' adventure only five months away, that I resolved to get back into shape. Using lifts and escalators became a thing of the past in favour of the stairs, and I joined my wife Lynn and daughter Sophie on that most ubiquitous of post-Christmas pursuits – the healthy-eating campaign.

In February I was offered an alternative role with the FM company I was working for and transferred across from the BBC account to a University College London Hospitals site. In addition to solving my employment worries, it afforded me the opportunity to step up my exercise regime – the walk back and forth between Waterloo station and WC1 each day being around 6 miles.

By March I'd managed to knock out about a stone in weight, but I was still a long way off what I considered to be my 'fighting weight' of around 16 stone. There were still a couple of months to go until my cross-country trek but with Easter looming and given my total lack of willpower, particularly when it came to chocolate eggs and hot cross buns, I seriously doubted whether I'd achieve my target weight in time.

Of far greater concern was my hip. The previous

summer, after a pleasurable but challenging day in the Brecon Beacons, I'd suffered a fair bit of pain in my left hip. It had dragged on for several weeks and only just eased up ahead of the Isle of Wight Challenge in late summer. Even then, I'd needed to pop a few painkillers en route, crossing the finishing line in an ibuprofen-induced daze. Following a company paintballing day one Saturday towards the end of March, the problem seemed to have returned and I'd spent the rest of the weekend with my leg up. If I couldn't do a day's paintballing without picking up a hip problem, how the hell did I expect to be able to walk across the whole of England!?

I am not, by nature, generally given to impromptu or spontaneous action, firmly subscribing to the old adage that proper preparation prevents piss poor performance – henceforth referred to as the 6 'Ps' principle – and with ten weeks to go, final preparations for my cross-country hike began in earnest. I'd booked my train journeys and the arrival of the tickets was a pleasant reminder that the trip was now only a few short weeks away. The outward journey to St Bees was on Saturday 6th June, returning from Scarborough, if all went to plan, two weeks later on 20th June, the day before Father's Day.

Wainwright's Coast to Coast walk is probably the best-loved and most popular long-distance trail in Britain and, given the remoteness of some areas on the route and the limited facilities in others, booking accommodation well in advance is essential, particularly during the peak walking season of May to September. I had booked my B&Bs across the whole route almost a year before, having discovered, during the initial planning stages, that some places were fully booked for the beginning of June this year even then.

To some extent, the need to reach a particular location each day rather flies in the face of a key objective of the walk, which Alfred Wainwright was adamant should "be done in comfort and for pleasure or not at all". When you have pre-booked accommodation, there is a tendency to focus on the destination rather than enjoying the 'here and now'. As part of my preparation I had read numerous books and articles, taking on-board a lot of very sound advice, but one piece which stuck in my mind was this – "Savour every step: it will be over before you know it". What a metaphor for life. How often we concentrate on where we *want* to be instead of taking the time to enjoy life's journey. How often we fail to realise that our journey is far more important than our destination which will, after all, be the same for every one of us. To quote journalist and travel writer Stephen Graham, "The adventure is not the getting there, it's the 'on the way'. It is not the expected, it is the surprise." I was determined to savour every step and allow myself time to enjoy the hike, the places, and whilst not being a particularly gregarious person, the people I'd encounter along the way.

For someone who enjoys the countryside and particularly water as much as me, it's quite surprising that I'd never been to the Lake District. Lynn and I had often talked about going but somehow never got around to it. I decided that my first trip to the Lakes should be with Lynn, so I booked us a weekend break in Keswick for shortly after Easter. Situated between the huge bulk of Skiddaw and the gentle beauty of Derwentwater, the bustling little town of Keswick has become the major centre for tourism in the northern Lake District and it's a great base from which to explore.

My wife is not a walker. But, despite her literally shedding tears of anxiety and with utterances such as "Why the fuck would anyone do this for fun?!" turning the air blue, I managed to coax her up and, more importantly, down Cat Bells. Arguably the most popular mountain in the Lake District, Cat Bells was described by Alfred Wainwright as "a family fell where grandmothers and infants can climb the heights together". Despite its modest elevation of 1,480 feet, it offers wonderful views over the lake and surrounding fells. Flushed with that success, the next day we took a stroll up Latrigg, one of the lowest fells but popular due to its convenient location overlooking Keswick and the beautiful views down the valley of Borrowdale from the summit. I was immensely proud of Lynn who made the ascent purely to please me – true love indeed!

Unusually fine weather and excellent and friendly service from our hosts Clare and David at the Thornleigh Guest House combined to make this an enjoyable trip and a marvellous introduction to the Lake District. If I was looking forward to my walk before, I was now positively champing at the bit.

The trip highlighted a possible deficiency in a vital item of my equipment. When it comes to rucksacks, size is most definitely important, and I seriously doubted whether my current backpack would be up to the challenge of a two-week, unsupported hike. So, taking the advice of the excellent *Country Walking* magazine, I invested in a new

Osprey Stratos 50, attracted by the 'AirSpeed' trampoline suspended mesh back system and the 'Stow-on-the Go' trekking pole attachment – yes, geeky, I know. Whilst we're on the subject, I must say I find it hugely diverting poking around in outdoor shops. For me, it's the equivalent of my wife shopping for floral frocks or shoes. I confess that I can spend hours looking at rucksacks, walking socks, compasses and maps, then go into another shop and look at it all again!

With three weeks to go and satisfied that I now had all the clothing, equipment, maps and guides I would need for the trip, I thought it would be a good idea to do a trial pack. Why then I left it to the night before was beyond me, but sure enough there I was at 10.00pm on the eve of my trip, forcing the last few items into every available nook and cranny in my pack. With a couple of litres of water, the overall weight of my backpack was close to 45 pounds, a not inconsiderable burden to be lugging across England and one which would have me questioning the wisdom of an unsupported trek on more than one occasion over the coming fortnight.

Chapter Two

I woke at 4.30am on Saturday 6th June to a perfect summer morning, the early sun giving promise of a fine day ahead. For the past few months I'd been like a mastiff straining at the leash. Now, at last, the day had arrived and the adventure was about to begin.

Heaving the weighty pack onto my back, I bid an emotional farewell to Lynn and set off to catch the 06.12 to Waterloo. Standing on the platform at Worcester Park station, under a cloudless, blue sky, I got some very funny looks from the other early morning weekend travellers. With the weather being so good, I decided to walk the three miles or so from Waterloo to Euston to acclimatise myself to the weight and balance of the backpack. Arriving in plenty of time to catch the 07.43 to Lancaster, I treated myself to a coffee and sausage and bacon baguette before taking my seat on the train.

I had planned to do a bit of reading up on the first part of the Coast to Coast walk and settled down with my breakfast and Alfred Wainwright's pictorial guide. However, any thoughts I might have had of a quiet read were quickly dismissed when three lively ladies occupied the seats across the aisle and, regardless of the relatively early hour, proceeded to crack open a bottle of champagne. Jane, Julie and Nikki had set off from Cambridge at about 3.00 that morning and were taking Julie on a surprise 50th birthday weekend trip to Whitewater Spa Hotel by Windermere. I declined the offer of a glass of bubbly but agreed to take on the role of official group photographer until we reached my change stop at Lancaster, at which point the ladies wished me luck with my walk and I switched to a two-carriage local service for the final leg of my journey.

The two-hour trip along the coast to St Bees in Cumbria passed pleasantly in conversation with Mike, a 72-year-old Aussie from Sydney, who, despite his advancing years, was clearly as fit as a butcher's dog. He was undertaking the Coast to Coast as part of a three-week trip to the UK and I would meet up with him several times throughout the walk.

Along the way we passed nearby to Sellafield, formerly known as Windscale, the site of the world's first commercial nuclear power station. It was here, on 10th October 1957, that a reactor overheated and caught fire. In the days that followed, a dangerous cloud of 'fallout' was carried towards cities in the North of England and Europe. As the technology was comparatively new, scientists were unsure how to deal with the raging fire and gambled on flooding the reactor with cooling water. They were aware of the risk that explosive hydrogen could be created which might then flash over causing an explosion, but there seemed no choice if they were to extinguish a fire that had now raged for three days. As this critical decision was being taken, the temperatures were climbing by twenty degrees a minute. Luckily, the gamble paid off. The water starved the fire of oxygen and the reactor was brought under control. A crisis had been averted but it was a disastrous public relations blow for nuclear energy.

Unusually for national rail, the entire journey had run exactly to schedule and shortly after lunchtime the train pulled in at the tiny station at St Bees and I made my way through the village to my first night accommodation. The Abbey Farm House B&B was run by Janet and Steve, who themselves met whilst walking the C2C some years before. I deposited my backpack in my room and settled down in the guest lounge, enjoying a complimentary cream tea whilst taking in the view of the Priory Church and a couple of pigeons copulating on the summer house roof.

St Bees has a long religious and academic history. The village name is a corruption of St. Bega who was, reputedly, an Irish princess who fled to this corner of Cumbria in the early Middle Ages to escape an enforced marriage to a Viking prince. There she settled for a time, leading a life of exemplary piety. Parts of the Priory Church of St. Mary and St. Bega date back to the 12th century and the ornate west doorway, erected in 1150, is widely considered to be the finest example of Norman architecture in the country.

The nationally renowned Grammar School was founded in 1583 by the Archbishop of Canterbury under a charter granted by Queen Elizabeth I. It sits opposite the church, both buildings constructed from the ubiquitous local red sandstone.

I was rather sad to learn that after nearly 450 years, the school was in danger of closing, due to falling pupil numbers and the high cost of their school fees. At the time of writing I believe the school, which counts actor and comedian Rowan Atkinson amongst its former students, has entered into a partnership with a South East Asian education group and that significant investment has been put into refurbishing the historic school buildings.

Feeling suitably refreshed after my home-made scones with jam and cream, I set off to explore the village, following a circular route thoughtfully provided by Steve, the proprietor of the B&B. The weather had become progressively threatening as I journeyed north and strolling along the beach I was barely able to stand as the wind and foam whipped in off the Irish Sea, reducing the promenade to something resembling the aftermath of an explosion in a detergent factory. Weather conditions, though, can change very quickly in this part of the country and within about half an hour the wind, having blown the clouds inland, subsided and the sun put in an appearance.

On the route back to Abbey Farm House I paid my respects to the statue of St. Bega and took a turn around the Priory churchyard, resplendent in the late-afternoon sun. Having enjoyed a relaxing soak in the tub, I strolled down to the Queens Hotel for a dinner of ham, egg and chips washed down with a couple of pints of *Cumberland* ale, then it was back to the B&B for an early night.

I started the first day of my cross-country adventure at 7.30am with an 'English Stack' – a variation on the full English breakfast – which Steve claimed to be his own invention. It consisted of a square of black pudding cooked in beer, served on a bed of thin white toasted bread (crusts removed), topped off with a fried egg and four rashers of streaky bacon. Satisfied that I'd taken on sufficient calories to sustain me for the rigours of the 14-mile day ahead, I set off for St Bees Seacote Beach and the 'Wainwright Wall'. This stone monument topped with its stainless steel banner was refurbished in 2013 in a joint project between the Wainwright Society and St Bees Parish Council. It provides information about the route and its creator and is the official start of the walk. After posing for the obligatory photograph, kindly taken by an Australian couple just starting their second C2C trip, I followed tradition and baptised my boots in the Irish Sea, collected a pebble as a keepsake to drop into the North Sea at the end of the walk and at 8.45am, suitably initiated and aroused with emotional feelings of hope, I headed up the steep path to the clifftop of South Head. The game was afoot!

The weather was sunny, with light cloud and just a hint of a sea breeze as I followed the coastal path around the 300-foot red sandstone cliffs in the company of a multitude of seabirds. Throughout the year these cliffs are home to puffins, terns and England's only colony of black guillemots. It is somewhat perverse that a trek which essentially follows a beeline across England from west to east should start by taking me north-west in the opposite direction! The wonderful clifftop walking and sea views more than compensated for this minor detour, though. In the clear Sunday morning conditions, I could glimpse the Isle of Man, 28 miles off the coast to the west with the mountains of Dumfries and Galloway in Scotland clearly visible to the north. The path dropped steeply down to

Fleswick Bay, then rose up onto North Head, passing St Bees Lighthouse before swinging east and heading inland.

The next few hours walking were fairly unremarkable and I can't help feeling a bit sorry for the small communities of Sandwith, Moor Row and Cleator, through which the route passes. Naturally, everyone raves about the spectacular Lake District, the beauty of Swaledale and the wide expanse of the North York Moors. Walkers are even quite vocal about the Vale of Mowbray, which is a fairly uneventful trudge by the standards of the Coast to Coast. But the flat coastal plain between the Irish Sea and the Lake District barely ever gets a mention. It was a pleasant ramble, though, and served as a tasty appetiser to the main course.

It was around lunchtime when I crossed the River Ehen at Blackhow Bridge just beyond the village of Cleator. This seemed like a good spot to take a break before starting the long, sweaty climb up to the summit of Dent Fell, the first real ascent of the trip. I found a shady spot by the river and, having removed my boots and socks to air my feet, tucked into the packed lunch provided by last night's B&B. The route up Dent Hill followed a winding forest track through a pine plantation, then spanned an open, grassy area up to the summit. The scene was fantastic. Behind me there were views right back to the sea with the enormous plant of Sellafield off to the south-west and the silhouette of the Isle of Man in the distance. Ahead, the Lakeland Fells.

The thing about steep *ascents* is that they are inevitably followed by steep *descents*. The total ascents on the Coast to Coast trail are equal to the height of Everest and the drop down to the valley below certainly tested the old calf muscles. While taking a quick breather I spotted a buzzard soaring high overhead and fell to wondering whether this was perhaps an ominous sign!

The path from the niftily named Nannycatch Gate, which heralds the start of the Lake District National Park, follows the line of a sparkling beck at the foot of Raven Crag, and provided wonderful walking in the afternoon sun. A couple of hours later I got my first glimpse of Ennerdale Water, and shortly after at around 5.30pm I arrived at Ennerdale Bridge, the first Lakeland village of the trip. As luck would have it, Thorntrees B&B, my accommodation for the night, was pretty much the first building I came to, but I was unable to resist the lure of the Fox and Hounds just beyond and a refreshingly cold pint of cider.

I unstrapped my pack, stretched out my weary legs and spent a very pleasant hour in the pub garden with Mike and Christine, a husband and wife from Manchester with whom I'd briefly chatted earlier in the day. Mike was a retired teacher and clearly the life and soul of the party but at 7.00pm, hard as it was to tear myself away, I decided I ought to make my presence known at Thorntrees.

Rosaleen and Billy had obviously spent a lot of money on the property and the en suite facilities were of a high standard. I had a double room which enabled me to spread myself out a bit. Having unpacked, showered, and changed into jeans and a clean shirt for the evening, I headed off to The Shepherds Arms Hotel for an excellent dinner of Cumberland sausage and mash with seasonal vegetables, washed down with a couple of pints of local ale.

By 9.00pm I was seriously flagging. I took a leisurely stroll back up to my B&B in the late evening sunshine and half an hour later I was tucked up in bed. Tomorrow, Lakeland, with it's picturesque patchwork of lakes, valleys, woodlands and fells. Undoubtedly one of the most beautiful and dramatic walking areas in the UK, it can truly be said that there is never a day with a bad view. The Lake District is a land of superlatives. Covering a total area of just over 885 square miles, it's the largest National Park in England, home to its longest and deepest lakes and nine of its ten highest mountains. In 2017 it became the UK's 31st World Heritage Site in recognition for the area's natural beauty, as well as its inspiration to writers and painters, such as John Ruskin, William Wordsworth and JMW Turner. It also happens to be holder of the national rainfall record, but fortunately the latest forecast indicated that the weather was set fair for the next few days at least.

Day two dawned on another dry and sunny day and, having reloaded my pack, I enjoyed a full English breakfast in conversation with a father and son from Chicago who were also on the Coast to Coast. While she was preparing the packed lunches for her walking guests, I had a chat with Rosaleen about the Fox and Hounds. The local village pub is an integral part of community life but many pubs, and indeed rural services generally, have struggled to operate as they used to and, in some cases, have faced closure. In such situations regulars often club together to run an ailing hostelry. The Fox and Hounds was West Cumbria's first community village pub and Rosaleen had been a shareholder. It seems the pub had been beset with financial problems and at one time was in danger of closing. I was very gratified to read that it's still going strong and has recently reopened following major refurbishment.

I set off at 8.00am on what would be a 15-mile day. About a mile and a half beyond the village, I arrived at the shore of Ennerdale Water. Ennerdale is the most westerly of the 16 lakes which give the Lake District it's name, and the most remote, possibly because it's the only lake that doesn't have a road running alongside it. The views down the lake past Angler's Crag to the peaks of Red Pike and High Stile were stunning in the morning sunshine. Taking the rough track along the southern shoreline, I set off around the water's edge, pausing at a rocky outcrop known as Robin Hood's Chair for an energy bar.

I chatted briefly to Steve and Janet, a couple from Burgess Hill near Brighton, who I had blindly followed round a perilous rock face overhanging the water. We realised afterwards that we could have taken an easier and safer route up and over the crag. At the head of the lake, the path crossed the River Liza and continued on at the side of the river through a plantation of conifers.

At this point, in clear weather, Alfred Wainwright recommends the High Stile alternative rather than continuing along the track to the Black Sail Hut, an old and much-cherished YHA hostel located in a wonderful remote valley. Failing to take note of the small print in his pictorial guide, which clearly states that this is a route for "very strong and experienced hill walkers only", I struck left off the main route and headed up Red Pike. The climb was exhausting with my heavy pack as I plodded on through the tussocky grass. Just as I was beginning to wonder whether I might have overstretched myself so early in the trip, I crested the final rise and found myself on top of the world amid an ocean of heaving summits. I could not recall having seen anything so beautiful as I surveyed the spectacular 360-degree view of Lakeland and the marvellous vista back over Ennerdale Water to the hazy blue of the sea beyond. In that moment, I knew I was hooked on the hills.

That afternoon, I enjoyed an exhilarating hike along the High Stile Ridge, which takes in a number of summits overlooking the lake and village of Buttermere. They include Red Pike at 2,476 feet, High Stile (2,648 feet), High Crag (2,441 feet), and Haystacks, which at 1,959 feet is the lowest but most interesting. I had been particularly keen to climb Haystacks and visit Innominate Tarn which was a favourite place of Alfred Wainwright. It was here that he took his last walk and the place where his ashes were scattered following his death in 1991 at the age of 84. He once said that "for a man trying to get a persistent worry out of his head, the top of Haystacks is a wonderful cure".

With the day rapidly disappearing, I didn't have long for contemplative thought and late in the afternoon I set off again along the roller coaster trail to where the high-level alternative rejoins the main route at a point known as Drum House.

Westmorland green slate was being quarried on an industrial scale on this part of the route from the early 1700s to the 1980s and Drum House, now little more than

The deep glacial lake of Ennerdale Water

Haystacks, from the High Stile ridge.

a pile of stones and slate, was so called because at one time it operated the cable of the tramway which lowered the bulk slate down to the cutting sheds in the valley below.

It was a steep descent to Honister Quarries, now a popular tourist attraction and the last working slate mine in England. I could have murdered a reviving cuppa in the Visitors Centre tearoom but alas, they were shut by the time I arrived at 7.00pm. With about 5 miles still to go to my B&B at Rosthwaite, I rang ahead from the YHA Honister Hause to let them know I'd be late but still needed my room (something I had to do several times on the trek!). Passing through the tiny hamlet of Seatoller, I arrived at The Vicarage, my accommodation for the night, just before 9.00pm after nearly thirteen hours walking, much of it over rough ground.

The Vicarage was a large and rather chilly old house but the proprietors, Gay and Terry, were very affable. Gay was the vicar of Borrowdale and as a sideline she took in a small number of walkers when the better publicised B&Bs in the village were booked up. I couldn't be bothered to walk down to the pub in Rosthwaite for an evening meal and would probably have been too late anyway, so I joined the only other guests that night, Ken and Phil from Australia, in the spacious sitting room and polished off a bag of crisps leftover from my packed lunch and tea and biscuits, thoughtfully provided by my host. I then took myself off for a hot bath, pondering what the difference is between 'village' and 'hamlet' whilst I soaked. The answer, according to American writer Bill Bryson, is quite simple – one is a place where people live and the other is a play by Shakespeare.

Day three began with a sunny dawn that promised another fine day and after missing dinner the night before, I was ravenous at breakfast and greedily tucked into porridge followed by toast and a full English. For most walkers, this would be a short 9-mile day to Grasmere, but following Wainwright's guide and schedule, I'd be combining this stage with the next one to Patterdale, adding up to a pretty demanding 18-mile hike.

I set off at 9.00am and, passing through the village of Rosthwaite, fell into conversation with Margaret from Harrogate who, having just been dropped off by her daughter, was walking solo to Grasmere. The route initially took us through pleasant fields alongside Stonethwaite Beck with the looming presence of Eagle Crag across the water. I met up again with Mike and Christine from day one and Steve and Janet whom I'd first encountered along the shores of Ennerdale Water, and we walked together until early afternoon. Janet was a keen 'cold water' swimmer and seized every opportunity to strip off down to her undies and immerse herself in the wonderful shallow pools along the beck.

The path soon began to climb steadily and crossing a prairie of 'drumlins' – mounds created by glacial action – ascended to Lining Crag where we took a well-earned break. From there the route took a fairly indistinct path on up to Greenup Edge which at 2,008 feet would be the highest point of the day, geographically speaking. At this point I faced a choice of routes: a ridge walk over Gibson Knott and Helm Crag, or the easier route following Far Easedale Gill. Had I been staying in Grasmere that night

I would have chosen the high-level alternative, but as I'd be continuing on to Patterdale I opted to save my legs for what I knew would be a tough climb to come.

From Far Easedale, an easy path threaded its way down into the village of Grasmere. Poet William Wordsworth and his sister Dorothy lived in Dove Cottage on the edge of the village from 1799 to 1808. It was here in the place he described as "the loveliest spot that man hath ever known" that Wordsworth wrote much of the poetry for which he is remembered today. My walking companions were all stopping off in Grasmere and so the conversation was turning towards a refreshing pint and a leisurely stroll around the lovely, if touristy, village. I knew I had another 9 miles to cover and needed to stay very focused on my objective that day. So, at around 3.30 in the warm afternoon sunshine, I bade farewell to the group and set off alone up the steep, grassy path beside Little Tongue Gill.

The strenuous hike was rewarded with wonderful retrospective views of Grasmere and Helm Crag. Ahead, along a stony path, lay Grisedale Pass and beyond that, Grisedale Tarn. Here, walkers are presented with a choice of three routes. To the north Helvellyn and Striding Edge beckoned, and to the south loomed the St Sunday Crag alternative. As I'd walked from Rosthwaite and it was already around 7.00pm, I elected to take the Grisedale Valley route, following a clear but often rough and rocky path past Ruthwaite Lodge, a small, stone-built climbing hut, eventually arriving at Patterdale around 9.30pm. I was rather disappointed to have missed out on two high-level routes, namely Helm Crag and Helvellyn, particularly given the fantastic weather conditions, but I would have had neither the time nor the strength given the overall distance of the day. I resolved there and then that should I walk the Coast to Coast again, I'd break the day at Grasmere and that I would return to Patterdale at the earliest opportunity to hike up Helvellyn.

After a swift pint in the White Lion Inn, I strolled on to my lodgings for the night. Old Water View B&B is a wonderful place and a favourite of Alfred Wainwright's. I'd rung ahead to let them know I'd be arriving late. Ian, the owner, had kindly kept the kitchen open for me so I was able to enjoy an excellent late dinner of steak with new potatoes in an onion and mushroom gravy, washed down with a couple of pints of *Wainwrights Ale*, before heading up to my room for a hot bath and bed.

Wednesday 10th June, Day 4 on the trail, was yet another beautiful sunny day. This would be a tough 16-miler which would see me leaving the Lake District National Park via Kidsty Pike, the highest point on the original Coast to Coast route at just over 2,500 feet.

I set off at 8.45am. First stop was the Patterdale Village Store, which lays claim to be the first place to sell Wainwright's Pictorial Guides. I bought a bottle of 'after-sun' lotion, not something I ever expected to be buying in the Lake District and judging by the dust on the bottle, not something they sold a lot of. Leaving the village, there was a steep climb up the hillside to Boredale Hause from where there were marvellous views back down to Patterdale and the southern tip of Ullswater, considered by many to be England's most beautiful lake. The track continued on and around the distinctively shaped shoreline of the idyllic Angle Tarn, the cool water very inviting in the warm sunshine.

Leaving Angle Tarn, the track levelled off for a while before another haul led me up around The Knott and along the path over Twopenny Crag to Kidsty Pike. From the top, facing west, I could see the mountain of Pillar looking down onto Ennerdale Water and the impressive peaks of Helvellyn and St Sunday Crag. To the south, a stunning view across to High Street, with its ancient Roman Road, the highest point in the Far Eastern part of the National Park, and the deep cleft of Riggindale in whose crags is said to be the eyrie of England's last golden eagle. The male eagle, nicknamed *Eddie,* has been resident since 2001. He has lived a lonely existence since the death of his elderly mate in 2004 and despite annual efforts, including elaborate flying displays, has failed to attract a new mate, a mission not helped by the fact that he resides about 40 miles south of the border with Scotland, where the nearest other golden eagles live. Sadly, *Eddie,* estimated to be around 20 years old, has not been seen for a number of seasons, leading RSPB staff at Haweswater to fear that he might have died from natural causes.

To the east, I got my first glimpse of the Haweswater Reservoir. At such a height there was a keen wind even on a warm day like this, but with the spectacular vista before me, it seemed the perfect spot to break for lunch and ponder the fate of Mardale Green. This picturesque village vanished in 1935, amidst a public outcry, when the valley below where I now sat was flooded to make way for the Haweswater Reservoir. Hundreds of people were evicted from their homes and most of the village buildings were blown up by Royal Engineers who used them for demolition practice. Farm buildings, pubs, and even a church and its graveyard were dismantled stone by stone. Meanwhile coffins were removed from the graveyard and buried elsewhere.

Considered something of an engineering feat at the time, the Haweswater Dam raised the water level by 95 feet, creating a reservoir 4 miles long and half a mile wide, which could hold 84 billion litres of water. Today, the reservoir supplies about 25% of the water needs for the north-west and occasionally, during particularly dry periods when the reservoir water levels recede sufficiently, the lost village of Mardale appears again from its watery grave.

The climb to Kidsty Pike had actually seemed rather effortless, approaching as I had across a couple of other 'peaks', but after lunch I set off on the fiercest descent of the whole route down to the shores of the reservoir. I was fortunate that the weather had been fine as I would imagine that this descent could be extremely slippery and treacherous in poor conditions.

At the foot of the hill I turned left over an old stone bridge and followed the clear but often rocky and undulating path along the whole four-mile length of the reservoir to the dam end. Passing through a wooded glade by the side of Haweswater Beck, I arrived at the 'model' village of Burnbanks, a small settlement comprising eighteen dwellings, originally built in 1929 to house the families of the men working on the reservoir dam.

After a brief respite on the village green, the route took me on through a beautiful woodland setting alongside Haweswater Beck and crossing Naddle Bridge I stumbled across my very first 'honesty box'. An enterprising local youngster had set up a box containing soft drinks and confectionery with a price list and Tupperware container for cash. It was by now late in the afternoon and the Snickers bar washed down with a can of orange Fanta really hit the spot and was well worth the two quid I popped in the box.

Suitably refreshed I plodded on through field and farmland arriving at Shap Abbey around 7.30pm. Located deep in the wooded valley of the River Lowther, Shap Abbey has the distinction of being the last abbey to be founded in England, in 1199. It was also the last to be dissolved by Henry VIII, in 1540. The best-preserved section is the western bell tower, built around 1500, although little else of the tower remains above first-floor level. I had a pleasant stroll around the remains of the various buildings within the grounds, wonderfully atmospheric in the orange hue of the early evening sunlight.

With the sun now starting to dip beneath the tree line, I crossed the bridge over the River Lowther, leaving the Lake District National Park in the process, and completed the final mile or so to the long, narrow village of Shap where I'd be stopping for the night. I arrived at The Hermitage B&B at 9.30pm and only just caught Jean Jackson, the owner, before she retired for the night. Clearly an evening meal was out of the question but she thoughtfully pointed me in the direction of the local Co-op where I managed to get myself a chicken salad sandwich before they closed.

I'd now walked across the whole of the Lake District, a distance of around 63 miles, and as I eased myself into a hot bath that night, my legs were feeling every mile of it!

Chapter Three

The Hermitage was a beautiful old house. Three hundred years old and furnished in a traditional manner, it had been highly recommended. The proprietor came from a family of butchers, and the locally produced sausages at breakfast the next morning were among the best I've ever tasted.

Shap is a village you can't help feeling a little sorry for. At just over a mile in length, it straddles the A6 high up on the moorland fringe of the Lake District. At one time all the main west coast traffic ran through the village, with the inherent benefit to local businesses. Then one day in October 1970, the M6 opened and the village was bypassed, signalling the loss of many jobs and livelihoods as hotels, cafés, shops, boarding houses, and other sundry services faced an immediate decline in trade. A number of these still remain, of course, to service Coast-to-Coasters, but the economy of the village now largely rests on the prosperity of the nearby granite works and quarries.

Rather than provide a packed lunch herself, Jean recommended a visit to a friend of hers who ran the local sandwich shop, thereby helping to spread business around. So as I set off on yet another warm and sunny morning, I called in to pick up some refreshments for later in the day, taking the opportunity to chat with a villager who was celebrating his 80th birthday. He had vivid memories of the time before the stroke of highway-engineering genius that brought peace and tranquillity to the village.

Leaving Shap, the scenery became noticeably different. I was now entering limestone country which would be quite a change from the rugged terrain of the Lake District. Today's hike across the Westmorland Plateau would be a little over 20 miles, but I was hoping that grassy strolls across the well-drained limestone bedrock would make it feel like something of a 'recovery day'.

Crossing the footbridge over the M6 signalled the fact that I had now completed a third of the walk and as I paused to celebrate this minor milestone with a swig from my water bottle, I fell into conversation with Mike. Like myself, Mike was on a lone Coast to Coast walk, although he was camping so had a bit more flexibility in terms of overnight stopping points. Originally from Leeds, he was slightly younger than me at 55 years old, and having made a bit of money from random business ventures, was now in retirement, currently living in Prague but of no fixed abode, and seemed to spend much of his time walking. We hit it off and in consequence 'buddied up' for the best part of the day.

Shortly after setting off we crossed a limestone 'pavement', a natural landform created when an advancing glacier scrapes away the topsoil, exposing horizontally bedded limestone and leaving behind a flat, bare surface. The limestone rock, being slightly soluble in water and particularly acid rain, is susceptible to corrosive draining along joints and cracks which then produces slabs often resembling man-made paving stones. On Crosby Ravensworth Fell, we passed an enormous, isolated granite boulder, deposited there by this same glacial action eons ago.

As lunchtime approached, Mike suggested a detour to the pretty Cumbrian market village of Orton, slightly off-route but well worth the visit. We slipped off our boots and rested our tired legs in the beer garden of the George Hotel, enjoying a couple of refreshing pints with our sandwiches. I could easily have sat there in the warm sunshine for the rest of the day, but with about 12 miles still to go to our destination at Kirkby Stephen, we needed to press on.

As the afternoon wore on, the combined effect of warm sunshine and lunchtime beverages began to take their toll on my pace. Chris, my eldest son, had rung to see how the walk was going, a conversation rudely interrupted by the noise of a Tornado jet screaming overhead and presumably heading to or from RAF Leeming in Northallerton. I was seriously slowing down and not wanting to hold Mike up, I urged him to go on ahead.

I'd been having a lazy day on the navigation front, preferring to leave the reasonably straightforward route-finding to Mike and his guidebook. Although he'd now moved off, he was pretty much always in view on the long, comfortable track, so I blindly followed on. Therefore, when he missed the turnoff to Smardale Bridge, so did I and before long, I was approaching the small town of Crosby Garrett, about 4 miles off course.

There were a number of things I'd particularly wanted

to accomplish on this walk. Among them was climbing Haystacks, Alfred Wainwright's final resting place. Spending a night at the Old Water View B&B in Patterdale, a particular favourite of AW's, was another. I was also keen to have fish and chips – which Wainwright claimed had been his staple diet for the best part of 80 years – in the 'Coast To Coast' chip shop in Kirkby Stephen. This establishment had been featured when Wainwright made a series about the Coast to Coast walk with Eric Robson in 1987, and again when Julia Bradbury had visited the town in her series on the walk in 2009. There was the sudden realisation that, being so far off course, I now wouldn't get to Kirkby Stephen before the chippy closed.

At times like this you need a little bit of what they call 'trail magic' and along it came in the form of Jim. Jim had been walking up the hill towards me from Crosby Garrett and as we drew level I stopped him to enquire as to my whereabouts. He confirmed that I was somewhat off course, and seeing my disappointment immediately offered to give me a lift on the relatively short distance into Kirkby Stephen. We walked back down the hill together and set off, picking Mike up en route, arriving at the 'Coast To Coast' chippy with about 40 minutes to spare before closing time. Jim wasn't dressed for walking and I never did find out where he'd been going before I met up with him, but I was extremely glad I had.

I can't say the cod, chips and mushy peas were up to the standard of my local chippy in Worcester Park, but there was plenty of it and after a long, tiring day, it was very welcome washed down with a couple of cans of ice-cold, cloudy lemonade. While we ate, the proprietor regaled us with tales of Julia Bradbury's voracious appetite when she'd visited back in 2009. When we'd finished, Mike and I strolled up the High Street and had a couple of pints together before he headed off to find a campsite and I set off for my B&B.

One of the great appeals of the Coast to Coast walk is that it passes through only two major towns and Kirkby Stephen is one of them. With a population of a little over 2,000, this pleasant and prosperous market town is hardly a heaving metropolis but it was pretty big compared to the small communities I'd been travelling through over the past few days. Needless to say, Brockram Cottage B&B was at the opposite end of the town and it was 9.00pm before I arrived on the doorstep. I was the only guest that night and once I'd settled myself into the comfortable double room and had a hot bath, I was treated to tea and fruit cake in the lounge. The owners, Denise and Mike, keen walkers themselves, had moved to Kirkby Stephen from Lincolnshire some years before and now just took in the occasional walker for a bit of extra cash and company. We chatted for an hour or so, Denise even offering to put a load of my dirty clothes in the wash that night and at 10.30pm tired and well fed, I took myself off to bed.

I was rather disappointed to have missed a number of key sights that day due to my navigational error: Severals Village settlement, said to be one of the most important prehistoric sites in Britain, the so-called 'Giant's Graves' (long, narrow mounds which, some say, may have been prehistoric rabbit enclosures), and Smardale Gill Viaduct among them. On reflection, though, it had been a good day.

Day 6, Friday 12th June, although a relatively short 13-mile stage, would be something of a red-letter day for three reasons. Firstly, I would cross the Pennines – the backbone of the British Isles – and in so doing would cross the 'watershed' on the Coast to Coast. From the summit at Nine Standards Rigg all rivers flow eastwards to drain into the North Sea, giving the somewhat optimistic impression that it would now be downhill all the way. Secondly, I would leave Cumbria and pass into Yorkshire, the largest county in the UK and finally, on arrival at Keld that evening, I would have completed half the trek.

I set off at 8.30am after another excellent full English breakfast (can you ever really tire of a good thing!?) crossing the River Eden and leaving Kirkby Stephen via the Grade II listed 'Frank's Bridge'. This 17th century stone footbridge, thought to have been named after local brewer Francis Birbeck, is reportedly visited by the ghost of Jangling Annas, an escapee from Hartley Castle who drowned in the river and now haunts the bridge jangling her chains.

The route, always on a steady incline, continued, essentially by quiet road, five miles to Hartley Fell. From here walkers are encouraged to take a particular colour-coded path, depending on the time of year, to help combat trail erosion and peatbog degradation. I followed the red route up the sprawling hill to Nine Standards Rigg, a group of nine stone cairns some of which are 10 feet tall. They stand at a height of 2,172 feet above sea level and there are a number of theories as to their origin. One is that they marked the former county boundary between

Westmorland and the North Riding of Yorkshire. Another more interesting tale is that the English built them in an attempt to persuade marauding Scots that an English Army was camped up there. My personal favourite is Alfred Wainwright's theory that the locals were just bored and it seemed like a good idea at the time!

It was another fine clear day and the breathtaking views from Nine Standards were the most far-reaching seen on the whole crossing and the perfect place for an early lunch. Beyond the summit, the path continued south across potentially boggy moorland – rumour has it that Julia Bradbury had to be rescued from here during the making of her television series – before picking up a more established track which I then followed down into Whitsun Dale, arriving at Ravenseat Farm in time for tea.

Ravenseat Farm, which sits by Whitsundale Beck at the head of the River Swale, is home to Clive and Amanda Owen, an astonishing couple with 9 children. Amanda, aka the 'Yorkshire Shepherdess', had become something of a minor celebrity following her appearance with Julia Bradbury, and in addition to running the farm, she is a writer, photographer and public speaker. She also provides very welcome refreshments to walkers and I couldn't resist one of her delicious cream teas before setting off on the last three miles to the hamlet of Keld.

Although it can be a bit 'midgy' in high summer, for an outdoor person keen on water, Keld is a wonderful place. Sitting at the head of Swaledale where the Coast to Coast crosses the longer, northbound Pennine Way, which celebrated its 50th birthday two months earlier, its name, derived from the Viking word Kelda, means 'a spring'. I was looking forward to visiting some of the numerous nearby waterfalls but first, a celebratory pint or two beckoned at the Keld Lodge pub. I'd walked the last couple of miles with Robert and his family and we joined forces to raise a glass of *Black Sheep* bitter to having walked halfway across England without needing to break out our waterproofs. If I needed an excuse for a second pint, I also celebrated arriving at an overnight stop while there was still a bit of daylight left.

Butt House B&B was conveniently situated across the road from the pub and after dinner I took a stroll out to have a look at the nearby waterfalls, known locally as 'forces'. The recent dry spell meant that the river level was fairly low but Catrake Force, just above the village, and East Gill Force below it, were nevertheless impressive and it was easy to imagine the roar of millions of gallons of peaty brown water pouring over them in times of spate. As Alfred Wainwright aptly wrote, "always, at Keld, there is the music of the river".

The accommodation at Butt House was excellent, as was the full English breakfast next morning. Jacqui and Chris were perfect hosts and this would certainly get my vote as one of the best B&Bs on the whole route.

About a mile east of Keld and high on the northern slope of Swaledale sit the intriguing ruins of Crackpot Hall. There is believed to have been a building on this site since the 16th century but the existing remains are of a mid-18th-century farmhouse, which may also have been used as mine offices at a time when the lead mining industry flourished in these parts. On a fine day, I would have been treated to marvellous views the length of the dale but I'd set off that morning in hazy conditions and the forecast for Saturday was cloudy, with mist on the high ground and a fair chance of rain around 4.00pm. Given the weather, I decided to eschew the original high-level route in favour of the valley path following the River Swale. This option amounted to about 11.5 miles of reasonably level walking and I looked forward to arriving at The Black Bull in Reeth by mid-afternoon.

I can't imagine that there is any place more alluring than a river on a summer's day. Moving water is, I think, an important component of mind-resting. Everything seems better by water. Whether it's the anticipation of the sight of a fish that might be lurking beneath the surface, behind the next rock or in the next pool, or whether it's to do with the calming influence of water's myriad rhythms and shapes, or any one of another hundred reasons or a combination of them all, I don't know. But, whatever the reason, I'm a sucker for a river walk and the route through the Swaledale Valley certainly didn't disappoint. Along the way I met fellow 'Coast to Coasters' Mike and Josh, a father and son from Cambridge who were wild camping their way across the country using hammocks, which they would suspend from a couple of trees each night. I shuddered at the size of their backpacks, realising that I'd probably be carrying a similar weight on my 'end-to-end' journey.

I arrived at the village of Gunnerside around lunchtime to find the streets lined with applauding spectators. Naturally assuming they had gathered to cheer *me* on through the village, I was somewhat disappointed to discover that my arrival had coincided with the annual Swaledale Marathon, then in its 36th year. The route covered 23 miles through some of Swaledale's finest scenery, finishing at Reeth Village Hall. Whilst less rugged than the Lake District, the terrain was nevertheless quite challenging for the competitors who have to self-navigate the route within ten hours, and later in the afternoon an air ambulance swooped in and landed nearby to carry off two entrants, one of whom had apparently suffered a stroke, the other a broken leg.

Before leaving Gunnerside I couldn't resist stopping off at the genteel Ghyllfoot Tearoom & Bistro, where I enjoyed a large slice of some wonderfully obscure cake (parsnip and orange, I think) and a pint of steaming hot Yorkshire tea. I continued along on a pleasant path crossing rich, green pastureland and a patchwork of walled fields containing sturdy stone barns and inquisitive cows. The route here was particularly memorable for what I can only describe as 'squeeze stiles' – awkwardly narrow stone stiles barely a leg wide, often fitted with tiny sprung gates and uniquely Yorkshire. They seemed perfectly designed to ensure that anyone who was either lame, stiff or, in my case, lugging a heavy backpack would get wedged in them.

Reeth, known as the 'capital' of Mid Swaledale, is a classic Yorkshire Dales village and I was hardly surprised to discover that the settlement was used as a location for many episodes of the 1980s Yorkshire TV saga *All Creatures Great and Small*, based on the books of rural vet James Herriot.

I arrived at my B&B late in the afternoon, just as the forecast rain put in an appearance. The village was awash with runners and spectators from the earlier marathon event and I was glad I had pre-booked accommodation. The Black Bull dates back to 1680 and has comfortable rooms with views overlooking the dominating village green and down Swaledale. Before checking in I parked my backpack at a table in the bar and downed a superb pint of *Theakston Old Peculier* in company with Mike and Josh (the wild campers) who arrived shortly after me.

I booked an early table in the pub restaurant to avoid the crowds later on and enjoyed an excellent roast beef and Yorkshire pudding dinner with all the trimmings. The rest of the evening was spent in the company of fellow Coast to Coasters Rod and Julia, retired GPs from Worcester, Rudi and his three friends from Germany, and several more pints of *Old Peculier.* Rod suggested an England v Germany pool tournament which he and I won comfortably 3–0. An international incident was thankfully avoided by a final round of single malt which ensured everyone went off to bed in good spirits.

Day 8 would be one of the shortest days of the trek at only 10.5 miles but it would give me a chance to recharge the batteries, as it were, before two consecutive days in excess of 20 miles. I left the pub at a leisurely pace around 9.00am under grey skies and with a light rain falling. My destination today was the town of Richmond, the largest settlement on the entire route. A mile or so into the walk, a muffled salutation from the undergrowth alerted me to the presence of Mike and Josh who had pitched camp overnight by the river and I gratefully accepted a cup of tea before bidding them farewell for the last time and heading off, leaving them to their ablutions.

About an hour out of Reeth, I arrived at Marrick Priory, an abbey founded by a local noble for Benedictine nuns around 1150. Despite the depredations of marauding Scots, the abbey thrived until 17th November 1540, when the Prioress and her 16 nuns were evicted as part of the Dissolution of the Monasteries. The site had been incorporated into a residential outdoor education centre and casual visitors were no longer allowed to visit the ruins, although on a damp Sunday morning I didn't think anyone would object to my having a stroll round.

On leaving the priory, I met Chrissie, a 68-year-old Aussie who was camping her way along the coast-to-coast route. She had suffered quite badly with blisters in the early stages of the walk and had been forced to take a few days out. She was now back on the trail and together we set off through a small, wooded area and up the 'Nuns' Steps', a flight of 375 well-worn medieval stone steps, believed to have been constructed by the nuns as a means of commuting between the abbey and the village of Marske. Crossing a couple of fields, we arrived in the tiny village of Marrick. I had hoped to find somewhere to get a cuppa and shelter from the rain, which by now, although relatively light, had become persistent. Alas, no such luck, and we made do with an early lunch on a bench partially sheltered by an overhanging tree.

From Marrick, the trail became a long, north-easterly plod up to Marske, through farmland punctuated by narrow pinch stiles with tiny gates perched atop the walls. In crossing one of these, I dropped one of my water bottles and an energy bar and was fortunate that a lone walker with his dog, who had been following on behind, recovered them for me. We somehow managed to miss the signs for Elaine's Farmhouse Kitchen so I was deprived of much-needed refreshment as we continued our march across damp fields, bidding farewell to the Pennines.

A short distance out of the village of Marske the road was once again forsaken in favour of moist, grassy pasture. The trail continued into Whitecliffe Wood and emerging about 20 minutes later we were treated to a rather hazy view of Richmond, with the dominating castle tower just visible in the distance. Generally regarded as the 'gateway' to and from the Yorkshire Dales, Richmond is far and away the largest town on the route and it came as a bit of a shock after the peace and quiet of the past week or so. I parted company with Chrissie as she went off in search of the tourist information office to find out about campsites in the vicinity, and I headed down to the River Swale and Richmond Bridge to locate my accommodation for the night.

The Old Brewery Guesthouse was an attractive Grade II Georgian building and the nerve centre for *Sherpa Van*, one of the major companies specialising in the movement of Coast to Coasters' baggage from one side of the country to the other. Regrettably, though, not mine. After checking in, having a nice cup of tea, a hot bath and changing into more civilised clothing, I decided to have a stroll around the town.

The castle grounds were closed by the time I emerged

from the guest house, but the circuitous Castle Walk at the base of the ancient walls was enjoyable. The castle stands in a commanding position above the River Swale close to the centre of the town. Construction of it was started in 1071 by Alan Rufus of Brittany, following the Norman conquest of England, and the structure is in remarkably good condition on the grounds that there is little historical evidence to suggest that it was ever tested in battle.

I wandered along the River Swale, here at its widest point, before going in search of some dinner. After the earlier rain, the evening sunshine was very welcome, and not wanting to eat indoors I parked myself on a bench in the town square and ate a fish cake and chips supper washed down with a refreshing can of *Tizer*. Then it was back to the guest house, TV, and an early night. The Vale of Mowbray lay ahead and tomorrow would be the longest section of the trip at 23 miles.

As a change to my usual repast, I decided on the smoked haddock at breakfast next morning before setting off at 8.30am in more fine and sunny weather. I faced the day with mixed feelings – on the one hand I knew this would be a rather uneventful trudge by the standards of the Coast to Coast, much of it conducted on minor roads and all of it fairly flat, but on the other hand I was quite looking forward to the placid, rural scenery.

Around lunchtime, I arrived at the hamlet of Bolton-on-Swale and took the opportunity to visit the 14th century St. Mary's Church. The churchyard here has become renowned on the route for its monument to one Henry Jenkins, whose claim to fame was that, from his birth at nearby Ellerton in the year 1501, he lived to be 169 years old. Although his birthdate is undocumented, the date of Jenkins's death is known to within days, as his burial is recorded in the parish register of Bolton-on-Swale as having occurred on 9th December 1670. The ancient obelisk in the churchyard, erected to his memory in 1743, seemed a fitting tribute to a colourful local character who, by all accounts, made his living from salmon fishing and thatching cottages. Even if the account of his age did seem rather far-fetched, it was a peaceful spot to kick off my boots and enjoy a bite to eat.

Leaving the village, I followed the springy track beside Bolton Beck, crossing lush fields and pausing to talk to a chap walking the Coast to Coast route from the opposite direction. A lengthy spell of fairly tedious road-walking led to my arrival at the small settlement of Danby Wiske, a stopping-off point for most people, which Wainwright rather cruelly claimed to be a low point in his project in more than just elevation. This may well have been prompted by the fact that the only pub was closed when he travelled this way, as indeed it seems to have been when Julia Bradbury passed through. Things had obviously changed for the better, though, and I enjoyed a pint of *Black Sheep* bitter at the White Swan Inn, with a couple of train drivers who were completing the C2C in stages fitting in around their shifts. It was by now quite late in the afternoon with still another 9 miles to go to Ingleby Cross. I phoned ahead to let the B&B know I would be late, heaved my rucksack onto my back, and with a tantalising view of the Cleveland Hills in the distance, plodded on up the road.

Nine Standards Rigg on the main 'watershed' of England

"Always at Keld, there is the music of the river"

The rest of the day was spent wandering along tracks and quiet backroads linking well-ordered farmland, hedgerows and coppices. After crossing a railway line and a beck or two, I finally arrived at the busy A19, beyond which lay my destination, Ingleby Cross. It was 9.00pm before I turned up on the doorstep of the Ingleby House Farm but the owners, Jackie and Malcolm, could not have been more welcoming. Jackie immediately set about making me a roast beef sandwich and I shared a chat and a beer with husband Malcolm before heading off to bed.

Chapter Four

Tuesday 16th June, Day 10, would be another lengthy stage which many walkers split into two. However, a lack of accommodation on the route itself, and my desire to spend the night at the isolated Lion Inn at Blakey Ridge, meant I faced the prospect of a pretty gruelling 21-mile trek. Jackie had kindly offered to prepare me an early breakfast for 6.00am to allow me to get on the road by 7.00am.

From here, the route entered the North York Moors National Park – the final lap. Over the next 50 miles, wonderful scenery, wide panoramas, and what is said to be the world's largest expanse of heather awaited me, and, in just four days, journey's end.

Having taken on sufficient fuel in the form of another first-class full English breakfast, I set off down the road and into Arncliffe Wood. Mount Grace Priory, built in 1398 by the Carthusian Order, is a popular stop-off point here but I didn't want to lose any time so early in the day so I pushed on up the steep track through the wood.

I was overtaken by Ian who was camping the Coast to Coast along with his dog 'Zen' and I recognised him as the chap who had thoughtfully recovered my dropped water bottle near the village of Marske a couple of days earlier. Shortly after, the route converged with the Cleveland Way, which was established a couple of years before Wainwright's original book was published and which I would follow for almost the entire distance to Blakey Moor.

The North York Moors is an open, unenclosed and virtually uninhabited expanse of high moorland. It is in fact not one but a vast collection of moors, almost 150, each with its own name, though quite where one ends and another begins is anyone's guess. I continued my relentless uphill slog through Arncliffe Wood before passing a telecoms station and emerging onto the first of them, Scarth Wood Moor, which, on this clear sunny day, afforded superb views back over the Vale of Mowbray. A steep climb through Clain Wood, led me to Live Moor, and upon reaching the trig point on Carlton Moor, I had my first hazy view of the North Sea far away to the east.

I had a late lunch break at Lord Stones Cafe, giving me the opportunity to refill my water bottles, before heading off along an undulating but predominantly paved route to Cringle Moor. From there I had a fine view across Cold Moor to a tumble of boulders and rocky outcrops known as the 'Wainstones' which sit atop Hasty Bank.

The path then dropped steeply down from Clay Bank Top, where almost everyone I'd encountered on my walk that day would be meeting transportation taking them to overnight accommodation in the nearby villages of Urra, Chop Gate or Great Broughton. My destination lay another 10 miles and almost four hours further east, and as I set off up the steep flight of paved slabs and steps, already pretty weary from the roller coaster morning, I seriously wondered whether I'd make it.

I tend to find that when the going gets tough something usually occurs to give one a bit of a lift. On reaching the top of Urra Moor, the gradient relented somewhat and the path eventually became the wide track of the former Rosedale Ironstone Railway, which served the nearby iron mines a century and a half ago. The walking now, although seemingly endless, was flat and firm underfoot and in the late-afternoon sunshine I plodded along almost on autopilot. When the Lion Inn finally came into view it was like an oasis in the desert. I nearly wept with relief. As a final twist of fate, though, I missed the short cut up to the Inn and instead walked another mile and a half of track and roadway before stumbling into the bar and ordering a very cold and refreshing pint of cider.

For everybody, be they walker or motorist, Blakey Ridge *is* the Lion Inn. This 16th-century free house is located at the highest point of the North York Moors National Park, and at an elevation of 1,325 feet it offers breathtaking views over the Rosedale and Farndale valleys. It's the fourth-highest inn in Britain and one of the most charming hostelries on the coast-to-coast route with its low-beamed ceilings and ancient fireplaces. I checked in at around 8.15pm and negotiated my way up the steep, narrow stairs to my room above the bar.

After following the well-rehearsed ritual of unpacking my gear in order across the floor, I showered and returned to the bar where I enjoyed an excellent dinner and a couple of pints of *Theakston Best* bitter before bed.

The last two days had been pretty strenuous but I knew that nothing as tough lay ahead. In my planning I'd thought long and hard about overnight stops for the last few days. After the challenge of two days in excess of 20 miles, I was looking forward to tomorrow's 10-mile stroll to Glaisdale, essentially downhill all the way as I dropped from about 1,300 feet to 500 feet above sea level. The penultimate day's walk, around 15 miles, would see me to the village of Hawsker before a final day of 12 miles to Robin Hood's Bay, bulked out by a detour off the main route via the seaside town of Whitby.

I was in no great hurry to set off the next morning. It was a heavily overcast and breezy day and with the prospect of a leisurely hike to Glaisdale ahead of me, I decided to take my time over breakfast of grapefruit segments, coffee, toast and a pair of Scottish kippers.

From the Lion Inn, the route took me north following the tarmac road before turning east onto the moors once again. Soon I passed a stumpy, white landmark known as 'Fat Betty', one of more than 30 prominent and named stone moorland crosses which are frequent occurrences on the North York Moors. Tradition dictates that walkers both take and leave a snack, sweet or cash, and I swapped an energy bar for a boiled sweet.

The rain, which had threatened from the start of the day, finally arrived just as an old shooting hut known as Trough House came into view and, although the building was locked, I was able to tuck myself in behind a low wall out of the keen wind to slip my waterproofs on for only the second time on the trip.

Crossing Glaisdale High Moor, with the extensive views down the wonderfully named Great Fryup Dale, I really got a sense of the wild remoteness of the moors and in the wind and rain, albeit relatively light, it was easy to imagine what a challenging terrain this would be in bad weather.

The easy track continued on across open moorland with the abundant heather gradually giving way to grass as height was lost. Soon after lunchtime I arrived at the sprawling village of Glaisdale which sits on a series of hillsides above the Esk Valley and which, a roadside sign proudly proclaimed, had been Northern Village of the Year 2002. I enjoyed a couple of pints of *Black Sheep* bitter and a chat with the landlord in The Arncliffe Arms before heading off down the road to my B&B.

The Beggar's Bridge B&B sits adjacent to, and takes its name from, the 17th-century 'Beggar's Bridge' and after settling in and enjoying a civilised pot of tea and toasted teacakes in the garden, I ambled off to explore this local landmark. 'Beggar's Bridge' spans the River Esk and was apparently the handiwork of Tom Ferris, a local man of modest means who fell in love with Agnes Richardson, the daughter of a wealthy farmer from nearby Egton. It seems that the night before Tom was leaving to seek his fortune he went to visit his beloved who lived across the river. Sadly, the river was swollen by heavy rain and his dreams of a romantic farewell were thwarted. To cut a long story short, Tom went off and made his fortune. When he returned, his future assured, he married Agnes and built his famous bridge in 1619 to ensure that other young lovers from the neighbourhood would not suffer the same torment as he had that stormy night.

I dined that evening at The Arncliffe Arms, ordering a double cheeseburger with chips and onion rings, appropriately named the 'Arncliffe Whopper', and then strolled back to the B&B for another early night. Tomorrow would be the penultimate day on the walk and I was particularly looking forward to visiting the North York Moors Railway at Grosmont.

I set off after breakfast (yes, another full English!) at 9.00am joining forces with a couple of mature gentlemen from Ireland who had been the only other guests at the B&B the night before. The route would take us up into Arncliffe Wood and on through the picturesque villages of Egton Bridge and Grosmont – both charming settlements easily on a par with the Lakeland villages of Borrowdale and Grasmere. It was no surprise to learn that nostalgic TV show, *Heartbeat*, was filmed nearby.

My companions, clearly experienced walkers, were aiming for the 'finish line' at Robin Hood's Bay, the best part of 20 miles distant. In consequence, their pace was a little smart for my taste and I wished them luck and bade them farewell at Grosmont.

Grosmont is essentially a one-street village, popular with tourists and steam rail enthusiasts. They're attracted by the old locomotives of the North York Moors Railway, the largest preserved heritage railway in the UK in terms of route mileage operated and passenger numbers, and I was keen to see at least one of the engines before departing. I called in at the local Co-op store and post office to buy my lunch and post back to Butt House B&B at Keld, the room key (accompanied by a suitably apologetic note) which, despite the enormous plastic fob, I had managed to walk off with. Chores complete, I bought a cup of tea at the wonderfully nostalgic Grosmont station and settled myself down on the platform to await the arrival of the next train. Engine '76079' – a 1957 BR Standard 4 MT locomotive – duly arrived and was greeted with celebrity status, a flash of cameras and the admiring attention of the assembled crowd.

I would have loved to take a trip down the line, which runs back and forth the 18 miles between Pickering and Whitby but I needed to move on, and having finished my tea, headed off over the level crossing. After a fierce climb up from Grosmont, I reached Sleights Moor and was treated to a wonderful view north-east to the ruins of Whitby Abbey.

After crossing the busy A169, the route dropped down to the picturesque hamlet of Littlebeck where I stopped for lunch on a bench by the village hall. Rested and refreshed, I continued on into Little Beck Wood, enjoying the vibrant green and lush vegetation of this sylvan glade beside May Beck. The track took me past the mysterious 'Hermitage', an enormous sandstone boulder hollowed out to form a small cave. It was apparently constructed at the behest of one George Chubb, the schoolmaster from Littlebeck, in 1790, and bears his initials, though quite *why* it was built appears to be unrecorded. It may be that Mr Chubb felt a strong spiritual need to escape from his pupils, although a more popular theory is that it was constructed as a 'folly' to provide employment for local people.

Despite being one of the most popular long-distance

walks in the world, Wainwright's Coast to Coast is not designated as a national trail and therefore doesn't benefit from official funding. As a consequence, way-marking varies considerably along the path and in many cases responsibility rests with local landowners. There is little in the Lake District National Park section, though for much of the time the path is well-trodden and fairly obvious, and where route-finding does become more challenging, small cairns (piles of stones) often help to keep walkers on track. Once over the Pennines and into Yorkshire the trail becomes much better signposted, although there are a number of areas where the ground can become so boggy that paths are not visible at all.

There seemed to be a distinct lack of signposting now in Little Beck Wood and shortly after moving on from the 'Hermitage', I somehow managed to take a wrong turn, becoming completely lost. I knew there to be a tea garden in the vicinity, alongside the former ruins of Midge Hall and after stumbling around aimlessly for a while in the dense woodland, I heard voices. Climbing to the top of a small rise, I caught sight of the Falling Foss Tea Garden through the trees. The route down was steep and pathless and I carefully picked my way through a tangle of undergrowth and fallen tree trunks.

Relieved to have got myself back on track, and as it was by now mid-afternoon, I treated myself to a cream tea and a view of the 30-foot-high waterfall known as 'Falling Foss' before leaving the woods and heading up onto Sneaton Low Moor. I took a short break to watch a young chap repair an old stone wall, utilising skills handed down from generation to generation, before a freshening breeze and gathering rain clouds reminded me that I still had about 4 miles to go. The final stretch of heather moorland across a section ambitiously named Graystone Hills soon gave way to a minor road into the village of Hawsker.

Hawsker sits astride the A171 Scarborough-Whitby road and is actually a two-part village, *High* and *Low*. From here, the end of my journey across England was actually only a couple of hours away as the crow flies, but I had planned an unofficial stopover at Hawsker in order to visit the seaside town of Whitby, with its famous abbey, and to ensure a more leisurely arrival at Robin Hood's Bay the next day.

I'd been pretty lucky with my accommodation on the trip having selected, almost without exception, from Mrs Doreen Whitehead's famous *Coast to Coast Bed & Breakfast Accommodation Guide* – in my opinion, essential reading for anyone planning to undertake this walk. I'd paid on average £44 per night, including the inevitable single-occupancy supplement, and the facilities had been good. In most cases I'd had a large, comfortable double room to myself, and most importantly they'd confirmed the booking and were expecting me.

My heart sank a little when I arrived at the Long Leas Farm B&B at 6.00pm that evening. It seemed that Brian and Jill McNeil, with whom I'd originally booked, had moved on a month or so before and the new proprietor couldn't find a record of my booking. As I stood in the doorway watching him feverishly thumb through his reservations book, the expected rain began to fall and I had visions of spending a damp night in a bus shelter alongside the busy A171. Eventually, he found a booking for that night in more or less the right name, and with great relief I was invited in and issued with my key.

The room, which was among a small row of chalets in the grounds of the farm, was basic and functional but lacked the homely charm I'd become used to on the walk, although at £30 it was certainly the cheapest. I ramped the small, electric heater up to full power to take the chill off the room before unpacking and hitting the shower. The light rain eased off after an hour or so and, although I'd almost made up my mind to have an evening in front of the tiny TV with a cuppa and a *Mars* bar, I relented and strolled down to the Hare & Hounds where I enjoyed a seafood platter and a couple of pints of *Theakston's Old Peculier*.

I was up bright and early the next morning and after carefully repacking my rucksack, wandered up to the main farmhouse where breakfast was served. I appeared to be the only guest and while working my way through the substantial meal, I checked out the route for the final day of the walk.

Following the official route would have entailed a mere 5-mile stroll, but I'd planned to extend the day by taking a minor road up to Whitby, then picking up the Cleveland Way and following the coastal path all the way around to Robin Hood's Bay. This amounted to a leisurely 12 miles and would see me at my destination shortly after lunchtime when I planned to meet up with my daughter-in-law's father, Pete, who had kindly offered to drive up and meet me.

I set off around 9.30am on the first short section up to Whitby Abbey. The weather, whilst overcast, was warm and dry and made for comfortable walking. I was overtaken en route by an elderly couple, clearly heading for one of the coastal holiday parks, who cut an amusing picture as they sped along on their mobility scooters each dragging a suitcase behind them. Arriving around mid-morning, I was looking forward to a relaxing cup of coffee. Alas, the abbey tearooms were closed for staff training – hopefully, a session on the importance of providing much-needed refreshment to knackered long-distance walkers!

Perched high on the clifftop overlooking the popular seaside town of Whitby and the North Sea, Whitby Abbey is a ruined Benedictine structure dating back to AD 657. It was Whitby's first monastic site and quickly became one of the most important religious centres in the Anglo-Saxon world. After a turbulent history, including its abandonment in the 9th century following Danish raids, the monastery was finally suppressed by Henry VIII in 1539. Set against the overcast sky it was easy to see why the haunting remains have inspired artists and writers for nearly 1,500 years and were said to be the inspiration for Bram Stoker's 1897 novel *Dracula*.

I took some time out to explore the abbey grounds and appreciate the stunning views, then set off south-east along the blustery clifftops. Shortly after passing a coastguard lookout station, the broad sweep of Robin Hood's Bay, with its charming red-roofed houses, finally came into view. I knew then that nothing could stop me and that within the hour I'd be at journey's end.

Known locally as 'Bay Town', Robin Hood's Bay is a quaint old fishing village with a dubious history in smuggling. Following the steep road down through the old town, I arrived at the slipway or 'Dock' as it's known, and at 2.00pm I stepped onto the beach to dip my boots in the North Sea and release the pebble I'd carried all the way from St Bees. Tradition honoured, I retired to The Bay Hotel where, having signed the book in the bar and received my completion certificate, I settled down for a well-earned pint of *Wainwrights Ale*.

Peter arrived around 3.00pm and we whiled away the rest of the afternoon at the hotel, seated on a bench under the sign proclaiming, "The End of The Coast to Coast Walk". I really appreciated him driving all the way up to meet me and it was good to see a familiar face at the end of the trip. My original plan had been to overnight at Robin Hood's Bay then take a bus to Scarborough the next morning where I'd pick up the rail connections back to London. But when Peter, himself a Yorkshireman, had made contact during the trip offering to drive up and collect me, I readily accepted. I had the feeling, though, that I was actually doing him a favour. He and his wife were in the midst of a kitchen refit and I got the distinct impression that domestic harmony was seriously lacking in the household.

Having taken on as much *Wainwrights Ale* as we could decently hold, Pete and I weaved our way back up the precipitous road to our respective B&Bs. After checking in at The Studio, unpacking and showering, we met up for dinner at the Victoria Hotel, only just arriving in time for food as Pete had rather overdone his late-afternoon nap.

We spent a very pleasant evening in the hotel bar. I met up again with Mike and Chris from Manchester, the Australian couple who'd taken the picture for me at the start of the walk on the beach at St Bees, and Mike, the mature Aussie I'd first met on the train up from Lancaster what seemed like ages ago.

I doubt whether many people sitting in the bar that evening would have had much understanding of our achievement – success is a very personal thing after all and most would probably have thought us mad. It was very satisfying to sit among this small group, drawn, like tens of thousands of others each year from all over the world, to complete a walk first devised by a retired borough treasurer over 40 years ago. I was content in the knowledge that I'd walked across the whole of England, coast to coast, and in so doing had completed the first part of my personal walking challenge.

Next morning, having repacked my rucksack for the last time and enjoyed my final full English breakfast of the trip, I bade farewell to Anne, the owner of the B&B, swung my pack into the boot of Pete's car, and headed south for home.

Tomorrow would be Sunday 21st June, officially the start of summer and more importantly Father's Day and I was looking forward to a leisurely afternoon on the patio with the family and no walking!

People have since asked me whether I'd do the walk again. The answer is an emphatic 'yes'. It was certainly challenging – despite the daily breakfasts I returned 9 lb lighter – but the Coast to Coast is a wonderful walk, full of variety and interest, and possibly a journey appreciated all the more the second time around. The marvellous weather made the trip, of course. I'd been incredibly lucky in that regard, experiencing only light rain for part of two days. This was something of a minor miracle given that I had walked across what is statistically the soggiest part of the wettest region in the land. Indeed, within six months of my completing the walk, Cumbria and the Yorkshire Dales were hit by 'Storm Desmond', suffering severe flooding following the heaviest rainfall ever recorded in the UK. So heavy was the rain that the waterfall at Malham Cove in North Yorkshire was brought back to life after being dry for hundreds of years and at 260 feet became, overnight, the highest unbroken waterfall in the country.

A well-earned pint at the end of the road

It was always my objective to complete the walk in accordance with Wainwright's schedule and as a lone, unsupported, single trip and I'm glad I did it that way. Next time around, though, I would extend the trip by possibly three days, splitting the stages between Rosthwaite and Patterdale, Patterdale and Shap, and Ingleby Cross to Blakey Ridge. Carrying so much weight had made one or two sections a test of endurance but I'd now completed my first long-distance trail and it had been a marvellous experience.

Chapter Five

For the first week or so after my return home I felt absolutely wiped out both physically and mentally. But it's amazing how mind and body recover from these 'traumas' and before the year was out I'd booked myself onto a charity hike up Ben Nevis, the highest mountain in the UK, raising a bit of cash for Macmillan Cancer Support along the way. I'd obviously exhausted my quota of luck with the weather on this trip, though, experiencing fierce winds and driving rain at the summit.

I had now walked the breadth of England and climbed the highest peak, and as 2015 drew to a close I was looking forward to the second part of my personal challenge – the ultimate long-distance walk in Britain – LEJOG.

2016 didn't get off to the best start. In the late summer of the previous year, my siblings and I had decided to sell our old family home which we'd been renting out for the last few years. We'd received and accepted a particularly good offer and the sale was going along swimmingly. Buoyed by the prospect of a financial 'cushion', I'd decided to throw caution to the wind and set a provisional date to kick off my 'end-to-end' adventure in April 2016.

I'd spoken to my boss, outlined my plans and requested

a 10-week sabbatical. Unsurprisingly, I was informed that this didn't fall within the company's policy and they regretted that they would be unable to support it. Undeterred, I decided that, as soon as my share of the proceeds from the house sale hit the bank, which was expected around mid-January, I would give my employer the contractually required three months' notice and leave around the second week of April. This would give me a few days for final preparations before setting off on Monday 18th April.

The timing seemed right. I'd have a bit of money in the bank to tide me over until I could get back into gainful employment on my return, and I'd done most of the planning and already acquired most of the maps, guidebooks and equipment I'd need. Leaving my job would not be a massive wrench and I felt that now was the time for a career break. In truth, I also wasn't getting any younger and having already started to experience the odd twinge in my knees and left hip, who could predict what might be around the corner on the health front?

A phone call from our estate agent late in the day on 30th December potentially blew my plans out of the water. The prospective buyer had withdrawn from the sale and we'd have to put the property back on the market. Walking out on my job, at my time of life, was scary enough but without the guarantee that I'd have a 'nest egg' to fall back on if required, it seemed rather foolhardy to commit to going in the coming spring.

The timing of my expedition, starting mid-April and finishing around the end of June, was decided on for three main reasons. Firstly, the weather, or at least the temperature, would, in theory, improve as I journeyed north, with the subsequent lengthening of daylight hours. Secondly, I wanted to limit my exposure to the midges, which habitually plague the Highlands of Scotland throughout July and August; and thirdly, to avoid any restrictions on access to the Scottish hills in the deer-stalking and grouse-shooting seasons between 12th August and the end of October.

The news from the estate agent was a body blow. I'd been mentally preparing myself for the trip for some time and the realisation that the whole show might now have to be postponed for another year was deeply disappointing.

On the plus side, I would have a full year to get myself into better shape and ample opportunity to test run my new tent, sleeping bag, and cooking equipment, not to mention the enormous Osprey rucksack I'd bought to carry it all in. It would also allow more time for the flood-ravaged North of England to recover from storms 'Desmond' and 'Gertrude' and the damage caused by the heaviest rainfall on record. The next year would see a late Easter, so I'd be looking to travel down to Penzance on Tuesday 18th April 2017.

If progress on the house sale was disappointing, at least there was some good news on the weight loss front. At the start of the year an acquaintance had started up his own *Slimming World* group. Lynn and I had piled on a few festive pounds so we decided to go along to support him in this endeavour. Through a combination of healthier eating, abstinence from 'fridge picking', plus my early morning walks, I'd managed to knock out over three stone by the end of March, picking up seven 'Slimmer of The Week' and three 'Slimmer of The Month' awards in the process. I had the dubious honour of being the group's 'Greatest Loser 2016' and to top it all, Lynn and I had even won the group 'Couple of The Year 2016' award. It has to be said, though, it was a very small group and there weren't many couples.

Having resigned myself to the fact that I wouldn't be able to undertake my journey this year, I was determined to use the time to get fully prepared, in terms of both equipment and, more importantly, mind and body. I had set myself a target to lose four and a half stone by the time I set off and this was a massive step towards it.

With bodily preparation in mind, I decided I needed to address my hip problem. Although it wasn't yet causing constant pain, it *was* getting steadily worse and the time had come to seek medical advice. My doctor had sent me for an X-ray which confirmed bilateral hip osteoarthritis in both hips but the left side particularly and as a consequence he'd referred me to a consultant orthopaedic surgeon. He, quite frankly, seemed rather stunned by my walking plans and seriously doubted whether the hip would withstand a 1,200-mile trek. Cancelling my walk was not an option, so a hip replacement seemed the only course of action. Membership of the company-provided healthcare scheme did, at least, ensure the operation could be planned. I had a busy summer coming up, culminating in the 62-mile South Coast Challenge at the end of August, so the surgery was booked for 24th September. This would give me almost 7 months' recovery time before I set off for John o' Groats.

In the spring Lynn had suggested another visit to the

Lakes and, sensing an opportunity to finally climb Helvellyn, I booked a four-night trip to Patterdale for the beginning of June, staying at the highly recommended Patterdale Hotel. The weather in London and the South East at the time had been dire, but as we entered the Lake District National Park the clouds parted, the sun came out, and that's pretty much how it stayed for the next four days.

At 3,117 feet, Helvellyn is the third-highest peak in England. My route from Patterdale took me along Grisedale on a steady ascent to Grisedale Tarn where I'd had to make the decision to take the more direct valley route in the other direction a year earlier on the coast-to-coast walk. I took a short break on the grassy hillside, drinking in the total silence with the sun glinting on the surface of the tarn below me. Then it was a sharp climb up Dollywaggon Pike across Nethermost Pike and on up to the broad summit of Helvellyn. So broad in fact, that on 22nd December 1926 two aviators, John Leeming and Bert Hinkler, landed an Avro 585 Gosport biplane on the summit and after a short stay managed to take off again.

The 360-degree views under the clear blue sky were stunning and made even more memorable by the acquisition of a mobile signal and a call from my brother confirming that the sale of our late parents' house had finally been completed. I knew then that I would be able to finance my LEJOG adventure in 2017. After a celebratory lunch by the stone shelter at the summit, I set off to tackle the most famous ridge walk in the Lake District – Striding Edge. The notorious ridge that flanks the south-eastern approach to Helvellyn certainly needs to be handled with care and respect, and even then, things can go wrong. Hundreds of people have died falling from the exposed mountain ridge, with five lives claimed in the previous year alone. I edged my way along the knife-edge summit high above Red Tarn, then, with some relief, joined a well-worn track affording me wonderful views along Ullswater on a steep descent to the small town of Glenridding. From here it was a short road walk back to the hotel where Lynn thoughtfully provided me with a refreshing pint of the ingeniously named *Patterd'Ale.*

I was keen for Lynn to experience and enjoy the great outdoors, particularly since the weather was so good and though she's not, by any stretch of the imagination, an enthusiastic walker, she did consent to join me on a relatively short stroll to Aira Force, a beautiful waterfall set amongst ancient woodland and landscaped glades, the site of which is owned by the National Trust. Although generally easy walking, some parts, particularly those in the vicinity of the impressive 65-foot cascade, were a bit rough underfoot. Poor Lynn, who likened the experience to a route march from an episode of the TV series *Tenko*, unfortunately suffered a foot injury which later resulted in the loss of a big toenail.

Our stay in Patterdale also gave me the opportunity to sample a stretch of the Ullswater Way. This new walking route, opened in April 2016, offered a 20-mile waymarked circular path around what is arguably the most beautiful lake in England, rekindling much-needed tourism in a corner of the Lake District hardest hit by the winter floods. Sadly, my time on this trip was limited but it would make for a wonderful day's walking on our next visit.

Physical preparations this year were proceeding well. By the end of June I reckoned I'd clocked up around 1,100 miles of essentially road-walking, losing 4.5 stone in the process and achieving my personal target weight of 15 stone. The battle would be to maintain this, particularly in the weeks following my hip operation at the end of September. My target was to be below 15 stone by the start of my journey, in 292 days.

I had one final walking challenge to tackle before the operation put me temporarily out of action, and at 7.20am on Saturday 27th August, the four-man team which included my brother, niece and son set off on the South Coast Challenge. The weather was glorious as we strolled along the front at Eastbourne on the first leg of a 62-mile trek which would primarily follow the beautiful South Downs Way to Arundel.

My son regrettably suffered a reoccurrence of a leg injury and was forced to drop out at the halfway stop in Brighton. The rest of the team continued on, crossing the finish line just under 32 hours after setting off. Around £2,000 was raised for my brother's chosen charity, Combat Stress, the leading UK charity for veterans' mental health.

The hip replacement operation towards the end of September went well and I'd 'escaped' from the hospital within four days. I was out walking again after only a week and within a month I was up to 5 miles a day.

I'd given a lot of thought to the route I'd be taking on my journey in 2017 and to the equipment required, but during my enforced convalescence my mind turned to the geography and history of the walk and, in particular, my reasons for wanting to do it. LEJOG is the traversal of the whole length of mainland Great Britain between two extremities – in the south-west and north-east. Land's End is *not* the most southerly point in England and John o' Groats is *not* the most northerly point in Scotland – these honours belong to The Lizard and Dunnet Head, respectively. The reason Land's End and John o' Groats are regarded as the end points of Great Britain is that they are the two points on the mainland that are the furthest apart from each other. The traditional distance by road is 838 miles, but my off-road route totalled about 1,200 miles.

The first recorded end-to-end walk (actually from John o' Groats to Land's End) was undertaken by brothers John and Robert Naylor in 1871. Since then, the walk has been tackled many times, more particularly since 1960, after a well-publicised road walk by Dr Barbara Moore. In the same year, the entrepreneur Billy Butlin organised a road-walking race, which gave further impetus to the idea. An account which has inspired many 'end-to-enders' is from 1968 by the travel writer John Hillaby, in his classic book *Journey Through Britain.*

Since then, the end-to-end business has never looked back. In addition to the cyclists and runners, there have been many 'novelty' approaches, often undertaken for charity fundraising purposes. Most of them have been along the roads, aiming to achieve a fast time, fundraising or publicity and, although I would be aiming to raise funds for SSAFA – the Armed Forces charity, my primary objective was to enjoy the journey for its own sake, adopting a more relaxed but nevertheless adventurous approach. The fastest passage between the two points was made in 1988 by a McDonnell Douglas F-4K Phantom jet, in a time of 46 minutes 44 seconds. I anticipated that *my* off-road journey of around 1,200 miles would take around 10 weeks.

Which brings me to the question of why I felt compelled to undertake this epic journey, when most people would consider me a little mad. People in general have seldom regarded walking as a pleasure and historically it has nearly always been viewed as the poor man's way of getting around, with 'pedestrian tourists' often regarded very suspiciously. In Morris Marples's *Shanks's Pony: A Study of Walking*, he relates the experience of a German pastor who visited England in 1782 and spent six weeks tramping from London to the Peak District in Derbyshire and back. He observed: "...in England, any person undertaking so long a journey on foot is sure to be looked upon and considered as either a beggar, or a vagabond, or some necessitous wretch, which is a character not much more popular than that of a rogue..." It may well have been that the perceived hostility was due to him being a foreigner, but it's certainly true that few long-distance travellers went on foot in 18th-century England and it illustrates how much attitudes have changed in the intervening years to the popular pastime enjoyed by so many people today.

We are fortunate to be surrounded by arguably the greatest walking country on earth. With around 3,000 miles of National Trails, 19,500 miles of coastline, and 140,000 miles of rights of way, our relatively small island has a staggering walking wealth, and to my mind walking is the only way to really enjoy it. By walking through a landscape, you enter into it, experience it with every one of your senses in a way that's not possible when it's simply viewed from a bus, car or train. As a complete novice to backpacking, I confess that the prospect of exploring the relationship between myself and the natural world was not without trepidation, but I relished the challenge.

I had read many accounts of long-distance hikes and other people's experiences and thoughts on their journeys through wild places. Now in my advancing years I felt the need, as the naturalist John Muir once put it, to "throw a loaf of bread and a pound of tea in an old sack and jump over the back fence". I wanted to experience for myself the joy of walking through the ever-changing though ever-constant natural world, the magic of waking to sunlight glinting on a mist-wreathed lake, or the contentment after pitching camp at the end of a long and satisfying day.

I'd dipped my toe in the water, so to speak, on the Coast to Coast in 2015, hiking in the wilds during the day but returning to the civilisation of B&Bs at night. Now I wanted to take the full, invigorating swim, to experience everything the countryside had to offer.

It was, in part, to fulfil a long-standing ambition and to achieve an objective, but it was also a desire to explore a world beyond my everyday life, and in doing so to challenge and explore myself. I needed an adventure that was both physically and mentally demanding, and potentially life-enhancing. Over the years there had been too many projects started but not completed, too many 'if onlys'. As I looked back from my armchair in later life, I wanted to remember this fondly rather than as one more uncompleted item on my 'bucket list'. I'd spent a lifetime watching films and reading books about other people's tales of adventure and derring-do and felt that I needed to go out and write my own story. Perhaps, most importantly, I hoped that by completing this challenge, I could gain something that I felt at the time was seriously lacking – self-respect and pride in myself. In short, my journey wasn't an indulgence, but a necessity.

The timing was also critical of course. I wasn't getting any younger and in 2017 I would hit the big 60. My hip operation had brought home the fragility of one's health and the question of how much longer I might be able to attempt the journey, let alone complete it. Also, from a work perspective, I wasn't so in love with my job that it would be a great wrench to leave it. With the sale of my late parents' house earlier in the year, I now at least had a small financial cushion should quickly getting back into gainful employment prove an issue. All things considered, if I was ever going to do it, April 2017 was the time.

It had been my original intention to undertake the journey in 2016 but when my parents' property failed to sell at the start of that year, I'd had to postpone. This, as it turned out, was no bad thing. It gave me a year to acquire the rest of my equipment and get myself in shape and as we moved into 2017, I was satisfied with progress in both regards.

I'd logged over 2,000 miles of mainly road-walking in 2016 and combined with an improved diet I'd lost around

4.5 stone, achieving my target weight of 15 stone. The hip surgery towards the end of September appeared to have gone well and I was confident that it would be suitably healed by the end of March. The outstanding small items of equipment had been received as Christmas presents, and apart from a few food items, which would be sourced nearer the time, at 'D' minus 99 days, I was good to go.

I was contractually obliged to give three months' notice to my employer, so on 9th January, having had one or two sleepless nights pondering it, I sat down with my boss to announce that I had decided to undertake my trek this year. He was actually very understanding and took the news pretty well. He recalled our conversation on the subject just over a year earlier, accepted that I'd given the matter serious thought and that it would be pointless to try to talk me out of it. I would take accrued annual holiday to leave at the end of March, giving me a couple of weeks for final preparations and to spend some quality time with Lynn. My official final day's employment, appropriately enough, would be Good Friday.

The Land's End–John o' Groats Association is an exclusive membership of people who have completed the journey in either direction by any means, in a single trip. I had joined during 2016 as an associate member (you can't be a full member until you've done it) and took the opportunity for a couple of days away with Lynn at the Toorak Hotel in Torquay at the end of January, for the Annual Dinner and Presentation Weekend. It also gave us the chance to meet up with some friends who travelled down from their home near Barnstaple – I'd planned to stay with them at the end of the first section of my trek. It was great to see people, who had completed their journey's the previous year, receive their certificates and awards, and it gave me the opportunity to discuss the trek with like-minded people who had actually done it – some a number of times!

With 11 weeks to the start of my journey, and with a view to conditioning myself to carrying a fully loaded pack, I decided I needed to step up the training regime. So, at 4.30am, on a damp and chilly February morning, I set off for my regular 4-mile walk carrying my Osprey backpack, loaded with sundry items to around 35 pounds in weight. My new hip felt worrying sore but I hoped that things would improve as my training progressed towards the big day. I resolved to continue the early morning walks at least until the end of March, with the addition of a loaded pack each day. The exercise certainly brought home to me the importance of selective packing.

Bearing that in mind, thoughts turned to the issue of resupply throughout the trek. Even though I'd be camping a lot of the time, I still planned to get an evening meal at B&Bs and pubs. But in more remote areas, this wouldn't always be possible. Over the preceding few weeks, I'd been stocking up on dried pasta and rice meals, ration packs, and ready-to-eat 'All Day Breakfasts' plus a variety of breakfast items such as muesli and porridge (all in convenient sachets) and cereal bars. To maintain my energy levels throughout the day I'd just taken delivery of a consignment of trail mix – a wonderful blend of dried fruit, raisins, nuts and seeds, kindly donated free of charge by the supplier RM Curtis Ltd. Known in the States as 'GORP', or Good Old Raisins and Peanuts, this snacking product would provide the nutrients I would need: 50% sweet carbs for energy; 50% nuts and seeds for protein, fat and sodium. All these items, together with condiments, tea bags, sugar and powdered milk, along with each section's maps, guidebooks and other miscellaneous necessities, would be loaded into individual resupply boxes and sent to post offices at each section end point. Unwanted items would then be returned home in the same box.

At the beginning of March, I completed an exercise to transpose the route from various guidebooks onto the 47 Ordnance Survey maps covering the entire journey. I'd been very undecided about my route on the final section from Fort William but having had the opportunity to discuss alternatives with other 'end-to-enders' at the LEJOG Association weekend in January, I'd now committed to a firm route.

My declared aim was to walk from Land's End to John o' Groats following paths, tracks and established National Trails rather than roads, to enjoy the best of the British countryside, and my chosen route was very much based on Andy Robinson's excellent *End to End Trail*. Setting off from Land's End on 19th April, I planned to follow the spectacular South West Coast Path as far as Barnstaple. From there, the trail headed inland across Exmoor, over the Quantock Hills, on past Bristol and across the Severn Estuary to Chepstow in South Wales.

From Chepstow, the route followed the first half of the Offa's Dyke Path along the beautiful Wye Valley and the

England-Wales border.

At Knighton, I would cut across north-east to follow the Staffordshire Way and the Limestone Way into the heart of the Peak District before joining up with the Pennine Way just beyond Hebden Bridge. It would be here, if all went according to plan, that I'd be meeting up with the family to celebrate my 60th birthday towards the end of May.

The Pennine Way would be followed to the Scottish borders. Then, turning north-west, St Cuthbert's Way, the Southern Upland Way, canal towpaths and a disused railway line would take me north-west of Glasgow, thankfully avoiding the urban sprawl, to pick up the West Highland Way which I would follow to Fort William.

The final section of my trek would take me along the Great Glen Way, threaded by the scenic Caledonian Canal and the massive expanse of Loch Ness. From Inverness, the self-proclaimed 'Capital of the Highlands', I planned to head north-east, taking in sections of the John o' Groats Trail, completing my epic journey, as it began, with a coastal walk to Duncansby Head and John o' Groats.

My chosen charity was SSAFA – the Armed Forces charity. Although never having served myself, my brother had had a long career in the Royal Navy, and my son and niece were both currently serving in the British Army. I'm also firmly with Theodore Roosevelt, who stated back in 1903 that "a man who is good enough to shed his blood for his country is good enough to be given a square deal afterwards". Regrettably, for any number of reasons, there are many serving and veteran service personnel in need, and SSAFA is committed to providing support to help them overcome whatever problems they face and rebuild their lives.

Meanwhile, planning was complete, my bag was packed, and having just finished reading Russell George's *Footsteps in Summer* – an entertaining account of his 950-mile solo charity walk from John o' Groats to Land's End in 2013 – for some last-minute inspiration, I was raring to go.

Chapter Six

Tuesday 18th April dawned on a lovely fresh spring morning. After an emotional farewell to wife Lynn and cat Rosie, I set off on the first leg of the expedition to Land's End, which involved a five-hour train journey from Paddington to Penzance followed by an hour-and-a-half bus ride to Land's End itself. Apart from being either the start or finishing point for 'end-to-end' journeys, Land's End has little to commend it. The 115 acres of rock and heathland at the south-west extremity of the British mainland was owned by a Cornish family until 1982 when it was sold to a Welsh property developer. Five years later, property magnate and entrepreneur Peter de Savary outbid the National Trust to purchase the site for almost £7 million. He turned it into a King Arthur theme park, expanded the onsite hotel and added other tacky extras. The present owners, Heritage Great Britain, which also own John o' Groats, the top of Snowdon in Wales, and The Needles Landmark attraction in the Isle of Wight, acquired the site in 1996 following the collapse of de Savary's business empire. I had booked to stay on the complex at The Land's End Hotel that night and following the long and uneventful journey, eventually arrived around 5.00pm, fortunately after most of the day's tourists had left.

That evening, I sat in the hotel bar watching the sun set beyond The Longships, a small group of rocky islets about a mile offshore, and pondered on the route ahead. For the first couple of weeks I'd be following the popular South West Coast Path which, at 630 miles, is England's longest waymarked long-distance footpath and a National Trail. It runs from Minehead in Somerset to Poole Harbour in Dorset, and I'd be walking the section along the rugged coastline of North Devon and Cornwall, in the opposite direction, the 167 miles as far as Barnstaple.

I would have preferred a much earlier start on Weds 19th, but keen to get an official photo at the iconic signpost and having to wait for the photographer to turn up, it was gone 10.00am before I set off with 'The Beast' strapped to my back, under a warm sun and clear blue sky. The hotel receptionist had stamped my journey verification sheet, a key element of proof of completing the challenge, and I'd considered some kind of ceremony to mark the start of my expedition. Being unable to come up with anything, and thinking back to my coast-to-coast trek, I picked up a small piece of stone from the 200-foot-high granite cliffs that rise out of the Atlantic Ocean to carry with me to hurl into the North Sea when, or if, I reached my destination.

The coast path was stunning with wonderful views at every turn. I picked up a sandwich at Sennen Cove and stopped for lunch up on the cliffs just before Cape Cornwall. It quickly became apparent that I had, perhaps, overestimated my abilities regarding my walking schedule, particularly with such a heavy backpack, and I struggled to reach the first night's destination at Zennor, some 16 miles from Land's End.

Ready for the off!

A mild and balmy dusk was ending a glorious spring day when I eventually arrived in the picturesque village, which writer and poet D.H. Lawrence once described as "a most beautiful place: a tiny granite village nestling under high, shaggy moor-hills with a big sweep of lovely sea beyond". I had an early introduction to the delights of wild camping when I discovered that the independent hostel and campsite mentioned in the guidebook no longer existed. Jon, the bar manager at the 13th century Tinners Arms, put in a call to a local dairy farmer's wife and a 'pitch' in the corner of her field was thankfully arranged. Having set up camp, I returned to the pub for a mackerel pâté compote and salad dinner washed down with a couple of pints of *Harbourside* beer. Then it was back to camp and bed by 9.30pm.

They do say you only get what you pay for, and good quality outdoor gear certainly can cost. My Osprey Xenith rucksack had set me back over £200 and that's not including the rain cover you need to be sure of keeping the water out. The tent had been my biggest indulgence at around £400 but the Hilleberg Akto had come highly recommended and combined with my Quantum 200 XXL sleeping bag and Therm-a-Rest self-inflating camping mat, I'd considered it worth the investment. Adhering to the well-known outdoor equipment adage "nothing new on the day", everything had been tried and tested over the past few weeks with the exception of my bright orange plastic 'poop' spade with which I could not honestly see much potential for malfunction.

It had been many years since I'd spent a night under

canvas, so to speak, with nothing but a few microns of nylon between me and the chill night air, and I was up at 5.00 the next morning following a restless night. After a cup of tea and a bowl of muesli, I set off along the coast path soon after 7.00am. The early morning haze soon melted away under the glorious sunshine, revealing stunning views in all directions. The wild and adventurous trail, which has inspired writers and painters for hundreds of years, led me round to St Ives, the first seaside resort of the walk, where I enjoyed a sandwich and a piece of seaweed and cider salami for lunch. During the afternoon, the route took me by the Grade I listed medieval St. Uny's Church in Lelant and I popped in for a bit of divine guidance and to offer up a prayer for the mental and physical strength to complete my journey.

Flagging in the heat of the afternoon, I realised that I wasn't going to reach my intended destination of Gwithian that day and decided to detour to a campsite near Phillack. The Beachside Holiday Park lay on the edge of the fabulous St Ives Bay, set amidst sand dunes behind what must be one of the country's finest golden sandy beaches. There were excellent wash facilities but, unfortunately, their bar and restaurant were not open that early in the season. After a refreshing shower I settled down in my tent with a cuppa and an All Day Breakfast ration pack for dinner.

After the fine weather of the previous day, it was another chilly night and I awoke at 4.30am on Day 3 to find that a sea mist had enveloped the campsite. I set off along the deserted beach a couple of hours later and by mid-morning, realising that I clearly hadn't learned the lesson of 'selective packing', I made the decision to send some of my gear home and source a lighter sleeping bag. A couple I met up on the cliffs recommended Penrose, an outdoors shop in Truro, pointing out that I could get a bus there from Portreath, only a few miles further on. So, having first called in at the village bakery for a couple of their celebrated pasties, I hopped on a bus to Truro.

Penrose Outdoors was situated conveniently close to the bus station and after selling me a lighter sleeping bag at a discounted price, Adam, the helpful assistant, allowed me use of the shop floor to spread out and sort through my gear, even giving me a box to load the surplus into. After a couple of hours and a visit to the post office, I was on the bus back to Portreath about 15 lb lighter. I was rather touched when I received a message from Adam towards the end of the year telling me that he'd been inspired by my quest. He planned to undertake his own journey and I readily agreed to his request to contact me if he needed any help with his planning.

My map had indicated the existence of a campsite just outside Portreath and on the journey back, having failed to get onto the website, I rang my wife who contacted them to secure not only a late booking but a free pitch as it was a charity walk. Mark, the bus driver, kindly let me off near the site and at 8.00pm having pitched camp I settled down to enjoy a cup of tea and one of the pasties I'd wisely saved from lunchtime. As I lay in my tent a couple of emails popped up informing me that donations had been made to my *JustGiving* page. I'd given a fair bit of thought to how I might handle donations along the way. A small amount of cash would not be an issue but hanging collecting pots off my backpack wouldn't be practical given the distance and the nature of the terrain and would add considerably to the weight I'd be carrying. I'd decided to have a few hundred small 'business cards' made up to promote the enterprise and give details of how people could donate online, and they had evidently started working.

I set off again the next morning at around 7.00. The weather was more overcast but perfect for walking. Before joining the coast path, I swung into the village shop in Porthtowan to pick up some supplies for lunch, then it was back up onto the cliffs. I hiked with enthusiasm and renewed vigour, buoyed by the fresh sea air and a lightened load. Although I was still carrying around 55 lb, it was manageable.

Despite the wonderful weather, I hadn't really seen many people on the trail so far, and those I had encountered had generally been following the SWCP in the opposite direction. Just before St. Agnes, I met Keith from Scotland. He'd set off from Plymouth 18 days before on a whim and just kept walking! I had a brief coffee stop in St. Agnes with him before heading on to Perranporth where I stopped for lunch, enjoying my sandwich and a takeaway tea on the beach. The path here shows much evidence of the area's rich tin and tungsten mining history, the cliff face displaying the vivid colours characteristic of metal ores, including green streaks of copper sulphate.

By its very nature, the South West Coast Path is rugged and in places can be quite treacherous. In a momentary lapse of concentration, gazing at the view, I stumbled on a particularly rocky section of path and fell heavily. With the weight of my pack, I struggled to get back onto my feet – if I'd still been carrying my original load, I'm not sure I'd have gotten up at all! Fortunately, I wasn't badly injured and apart from my wounded pride – I'd managed to time my faux pas just as a couple were approaching from the opposite direction – and a bruised thumb, which was rather uncomfortable for the next week or so, no harm was done.

I arrived in Holywell around 4.30pm and decided to stop for the day. After enjoying a couple of pints of *Doom Bar* I strolled on to Holywell Bay Caravan Park where I managed to get a 25% discount on a night's pitch. After putting up my tent, and with the sun still shining, I washed out a few items of clothing and hung them out to dry while I headed off to The Tresuth, a local 13th century pub, for a steak burger and chips washed down with a pint of *Tribute* and *Doom Bar.*

Day 5 dawned on another crisp and bright morning and I was on my way soon after 7.00am. The first part of my walk today took me along the beach and through the dunes beyond Holywell Bay before crossing the footbridge over The Gannel, a tidal estuary that separates Crantock village from the major holiday resort of Newquay. Having no need or desire to sample its delights, I managed to bypass the town, partly along the wide, sandy beach, as far as Watergate Bay where I stopped for lunch.

From here it was only a couple of miles to Mawgan Porth which I reached around mid-afternoon, and despite being a short day, both in terms of time and mileage, I was drawn by the lure of a cool pint of *Tribute* in The Merrymoor Inn. From there, it was a short stroll to The Magic Cove Touring Park, a small but excellent site where Brian, the owner, let me pitch for free. I had a refreshing shower in the first-class facilities, and later in the evening wandered back to The Merrymoor Inn for a substantial Sunday carvery roast and a couple more pints of *Tribute.* Suitably fed and watered, I ambled back to camp to check out my route for the next day.

Thankfully the weather forecast, which had predicted cooler, more overcast conditions, proved spot on and the next morning I set off early in what I considered perfect walking conditions. My destination today was Wadebridge, some 17 miles away. The coastal path scenery was again wonderful, and as I had finally acclimatised to my hefty backpack, not too strenuous. The air was full of the jangling, keys-like calls of the corn bunting, as I rounded Park Head, before dropping down to the small village of Porthcothan. Here I picked up lunch for later from the Bay Stores and had a coffee break.

The trail would leave the SWCP at a couple of points today. The first departure, cutting out the wide sweep around Trevose Head, came at Constantine Bay where field paths led me to Harlyn. From here it was back on the coast path to Trevone where I stopped for a granary bap cheese ploughman's and Chough Bakery fudge flapjack lunch, all washed down with a tepid can of ginger beer.

After lunch, I cut across inland to arrive at the popular town of Padstow on the River Camel estuary, at the mouth of which lies the treacherous Doom Bar sandbank, the inspiration for one of my favourite amber ales of the same name. I thought it rather too early for a beer, so instead I treated myself to an ice cream by the picturesque harbour, before joining the Camel Trail. This 5-mile disused railway line took me along the River Camel estuary. Although, at times, a rather monotonous trudge compared to my walk thus far, it was easy underfoot, gave great views of the estuary and brought me right into the heart of Wadebridge, the first proper town on the route since Newquay.

A mile or so beyond the town centre and at the top of a steep hill, I arrived at the Little Bodieve Holiday Park, paying £4 for a pitch for the night. There were no refreshment facilities onsite, so I was forced back down the road to The Ship Inn, where I ordered a burger and chips with Bakewell tart and clotted cream to follow, accompanied by a couple of pints of *Two Tides* bitter. While I was enjoying my dinner, the first light rain of the trip fell, with more forecast for the next day.

After a windy though dry night, I broke camp and set off at 6.45 intent on reaching Boscastle, around 19 miles away. The first 6 miles took me north, inland, along wooded paths, through meadows and across a line of hills to the quaint and typically Cornish fishing village of Port Isaac, the location for TV series *Doc Martin.* After a mid-morning coffee break, I headed for the Pasty Shop. The girls serving were extremely interested in my charity walk and by way of a donation they returned the £5 I'd paid for my large steak & Stilton pasty and can of pop.

Now back on the coast path the views were magnificent, with the vibrant colours of the yellow gorse harmonising beautifully with the deep blue of the ocean beyond and the paler blue of the sky above. I could have spent all afternoon drinking in the vista, and as the day wore on I realised that reaching Boscastle was probably a bit ambitious, particularly having to negotiate a series of steep ascents and descents to cross streams, the last one by Jacket's Point being the most severe. On reaching Trebarwith Strand, I swung into The Port William Inn for a refreshing pint of iced Coke and after consulting my map, decided on a change of plan and headed for the youth hostel at Tintagel. Surprisingly, I'd waited until my 60th year to sample the delights of youth hostels, and having joined the YHA earlier in the year, I was keen to try them out.

The youth hostel sits right on the SWCP on the cliffs above the village of Tintagel and appeared like an oasis in the desert late in the afternoon. Fortunately, they had vacancies and I booked into a dormitory with three other guys. Here I met Dave, a retired warrant officer, late of the 7th Para Royal Horse Artillery. He was an experienced 'thru-hiker' who had walked the Appalachian Trail and Pacific Crest Trail in the United States, as well as the Camino de Santiago in France and Spain. He was currently working his way round the whole of the South West Coast Path.

As the youth hostel was self-catering only, Dave and I decided to take a stroll down to the village for a fish and chips supper. We only just made it before the chippy closed at 8.00pm but were rewarded with a delicious meal of cod and chips washed down with a couple of cans of cloudy lemonade. It brought back fond memories of my visit to the 'Coast To Coast' chip shop in Kirkby Stephen on my

C2C adventure two years before.

Dave was a real 'weight geek', carrying ultralight cooking equipment and even lightening his load by cutting his toothbrush in half and removing unused straps and flaps from his backpack. He kindly gave me a small water filter and suggested I top up from the many streams along the route, thereby halving the amount of water I had been carrying. On the basis that a litre of water weighs approximately 2 lb – and in the warm weather I'd been setting off each day with 4 litres – this amounted to a considerable weight saving.

Back in the youth hostel dorm, we chatted until past 11.00pm before lights out. As I lay in my bunk, I reflected on the fact that I'd now been walking for 7 days and covered 100 miles. My planned schedule had very quickly gone adrift but, as German military strategist Helmuth von Moltke sagely noted, "No battle plan survives contact with the enemy". When your plan meets the real world, the real world wins.

After a bit of a lie-in and a bowl of muesli for breakfast, it was 9.00am before I bade farewell to Dave and the others and hit the trail on another beautifully sunny day. A short walk round from the youth hostel I got my first view of the ruins of Tintagel Castle, a medieval fortification perched on the fringe of The Island at Tintagel Head. The castle is the legendary birthplace of King Arthur, and while there is little real evidence to support the Arthurian claim, the site has at least 2,000 years of history behind it.

Around mid-morning, I descended to Boscastle Harbour, described by Elihu Burritt, the founding father of Land's

End to John o' Groats walks, as "one of the neatest, most romantic little harbours in the world". I picked up the inevitable pasty for lunch and enjoyed a coffee break in The Harbour Light Tea Garden. The tearoom had a wonderfully 'olde worlde' charm and atmosphere about it, and I was surprised to discover that the building was less than ten years old. The original 16th-century structure was faithfully re-created in 2006 having been destroyed in the wake of flash floods in August 2004, later described by the Environment Agency as being among the most extreme ever recorded in Britain.

I stopped for lunch shortly after on a clifftop bench. The air was sweet and fresh, and down below the cliffs the sea battered the rocks in an impressively tempestuous way. As I sat, with my boots and socks off, soaking up the glorious sunshine and enjoying the wonderful view, I couldn't help but spare a thought for all those poor souls eating their lunches staring at blank walls in busy workplaces back in London. I was reminded of Kenneth Grahame's observation in *The Wind in the Willows,* that "...the best part of a holiday is perhaps not so much to be resting yourself, as to see all the other fellows busy working".

Despite it being midweek, the fine weather had brought out a lot more walkers, and throughout the afternoon I chatted to several people on the trail, including James and Claire, a young couple from Preston in Lancashire. As we walked, I disturbed a sizeable adder which had been basking in the sunshine on the path just ahead of us. Thankfully, it took no great offence to this interruption and slithered off into the trackside gorse.

Ruined mine buildings and secluded coves on the wild and dramatic South West Coast Path.

I ran out of steam around 5.00pm and booked into the Coombe Barton Inn at Crackington Haven for the night, negotiating a 20% discount for being a senior citizen on a mission. My room had a bathtub and I had a relaxing soak while washing out my sweat-infused underwear and shirt. Refreshed, I donned my SSAFA 'tech tee' and settled down in the bar, ordering a smoked mackerel salad for dinner, accompanied by pints of *Tribute, Harbour Special* (from Tintagel Brewery) and *Golden Hare* (a Bath Ales pale ale). After dinner, I updated my journal and checked out the route for the next day, alternately studying the map and appreciating the stunning sunset through the bar window. Before heading off to bed, I chatted with a holidaying couple who, after hearing about my walk, kindly donated £5 to the charity.

Day 9 was another fine day and I set off at 9.00am after my first full English breakfast of the trip. From Crackington Haven – a rocky cove popular with geology students – the path followed a tough series of valleys and headlands before shifting onto a wooded slope at Dizzard Point. Around lunchtime, I dropped down into Widemouth Bay and stopped off at a café for a pasty, conscious of the fact that this would be one of the last opportunities for a genuine Cornish pasty, as tomorrow I would be in Devon.

The approach to Bude, after lunch, was along a pretty dreary stretch of coastline. Gone were the dramatic high cliffs that had dominated the route thus far, and even the sand changed colour to a rather dirty brown. The weather had become overcast with a suspicion of light rain as I arrived at the holiday resort around 3.30pm, so my first port of call was a beachside café where I had a refreshing cuppa and made enquiries about a campsite for the night.

The café owner recommended the Bude Holiday Park, situated just outside town, but on arrival I discovered that their 'touring' section hadn't yet opened for the season. I was forced inland for another couple of miles to the Wooda Farm Holiday Park at Poughill, ringing ahead en route as I wasn't expecting to arrive before 6.00pm. This well-appointed site gave me a 50% discount, so I pitched camp for the night for a very reasonable £7. The weather deteriorated somewhat while I was setting up my tent, becoming very overcast and, with a keen wind, rather chilly, so I was pleased to get into the onsite bar and grill for a plate of ham, egg and chips and a couple of pints of *Tribute* before bed. Tomorrow would be a tough day.

The section of the SWCP between Bude, Hartland Point and Clovelly is one of the most strenuous stretches on the whole end-to-end trail, with a lot more climbing (about 7,800 feet) than any other day. The coastline here is remote with few amenities so I had decided to split this stage into two days, taking a break at the Elmscott Youth Hostel.

It was overcast but dry as I set off on the 11-mile stretch to Elmscott. I stopped for a light lunch at The Bush Inn, a wonderful 13th-century free house just inland at Morwenstow. The coast here is steeped in a history dominated by Parson Hawker, who was vicar at Morwenstow for 40 years until his death in 1875 and was perhaps the most memorable of 19th-century West Country clergymen. A Romantic poet, and professional eccentric, The Reverend Robert Stephen Hawker was a diverse, free character quite unfettered by Victorian social attitudes. He built a little hut on the cliff using timbers washed up from shipwrecks and there he would sit composing his poetry, smoking opium and, during stormy weather, scouring the waters for ships in distress. The hut can still be visited and is, I believe, the smallest property belonging to the National Trust.

Leaving the village on the footpath back to the clifftop, I passed the beautiful Grade I listed Norman parish church and, shortly after, crossed the stream at Marsland Mouth, which signalled my departure from Cornwall and arrival in Devon. I reached the youth hostel around 5.30pm and was billeted in a dorm with Richard. One of the great things about hostels is the colourful characters you tend to meet and Richard was certainly that. This 70-year-old 'free spirit' seemed to spend all his time travelling – at home and abroad. He stayed in hostels and cheap hotels and once, apparently, spent three months wild camping in a wood on the outskirts of Swansea. He claimed to be writing a book and his aim was to move to his beloved South America, specifically Brazil. Another guest was a Dutch lady called Remmy. She was staying at the hostel for two weeks whilst working as a supporting artist on a film being shot locally. We chatted whilst I ate my dinner of canned sausage, beans and meatballs – purchased in the hostel shop – but by 8.30pm the exertions of the day had finally caught up with me and I turned in for the night.

Remmy took a great interest in my epic walk and before I set off the next morning, under a clear blue sky bound for the classic 'chocolate box' fishing village of Clovelly, we swapped contact details so she could follow my progress. She had been very tight-lipped about the film she was working on, as they had all been sworn to secrecy, revealing only that it was a period drama, but a short distance out of Elmscott, I wandered through the set of *The Guernsey Literary and Potato Peel Pie Society,* a film based on the international bestselling novel by Mary Ann Shaffer and Annie Barrows. The story is set on Guernsey island during the German occupation in World War II and I was reliably informed that it would feature several *Downton Abbey* stars, including Lily James, Penelope Wilton and Matthew Goode, though I can't say I recognised anyone on set.

The path from Hartland Quay to Hartland Point is, to say the least, dramatic, with wild cliff scenery and strenuous walking. A spectacular waterfall shot across Speke's Mill Mouth, a mile south from Hartland Quay, where Milford Water plummets 150 feet down to the wave-scoured beach below. Hartland Point itself is a headland of savage cliffs with a lighthouse perched precariously on the end, from which flat-topped Lundy Island was clearly in view out in the Bristol Channel. As I rounded the point, I immediately happened upon a wonderful little café operating out of a wooden hut. I enjoyed a very welcome mug of hot chocolate and purchased a ham and cheese sandwich, a pasty, and a can of fizzy orange for my lunch later.

The terrain levelled out during the afternoon and included a delightful stretch of bluebell wood at Brownsham just before the picturesque, privately owned harbour village of Clovelly. I had intended to pitch camp in the Clovelly area, but as it was still quite early, I decided to press on for a couple of hours, aiming instead for a campsite at Steart Farm, just inland from the charming hamlet of Bucks Mills. Devoid of both pub and shop, this pretty retreat seemed immune from the trappings of the 21st century but was an ideal location for anyone wishing to explore the beautiful coastal scenery and lush green woodland that surrounded it. Its history dates back to the days of the Spanish Armada when survivors of a shipwrecked Spanish galleon took refuge and settled here. It is said that local women married the survivors and together they formed a close community self-sufficient from fishing, farming and lime-burning. The population was also said to be extremely hostile to newcomers, though, fortunately for me, they seemed to have mellowed over the years.

I happened to call at a house in the small settlement, to top up my water bottles, only to discover that the campsite I was aiming for no longer existed and the land was being developed for a new school. Julia, the houseowner, noted my disappointment and took pity on me, offering use of the summer house in her garden. The cabin was chock-a-block with boxes of household items being stored for her son, but it contained a sofa, electric kettle, a radio and even a toilet and shower. Julia threw in a couple of pillows and fresh milk for my morning tea and I was sorted for the night. I ate my simple supper, consisting of half a sandwich and the pasty saved from lunch, whilst listening to a discussion about the day's footballing prowess on the radio. Then, after a nice hot cuppa, I turned in. Heavy rain was forecast for about mid-morning the next day and I wanted to get an early start.

I don't sleep particularly well at the best of times, and I arose at 5.00am following another restless night. After a cup of tea and bowl of muesli, I set off, leaving a note for Julia thanking her for the use of the cabin. It was already heavily overcast at 6.45am as I climbed up through the woodland beyond Buck's Mills. The Devon coastline is noticeably different from Cornwall, being distinctly greener and more 'rolling' than its dramatic neighbour, but for all that, there were still a few strenuous ascents and descents, and on this Sunday morning, I had the coast path pretty much to myself. My planned destination today was a café at Fremington Quay, just before Barnstaple. I was looking forward to meeting up with friends who lived nearby, and tomorrow would be my first rest day.

The predicted rain, the first downpour of the trip, arrived late morning just as I hit the outskirts of Westward Ho! This unusual village name, complete with exclamation mark, comes from the title of Charles Kingsley's 1855 novel *Westward Ho!* It was set in nearby Bideford, where my route now headed, and was such a bestseller that entrepreneurs saw the opportunity to develop tourism in the area. A perhaps less-known fact about Westward Ho! was the part it played in the downfall of what had to be the craziest, most explosively unsuccessful invention of World War II.

War has a long history of sparking and accelerating invention and when the War Office wanted something which could be used to breach the massive concrete coastal defences as the troops stormed ashore on D-Day, the Directorate of Miscellaneous Weapon Development, known affectionately as the 'Wheezers and Dodgers', came up with the Great Panjandrum. The name derived from a reference to a character in a nonsensical piece of 18th century prose, and the project leader was aeronautical engineer and novelist Nevil Shute. The device consisted of two wooden wheels, 10 feet in diameter, joined by a central drum. It was propelled by sets of rockets attached to each wheel like giant Catherine wheels, and it was intended to carry 4,000 pounds of high explosive at 60mph up the beach and through Field Marshal Rommel's defences. Unfortunately, the device was found to be very unstable, and the final trial on the beach at Westward Ho! in January 1944 ended with a dog chasing an errant rocket and the cameraman and assorted admirals and generals running for their lives. Unsurprisingly, the project was scrapped over safety concerns and the Panjandrum never saw battle. It has since been suggested that the entire project was a hoax devised as part of 'Operation Fortitude' to convince the Germans that plans were being developed to invade more heavily fortified defences surrounding the Pas-de-Calais, rather than the Normandy coastline. Given the almost farcical nature of the device and the fact that it was initially tested in full view of the general public on a busy beach, perhaps there's some truth in that.

I had a coffee in the Pier House and by the time I set off again, it was clear that the rain had set in for the day. I'd been slow to don my waterproofs and had a rather soggy trudge to Pusehill where I stopped off at the Pig on The Hill pub. I'd only intended to have a Coke and sort out my wet gear, but the pub was warm and dry and I succumbed to the temptation of a pint or two of *Old Pig* bitter, convincing myself that, as it was Sunday, I was entitled to a half-day.

I made a call to friends Kevin and Sue who drove over to collect me, bringing with them my first resupply box containing the next section's maps, food and sundry items. Sue was a most attentive host and whenever my wife and I came to visit, she could never do enough for us. I knew she'd want to spoil me on my flying visit but had, sadly, been undergoing cancer treatment and wasn't in the best of health. I hadn't wanted to impose upon them and consequently, after catching up on their news over another pint of *Old Pig*, they dropped me off at the Barnstaple Travelodge, which would be my accommodation for the next couple of nights. Here I was able to have a long, relaxing soak in the bath and wash out a few items of clothing, before rejoining my friends for an excellent meal of ham, egg, chips, and *Tribute* ale in a lovely old pub in Newton Barton.

Heavy rain overnight had, thankfully, subsided by the morning and my first job of the day was to locate a pharmacy. For about the last week, I'd been experiencing extreme soreness on a sensitive part of my anatomy, presumably caused by sweat. To put it mildly, it felt like I was urinating razor blades! Fortunately, there was a supermarket just around the corner from the Travelodge and after a brief consultation with the pharmacist I was smearing on the first application of Canesten hydrocortisone cream. It was a couple of weeks before the problem cleared up, though.

Kevin and Sue picked me up around 11.00am and after a pleasant pub lunch, I had a relaxing afternoon in their beautiful garden helping Kevin prepare his raised beds and sow his vegetable seeds. It reminded me of how neglected my own garden would be this year whilst I was away. Later in the day after a tasty bacon sarnie and Chelsea bun tea, I was dropped back at my hotel.

After the squally rain on Sunday night and the early hours of Monday morning, it was encouraging to awake on Day 14 to a fine dry day and the prospect of good weather for the week ahead. I'd broken off earlier than planned on Sunday so today I needed to complete the last stretch of this section, from Pusehill to Barnstaple. Kevin kindly picked me up at 7.45am on the way into his office, and dropped me back at the Pig on The Hill pub.

My 12-mile route today took me across rather damp farmland to Bideford – rather than following the wide sweep of the coast path around the River Torridge estuary – then by way of the SWCP and Tarka Trail back to Barnstaple. The weather was superb and the walking was all on the level for a change. I stopped off in the lovely little seaside village of Instow for a coffee late in the morning and enjoyed an excellent ham and cheese baguette at Fremington Quay at lunchtime. By 2.30pm, I was back at the Travelodge, having picked up my lunch for the next day, and relaxing with a cuppa in my hotel room I reflected on the first part of my journey.

I'd now completed Section One – after fourteen days and 166 miles. Tomorrow, I'd be leaving the South West Coast Path, the route now heading inland for the hills, rather than taking the long detour round the North Devon coast to Minehead. I'd been treated to some wonderful weather and, whilst certainly being challenging in places, I can't imagine that any other stretch of British coastline compares for scenic splendour, interest and history. It had been an absolutely wonderful start to my end-to-end adventure.

Chapter Seven

My navigational skills had never really been tested in the field. For the past two weeks I'd enjoyed straightforward wayfinding – after all, how hard *is* it to follow a coastal path? Providing I kept the sea on the left, I couldn't go far wrong. For the next week or so I'd be following my Ordnance Survey maps and the strip maps in my 'End to End' guidebook and, even though I was also equipped with a good quality GPS and compass, I was still a little nervous about navigation.

I set off from the Barnstaple Travelodge at 5.30am on Wednesday 3rd May on a route that ascended steadily out of the town. Once beyond the suburb of Pilton, I found myself on forestry tracks and muddy paths lined with swathes of aromatic wild garlic, as I skirted the woodland above the River Yeo. At Loxhore Mill Bridge, I stopped briefly to chat to the owner of a wonderful little cottage, who asked me if I was going to John o' Groats. When I expressed surprise at his perceptive question, he cast a wary eye over my enormous backpack and simply said, "Well, the path's on the route to John o' Groats and you look like you're going all the way!"

A little further on, I passed through the uninspiring

village of Bratton Fleming, whose main claim to fame is that P. G. Wodehouse's uncle was rector here for nearly 40 years and the author used to spend his school holidays there. Having fortified myself with a steak and ale pie from the village shop, I continued along minor roads up to the village of Challacombe, where I managed to purchase a can of ginger beer and get my journey verification sheet stamped just before the post office closed at 2.00pm.

Although I'd only covered about 14 miles that day, I'd set off pretty early and a lot of the walk had been uphill. Consequently, by mid-afternoon I was running out of steam. I decided to pitch camp on a reasonably flat, if rather breezy, piece of moorland known as South Regis Common which lay just beyond Challacombe. A cup of tea and an All Day Breakfast ration pack hit the spot and shortly after I settled down for an early night.

I broke camp and headed off at 7.00am the next day, on a dry but overcast morning. My route today would be entirely in the Exmoor National Park, following the Tarka Trail and Macmillan Way West. The first objective was to replenish my water supply at Warren Farm, which was situated in a particularly isolated location, at nearly 1,313 feet elevation in the middle of the hills. I stopped for an early lunch in an old farm outbuilding, partaking of an unheated ration pack and an apple, due to the absence of any local shops.

The route continued east across the high moors, over Almsworthy Common to Exford Common and it was here that I experienced my first real navigational malfunction. Whether it was due to confusion brought on by dehydration, fatigue or simply stupidity, I don't know, but I found myself on a very indistinct track, unable to determine not only my current position, but also even what direction I was travelling in. For what seemed like an age, I stumbled around in tussocky grass and knee-deep bog, filled with mild disquiet and that slightly uneasy feeling you get when you realise you're swimming too far from shore. Eventually, with the aid of my trusty GPS, I managed to reorientate myself, but for a while minor panic had set in and it was easy to see how, without the benefit of map or compass, people get completely lost on these open and sparsely populated moors.

By 5.00pm I'd been on the go for nearly ten hours and after the stress of my earlier navigational error, I decided to call it a day and set about looking for a suitable spot to pitch camp. A long, narrow field offered moderately flat grassland and after putting up my tent, I enjoyed another All Day Breakfast washed down with a mug of hot chocolate. As I brought my journal up to date, alternating between scribbling notes and taking in the extensive view in the late-afternoon sunshine, I pondered on the day's events and hoped that my wayfinding would improve tomorrow!

Rising to 1,705 feet, the sandstone hill of Dunkery Beacon was the highest point on the Trail before the Black Mountains in Wales, and I'd purposely stopped just short of it to make the ascent refreshed early next morning and enjoy the panoramic views undisturbed. This, as it turned out, was a mistake. The fine, clear weather of the previous evening had been replaced with a stiff breeze and a thick blanket of mist. Views there were none!

Today, I would leave Exmoor and enter Somerset, initially by woodland paths and then by reasonably well signposted and beaten tracks such as the Coleridge Way. Around lunchtime, I arrived in the parish of Luxborough which is split between two villages – Churchtown, which has the church, and Kingsbridge, which got the pub. In the toss-up between spiritual guidance and a beer, the beer won and I headed to the Royal Oak for a steak baguette and a pint of *Exmoor Ale*. The only other person in the bar was fascinated by tales of my walk and kindly donated £5 for the charity.

After a couple of nights' wild camping, and with my resolve weakened by the midday beverages, I decided to have an early day and treat myself to a B&B. So, after lunch, I set off on a short 5-mile trek, climbing out of the Washford Valley before descending through Langridge Wood to the Washford River and on, by way of a quiet road, to the village of Roadwater. I arrived at around 2.30pm to find that the pub, The Valiant Soldier, had just closed for the afternoon and wouldn't reopen until 6.00pm. I headed off up the road to the community shop and post office, where I bought a couple of cans of pop and got another stamp on my verification sheet.

Sitting on a bench outside the shop, I swigged ginger beer and pondered my next move. I'd fancied the pub but didn't know for sure whether they'd have any accommodation available. My map indicated the location of a YHA Camping Barn at Wood Advent Farm about a mile off-route up a very steep minor road, and not wanting to hang around waiting for the pub to open, I headed off in search of it. I discovered the camping barn had long gone and, although the farm did cater for B&B, it appeared to be of a very 'upmarket' – and consequently expensive – variety. In any event, there didn't seem to be anyone around and despite circling the building a number of times and ringing on the front doorbell, I succeeded only in arousing the suspicions of a couple of rather large and energetic dogs. Discretion being the better part of valour, I decided to call it a day.

I trudged dejectedly back down the road to the village where, unable to find anyone who knew of the existence of alternative accommodation, I sat for an hour and a half waiting for The Valiant Soldier to reopen. Thankfully, they had a room available at a very reasonably priced £35. After having a much-needed shower, washing out a few items of clothing and putting various electrical devices on charge, I repaired to the bar where I ordered a pint of *Exmoor Ale* and a gut-busting 20 oz mixed grill. As it arrived at my table, I wondered for a moment whether the barman had mistaken me for a gang of hungry navvies, but I greedily tucked into the delicious provender and afterwards sat slumped with another pint of *Exmoor Ale* and a happily distended stomach.

The downside to staying in pubs is that, short of skipping breakfast, you can't always get on the road as early as you'd like. People running pubs tend not to get early nights, so can't really be expected to be up early in the morning just because I want to set off at 'sparrow's fart'. The earliest I could get breakfast on day 18 was 8.00am, so it was nearly 9.00am before I set off in dry, overcast, ideal walking conditions.

Following another visit to the Roadwater community shop for supplies, I set off along a minor road and through a patch of woodland on the first of the day's ascents. After crossing a hill my descent brought me into a secluded valley and down to Nettlecombe Court. This Elizabethan country mansion is now a field centre but was once a seat of the Raleigh family, their spiritual needs catered for by their own private church. The grounds are a marvellous blend of heritage parkland and ancient woodland, and the centre is used by field scientists wishing to study the surrounding natural environment considered to be the best example of this type of ecosystem remaining in England.

Shortly after, I passed through the village of Monksilver, leaving Exmoor National Park in the process. The village had no shop and its only pub was closed for renovation work, but it did have an old red telephone box which had been converted to a 'book exchange' – interesting use of an instantly recognised feature of the British landscape.

Two and a bit miles beyond Monksilver, I crossed the West Somerset Railway, the longest standard-gauge independent heritage line in Britain, which runs for around 20 miles through prime Somerset countryside from Bishops Lydeard to Minehead. It would have been wonderful to have timed my crossing with the arrival of a steam train, particularly with the distant Quantock Hills for a backdrop, but sadly it wasn't to be. I arrived in the pretty village of Bicknoller around lunchtime and, although I'd already bought my lunch in Roadwater, I was tempted by the tasty-looking chicken, ham, and pork pie I spotted in the small village shop.

Fed and watered, I felt ready to tackle the steep climb which led to the main ridge of the Quantocks, a compact group of moorland hills running north-west to south-east for about 12 miles from the coast near Watchet. From the highest point, at Wills Neck, the route brought me down to the small hamlet of Enmore just over 3 miles short of the sizeable town of Bridgwater. Late in the afternoon I stopped off at the Tynte Arms to weigh up my options for the night over a pint of *Exmoor Fox* and a packet of salted peanuts. Being unable to secure accommodation in the pub, I decided to 'wild camp' in the vicinity and hopped over a fence to pitch camp in a sheltered roadside copse by the side of a small stream.

I'd now covered around 225 miles and was finding my new '3-month' schedule – averaging around 15 miles per day – much more manageable. Also, now it was early May, the nights were noticeably warmer, particularly when camping out.

I set off at 7.45 the next morning, after a cup of tea and bowl of muesli, on a bright, sunny day. The first leg of the route would take me right through the middle of the large market town of Bridgwater – not particularly inspiring – but on this quiet Sunday morning I was thankfully through, out the other side, and over the M5 motorway by 10.00am, including a stop-off at a local convenience store to pick up a sandwich for later.

Most of the day's walking would be across vertically challenged terrain sitting only just above sea level on an area known as the Somerset Levels. This is land that was originally salt marsh and historically has frequently flooded. Indeed, the name Somerset is thought to derive from *Seo-mere-saetan,* meaning "settlers by the sea lakes". Drainage work in the area started at least 1,500 years ago, much of it done by the monks of Glastonbury. Although there are still floods occasionally, the Levels are now drained by a criss-cross pattern of straight ditches and wider rivers, with pumping stations at intervals. In recent years, a halt has been called to further drainage to try to retain the traditional character of the Levels, which depend on seasonal freshwater flooding and the area will now be allowed to continue to flood regularly, as it has done for hundreds of years.

It was another warm day and before I headed across the Levels, I paid a visit to the Red Tile Inn at Cossington for an iced Coke and roast beef sandwich. Mac, the landlord, worked as a part-time volunteer for SSAFA so was very interested in my venture and promised to spread the word.

Given the nature of the terrain, there are few public footpaths on the Somerset Levels, so my route, in the warm afternoon sunshine, followed good farm tracks and quiet minor roads. It was on one of these that I happened upon a farmer moving his entire herd of cattle between fields and in order to avoid a stampede he strongly advised me to stand very still by the roadside whilst around 200 cattle trotted past, eying me suspiciously.

Late in the afternoon, I decided to head for the wonderfully named Splott Farm, where a campsite was indicated on my map. The site was basic but had good shower facilities and at £5.50 was very reasonably priced. Having pitched camp and cleaned up, I took a stroll along to the Sexeys Arms in the village of Blackford, about a mile down the road, where I enjoyed a couple of pints of *Exmoor Ale* and probably the best ham, egg and chips I've ever eaten. The hike back to camp was a little wearisome and I was glad when I finally crawled into my tent and settled down in my sleeping bag for the night.

I'd struggled, at times, with wayfinding on what Andy Robinson describes as "invisible paths". Indeed, I recently read that almost 10% of paths in the 140,000-mile UK network were difficult or impossible to use, according to a survey by volunteer 'citizen surveyors'. Footpath signs and stiles hadn't always been particularly well-maintained and were often overgrown and easily missed. So today, I decided to keep to minor roads and tracks rather than the more obscure footpaths dictated by the main route. My target was Sandford about 17 miles away but my first objective was Cheddar with its famous gorge, and I plotted a route accordingly. I broke camp and set off from Splott Farm at 7.30am on another glorious day. I couldn't believe how lucky I'd been with the weather, having had only one wet day since I set off from Land's End three weeks before.

A pleasant stroll along quiet roads brought me to the village of Cheddar, known throughout the world as the birthplace of Cheddar cheese. It has been produced here since the 12th century and to this day is still stored in the Cheddar caves to mature. I didn't partake of any myself, but I did enjoy a late morning coffee in a small café at the foot of the gorge before starting the climb. Considered by many to be one of the most spectacular places in England, the vertical limestone cliffs on either side of the narrow gorge are nearly 400 feet high in places. It was a long, steep haul up the southern edge of this ravine which cuts deep into the edge of the Mendips, a range of hills stretching inland for about 25 miles from the Bristol Channel. It certainly wasn't as strenuous as I would have expected, though – my fitness levels were obviously improving – and I was rewarded with some stunning views back across Cheddar to the shimmering blue waters of the massive circular reservoir in the distance. With a capacity of 135 million gallons, this artificial lake was completed in 1937 and in addition to being designated as a Site of Special Scientific Interest due to its wintering waterfowl, it was the first British reservoir to permit sailing.

From the scrubland at the top of the gorge, I passed a number of points from which I was able to peer down into the very bottom of it before heading off through the wooded valleys of Black Rock and Long Wood nature reserves. A stiff climb brought me up onto the moorland and Beacon Batch, which at 1,066 feet, is the highest point on the Mendip Hills. From the summit of Beacon Batch I continued along the ridge before descending into North Somerset, and the small town of Sandford.

My route through the town took me past the Thatchers Cider Brewery and in the heat of the afternoon I was tempted into the Railway Inn, right next door, for a thirst-quenching pint of *Thatchers Haze*, a sparkling, cloudy, sweet cider.

Enquiring about accommodation in the area, I was directed to Sandford Cottage B&B, just over the road. Alison, the owner, showed me to, not just a room, but a whole cottage, for which she charged £25 for the night, returning £5 as a donation to SSAFA. I had a relaxing soak in the bath, where I was able to wash out some clothes, then I headed back over the road for a tasty, if pricey, fish and chips supper washed down with a further couple of pints of *Thatchers Haze*. Does it get any better? – the B&B, next door to the pub, which is next door to the brewery!

I set off the next morning, after a muesli breakfast, in dry, slightly overcast conditions on a 17-mile stretch that would bring me to the suburbs of Bristol – by far the largest urban area I would encounter on the entire trip. The area around Sandford is big cider country, and the route initially took me through the brewery grounds and an orchard. It then joined the Strawberry Line, a disused railway line which used to run from Yatton via Cheddar to Wells before the 'Beeching Axe' closed it in 1963. This section is now a footpath known as the Cheddar Valley Railway Walk and I followed it for 4 miles to the station at Yatton, where I treated myself to a coffee and bacon bap in the Strawberry Line Cafe.

After picking up some supplies in the local shop, I opted for a minor road route up towards Clevedon. Then turning north-east, I followed a low, wooded ridge which took me over the M5 motorway to a lunch stop at The Black Horse in Clapton-in-Gordano. Refreshed, after a pint of *Tribute* and a ploughman's lunch, I set off on the last few miles to my destination at Easton-in-Gordano.

The guidebook made reference to a pub and a B&B near the route. As it turned out, the pub didn't open until 5.00pm and the B&B, which had once sat right opposite, had been sold as a family home. Undaunted, I pitched camp under a tree on the fringe of a cricket pitch behind the pub and later enjoyed a couple of pints of *Doom Bar* in the garden, from where, in the wonderful evening sun, I could keep an eye on my tent.

The items bought for lunch served as dinner and by 7.30pm I was back in the tent updating my journal before lights out. Tomorrow would be a challenging day which would see me crossing the Bristol Channel to Chepstow in Wales, and the start of the Offa's Dyke Path. I'd been keen to walk the ODP since watching a film some years before called *Arthur's Dyke* – an amusing tale about a rather downtrodden housewife, wonderfully played by Pauline Quirke, who, despite being totally ill-prepared, is inspired to walk the path after watching a TV programme about it. I recalled the wonderful scenery and I was looking forward to getting back on a waymarked national trail.

10th May, Day 22 on the trail, was another fine and sunny day as I broke camp and set off at 7.00am on this 19-mile section of my journey. There would be three obstacles to overcome before arriving in Chepstow that evening. The first was the River Avon, the second, the industrial and suburban sprawl of Bristol, and the third, the Bristol Channel itself.

After a brief trek through a housing estate and along the cycle track of the M5 over the River Avon, the route took me up into woodland at Kings Weston Hill and the Blaise Castle 'folly', a miniature, Gothic-style castle, built by Thomas Farr in 1766, that historically played summer house to the Blaise Castle Estate. Dropping down into Henbury, I stopped for a coffee in the café in the castle museum parkland before discovering a hidden gem in the form of the Blaise Hamlet. These nine attractive 'Hansel and Gretel' cottages were built in 1811, and once housed pensioners from the Blaise Castle Estate. As I strolled across the small green around which the cottages are grouped, it was easy to imagine myself in a remote village somewhere rather than being almost in the shadow of a tower block on the outskirts of the major conurbation of Bristol.

Leaving the tranquillity of the Blaise Hamlet, I headed across the M5 and up Spaniorum Hill, which provided the last good viewpoint of the day. Around midday, I called in at The Fox in Easter Compton, for a tuna mayo sandwich and chips washed down with a couple of pints of iced Coke. My enormous backpack and dishevelled appearance again proved a good talking point and another £5 donation was received for the charity.

After lunch I headed off for Aust and the crossing to Chepstow. The weather had been beautifully sunny all day and by the time I reached Aust, I was in serious need of some liquid refreshment. I was tempted into The Boars Head pub where I enjoyed a pint of *Razor Back* from the Ringwood Brewery. Billed as "an exceptionally refreshing craft ale" it certainly hit the spot and I was soon striding along the pedestrian walkway of the M48 road bridge across the Severn Estuary with renewed vigour. It wasn't the most inspiring 45-minute stroll of the trip but as I'd read that it could be hard work in poor weather, I took comfort that at least the sun was shining.

View across to Cheddar reservoir from atop the gorge

'Hansel & Gretel' cottages at the Blaise Hamlet, Bristol

By the time I reached the end of the bridge, I had crossed a county boundary into Gloucestershire and then entered Monmouthshire in Wales as it crossed the River Wye. Once off the bridge I followed a route through housing estates to reach the centre of Chepstow. Here, I booked into the Beaufort Hotel getting a discount for my charity walk and the prospect of a good breakfast the next morning. I washed out some gear and took a refreshing shower, noting with surprised gratitude that my body had taken on a considerably slimmer profile. I then headed for the hotel bar where I sampled a pint of Butcombe *Rare Breed* and the ever popular *Doom Bar* whilst contemplating the fact that I'd now completed just under 300 miles of my journey and most of it in glorious sunshine.

Chapter Eight

Offa's Dyke was built by the powerful King of Mercia in the late-8th century to establish the western boundary of his kingdom. This great linear earthwork became the inspiration for a 170-mile National Trail, crossing the border country of England and Wales from Sedbury Cliffs in the south on the River Severn close to Chepstow, to Prestatyn near the estuary of the Dee on the north coast of Wales. My route would take me along about 80 miles of it as far as Knighton and after a hearty full English (or should I say Welsh?) breakfast, I set off at around 8.00am under light cloud and with a weather forecast which predicted the arrival of heavy rain later.

Leaving Chepstow by the old bridge, I followed a well-marked path up into the woodland above the Wye Valley, passing within sight of the beautifully preserved Chepstow Castle, dating from 1067 and believed to be the oldest surviving post-Roman stone fortification in Britain. Around mid-morning I glimpsed Tintern Abbey through the haze from high up at a spot known as the Devil's Pulpit, a 10-foot-high column of rock found just off the path. Legend has it that the Devil used this limestone outcrop to preach to the monks below, tempting them to desert their order. Deciding the abbey was worth a visit, I dropped down the steep track into the village of Tintern, stopping off for a coffee and a slice of cake at The Filling Station Café. They were obviously regularly visited by 'end-to-end' walkers and cyclists, and had a small board affixed to the top of their sign proclaiming John o' Groats 726 miles, in one direction, and Land's End, 245 miles in the other. The café proprietor expressed a great interest in my journey and insisted on taking my picture beneath her sign, promising to try to promote my charity on their Facebook page.

Duly refreshed I paid a flying visit to the abbey ruins. Tintern Abbey was founded by one Walter de Clare, Lord of Chepstow, on 9th May 1131 and was only the second Cistercian foundation in Britain (after Waverley Abbey) and the first in Wales. Falling into ruin after the Dissolution of the Monasteries in the 16th century, the remains have been celebrated in poetry and often painted by visitors, and the site welcomes some 70,000 people every year.

From Tintern, there were a couple of route options. One involved a hefty climb back up into the woodland above the valley, the other following the river, picking up the 'official' path further on. I decided on a riverside ramble and, leaving the Abbey, set off along the wide, slow-moving River Wye in the direction of Bigsweir Bridge where the trail rejoined the main Offa's Dyke path. An hour or so later I reached an important (but invisible) milestone – 300 miles walked and 25% of my journey completed!

The Offa's Dyke Path, and on this section more specifically the River Wye, forms the border between

England and Wales and for most of the day I'd been walking in Gloucestershire. On arrival at Redbrook, down a steep, bluebell-carpeted slope, I left Gloucestershire for good and re-entered Wales. This in itself warranted a minor celebration, so not needing any further excuse, I called in at The Boat Inn for a revitalising pint of cider and a packet of salted peanuts.

Setting off on the last 3-mile stretch to Monmouth – my destination for the night – a series of ascents led me to a National Trust property called The Kymin, a hill overlooking Monmouth, with its turreted Roundhouse and Naval Temple. Constructed between 1794 and 1800, the Roundhouse, with its commanding view of the town, was built by a group of local gentlemen to provide "security from the inclemency of the weather" during their weekly social gatherings. The Naval Temple was added in 1800 and bears the names of no less than 16 admirals who distinguished themselves by their glorious victories for England in notable sea battles of the time.

The heavily overcast sky became more threatening as the afternoon progressed and on my descent into the town of Monmouth the forecast rain arrived with a vengeance. I had planned to pitch up at one of the two campsites marked on my map but with the rain now falling like stair rods, I bottled it and instead checked in at the Queens Head Inn. This Grade II listed building dates back to the 16th century and it is believed that, during the English Civil War, Oliver Cromwell stayed there on a number of occasions. The building has undergone many changes since it was first built and now seemed to be primarily a live music venue. I found it rather tatty and in need of renovation but my room was at least warm and dry.

After a shower, but no shave as I had made the momentous decision at the very start of my Journey to grow a beard, I wandered along to The Punch House for a fish and chips supper washed down with a pint of Brains *Rev. James Gold,* before heading back to my room for an early night.

It was raining quite heavily as I prepared to leave after breakfast the next morning, so I spent a lengthy period struggling into waterproofs in the pub lobby. There followed a good fifteen minutes crashing into walls and furniture before finally getting underway. Needless to say, by the time I'd called in at the local convenience store for some supplies the rain had stopped so I then spent another quarter of an hour removing my waterproofs and packing them away. The weather is, of course, one of the great preoccupations of the British and I'd recently spotted a weather forecast in a local newspaper which stated "Outlook – dry and warm, but cooler with some rain". In that line they'd captured the British weather to perfection, with a forecast they could use every day and probably never be wrong!

My route out of Monmouth took me through Agincourt Square, an open space in front of the Shire Hall. The hall is adorned by a statue of Henry V, also known as Henry of Monmouth due to his being born in the tower above the gatehouse of Monmouth Castle. Henry V was King of England from 1413 until his death in 1422. During his short reign, he presided over the drubbing of the French at the Battle of Agincourt in 1415, one of

England's most celebrated victories, earning himself his own Shakespearean play 180 years later. Also prominent in the square is an impressive statue to the memory of Charles Rolls, the Welsh motoring and aviation pioneer and one half of the Rolls-Royce automobile company, who like Henry achieved a fair bit during his 'short reign'. In addition to his motoring prowess, he became the first man to make a non-stop double crossing of the English Channel by plane on 2nd June 1910. Sadly, he was killed a month later on 12th July when the tail of his biplane broke off during a flying display over Bournemouth, making him the first Briton to be killed in an aviation accident in a powered aircraft. He was only 32.

One of the great pleasures of a long-distance walk is the variety of terrain one crosses, and today my route would essentially take me through a gently rolling landscape by field paths and quiet lanes, the rivers Monnow and Trothy replacing the great waters of the Wye. This is sheep country and I came upon one of the silly creatures with its head caught in a wire fence. I took a slight detour off-route into the next field to extricate the animal from its dilemma then took great satisfaction as I watched it scamper off bleatingly to rejoin its mother and sibling.

About 11 miles into the day, I passed the White Castle, a 12th-century Norman fortress which retains most of its walls and moat – still filled with water. The castle takes its name from the white rendering still visible on parts of the exterior walls, and its sturdy construction is a vivid reminder of how unassailable these strongholds must have been in their time.

The rain put in an appearance again around 3.00pm and fell intermittently for the last 5 miles of the day. I arrived at the scattered community of Pandy soon after 5.00pm and headed just off route along the A465, the Hereford-Abergavenny trunk road, for The Rising Sun, a pub with a handy camping field out back. It was basic, but at £8 for the night I couldn't complain and the steak and ale pie accompanied by a couple of pints of *Doom Bar*, went down a treat. I was also able to order a packed lunch for the following day as there would be no shops on the trail.

Following some overnight rain, day three on the Offa's Dyke Path started out cloudy but thankfully dry. I would be in the hills all day and I set off at 7.00am on the long ascent up into the Black Mountains – part of the Brecon Beacons National Park – en route to Hay-on-Wye some 16 miles distant. After the initial climb up from Pandy, the route followed the Hatterall Ridge with relatively clear paths and gentle walking. Alas, with the low cloud, potentially wonderful views were somewhat restricted and throughout the morning the weather deteriorated to the point where squally rain and wind forced me to don not only my waterproofs, but also my beanie hat and gloves.

I was beginning to wonder at how few other people I'd seen along the trail so far. That, however, was about to change as I suddenly found myself in the middle of a walking event in aid of the local mountain rescue group. By lunchtime, in excess of 1,000 walkers were streaming past me in the opposite direction and I soon found it rather irksome having to queue to cross the frequent flagstone 'bridges' over particularly boggy sections of the path and maintain an amiable smile. If I'd particularly wanted the hills to myself, I'd certainly picked the wrong day.

The route along the ridge took me past three separate triangulation points, topping at 2,306 feet, the highest point I would reach in Wales and indeed, the highest on the 'end-to-end' trail so far. Just beyond the final trig point, at a spot known as Hay Bluff, the trail dropped steeply over the edge and I started the long, although not continuous, descent for the final four and a quarter miles to Hay-on-Wye.

Apart from a brief lunch stop at a grassy spot along the ridge, I'd pushed on all day and eventually arrived in Hay around 4.00pm. Hay-on-Wye is a small Welsh market town, full of character and famed for its many second-hand bookshops. Since 1988 it has also been the venue for a literary festival which draws a claimed 80,000 visitors over ten days at the beginning of June to see and hear big literary names from all over the world. I wondered whether I might one day be one of them once this outstanding work of literary genius was published!

I happened upon the Tourist Information Centre and called in to enquire about accommodation for the night, and get recommendations for a good hostelry. Cynthia, the volunteer manning the office, not only ran a B&B at £35 for the night but was also able to point me in the direction of The Blue Boar. Both of my immediate requirements satisfied, I thanked her, told her I'd be round at 5.30pm and headed off for a pint.

After settling in at Cynthia's and enjoying a relaxing soak in the bath, I headed back into town. Being a Saturday, I'd earlier taken the precaution of booking a table for dinner in The Blue Boar and after picking up tomorrow's lunch from the local SPAR supermarket, I enjoyed a very passable Welsh ribeye steak dinner and a couple of pints of Timothy Taylor's Landlord bitter, before strolling back to my B&B for the night.

Over an excellent breakfast the next morning, Cynthia and I chatted about the weather, which was dry and bright in the wake of more overnight rain, and her garden, which looked a picture. She was looking forward to the literary festival a week or two away, an event which clearly brought a lot of additional tourists to the town with the ensuing economic benefits.

The main schedule in my *End to End Trail* guidebook had today down as a long, 28-mile stretch to Knighton, but as I had long since settled into the alternative 3-month schedule, my destination today would be Kington, a more manageable 15 miles away. The trail would follow the Offa's Dyke Path again all day and began with a leisurely level stroll along the River Wye, before heading up across farmland. Along the way, I met up with fellow walkers Pete and Judy from Cheshire, and Bernard from Melbourne, Australia. Pete and Judy had walked the northern half of the ODP from Knighton to Prestatyn the year before and were back to complete the southern half from Chepstow to Knighton. It made a pleasant change to have some walking companions and someone else to navigate.

Soon the route began to take us on a long, steady ascent up over the somewhat pretentiously named Little Mountain, and on to Disgwylfa Hill before dropping down into the small hamlet of Gladestry just in time for a welcome lunch stop. We sat in the garden of the Royal Oak where a pint of *Three Tuns* bitter went down very well. I also had the bonus of finding a £5 note inside my promotional packet of crisps!

Rested and ready we set off after lunch and almost immediately were climbing up to the highest point of the day along the Hergest Ridge. At 1,398 feet, the ridge was immortalised by Mike Oldfield in his 1974 album of the same name and is considered to be one of the finest sections of the Offa's Dyke Path. Although overcast, the weather had held and the views from the ridge were spectacular.

In conversation with Judy, I discovered that although she and her family now lived in Cheshire, she was born and bred only a mile up the road from me in North Cheam. Together we developed what became known as the 'Cheam Stroll' which basically involved walking half a mile an hour slower than everyone else, much to the annoyance of her husband Pete. He had set a smart pace since leaving Gladestry and as a result we found ourselves descending into the town of Kington at around 4.00pm.

I'd spotted a youth hostel on my Ordnance Survey map and planned to book in there for the night. As luck would have it, my companions were staying in a B&B only three doors along, so as we parted we arranged to meet up again the next morning. The hostel didn't officially open until 5.00pm, so leaving my weighty backpack with the volunteer wardens I set off to sample the local ales. I caught the tail-end of 'happy hour' at the Royal Oak Inn and quaffed a couple of pints of *Hereford Pale Ale* (from the Wye Valley Brewery), before paying a visit to the local supermarket for tomorrow's lunch.

After checking in at the youth hostel and feeling mildly drowsy from my session in the Royal Oak, I decided on a quiet evening in. As most hostels are self-catering and in anticipation of picking up my next resupply box tomorrow, I cooked up my last two sachets of All Day Breakfast, had a refreshing cuppa and was in bed by 9.30pm.

Monday 15th May would be my last day on the Offa's Dyke Path. I met up with Peter, Judy, and Bernard before setting off at 8.45am on a dry but overcast day. Today would be a 14-mile trek to Knighton following the line of the ancient dyke across hilly farmland – the dyke's direction indicated by a ditch and ridges through the fields. There would often be a line of trees growing along it and around lunchtime we took shelter under the canopy of a large oak tree as a light rain began to fall.

It was after lunch and whilst plodding uphill through a moist field, that I decided to test the traction on my boots with the aid of a fresh cowpat. I slipped, and unbalanced by the weight of my backpack, ended up arse over tit on the damp grass with a red face and an unpleasant greeny-brown smear up my right leg. As we neared our destination, having crossed the border between Powys and Herefordshire *four* times throughout the day, the route took us up Hawthorn Hill which, at 1,335 feet, was the highest point reached that day. It was late-afternoon before we began the steep descent into Knighton and I breathed a sigh of relief that the light rain we'd had throughout the day had not developed into anything heavier. I headed straight for the post office, conveniently located inside the local supermarket, to collect my second resupply box before joining my walking companions for a very welcome beer in the George & Dragon, a 17th-century inn situated in the centre of town.

The rain became more persistent as I supped my pint of *Station Bitter*. To celebrate reaching the end of this section of the journey, I decided to have a rest day and booked myself into the pub for the next two nights. Later, in the restaurant, I opted for the fish and chips, a meal which, after around 150 years remains a firm British favourite. If in doubt, this is generally my default dish and with over 250 million fish and chips meals being sold each year in the UK, who I am to fly in the face of popular opinion?

Knighton is a small market town located about halfway along the Offa's Dyke Path beneath the steep slopes of Kinsley Wood, and is only just in Wales. After boxing up unwanted maps and other miscellaneous items and dropping them off at the post office to send home, I spent the morning sightseeing. I ran into Pete and Judy and joined them for a cuppa before they boarded their train home to Cheshire. I'd enjoyed walking with them for the last couple of days. They'd set the pace to a certain extent, compelling me to stop 'ambling' which I'm inclined to do when left to my own devices.

Late in the day, I returned to my room to sort out my gear and after a couple more pints in the George & Dragon, so appropriately named given its proximity to the border, I hit the hay for an early night. Tomorrow I'd be back in England, heading north-east into Shropshire and the start of section three of my journey which would take me to

Hebden Bridge in West Yorkshire over the next two weeks.

The landlady of the George & Dragon kindly gave me a £20 discount for the charity walk as I checked out the next morning and after breakfast, I headed out of town and up around the steep contours of Kinsley Wood. Today's walk of around 14 miles would take me through the hills of southwest Shropshire, following paths and tracks over hummocky hills and through forestry plantations. Forecast rain started soon after I set off and turned into an insidious drizzle – that uniquely British kind of drizzle that hangs in the air, drains the spirit and has a tendency to last all day. This made for very muddy going through the forestry sections, the paths of which had been churned up by the recent passage of heavy logging machinery.

Around lunchtime, with the rain still falling, I took shelter in the porch of the Church of St. Mary in the small village of Hopton Castle. In addition to 11 listed buildings, the village is home to the remnants of Hopton Castle itself. In 2010, this 13th-century structure was the subject of a three-day excavation in an episode of *Time Team*, a long-running archaeological television programme presented by Sir Tony Robinson. As a result, a fair bit is known about its turbulent past and a particularly notorious siege during the English Civil War. It seems that in 1644 a Royalist force of around 500 men, led by Sir Michael Woodhouse, laid siege to the castle, which was defended by about 30 Roundheads under the command of Samuel More. Following a three-week siege, More surrendered to Sir Michael Woodhouse, who at his discretion decided *not* to grant the majority of his prisoners quarter and they were killed by their captors. This gave rise to the term "Hopton Quarter", referring to the treacherous treatment of captives by their opponents.

Mid-afternoon, I arrived at the picture-postcard Bird on The Rock tearoom at Abcott. It came highly recommended, with my guidebook declaring it to be "the best café between Land's End and John o' Groats". I had been looking forward to a cup of 'proper' tea and a home-baked cake, but regrettably, on this damp Wednesday afternoon they were closed and I trudged on, dispirited. My destination today was the small market town of Craven Arms and having been denied my afternoon refreshments, I made a slight detour from the route in my guidebook and headed straight for The Craven Arms Hotel and a pint or two of *Jennings Cumberland*. There were no campsites marked anywhere nearby on my map but Wade, the genial bar manager, pointed me in the direction of the Woodville B&B, which at £35 for the night seemed a reasonable bet.

Richard and Wendy, the owners of the B&B, made me very welcome and after settling into my room, which was in a small annex in the garden of the main house, I cooked up an All Day Breakfast from my food stock, watched a bit of telly and turned in for the night.

I awoke at 5.00am. The slate grey skies of yesterday had given way to a beautiful sunny morning. I'd now covered just over 400 miles of the trek and today would be an 18-mile stretch to Much Wenlock. The 'official' route took me along the wooded escarpment of Wenlock Edge, virtually all the way, but I'd read that some sections can get very muddy and after the previous day's rain I decided to take a parallel minor road route. First, though, I wanted to visit a place I'd missed by taking the minor diversion yesterday, and after an early full breakfast I set off for Stokesay Castle.

Stokesay is somewhat deceptively named, as its actually a fortified manor house. Built in the late-13th century it has pretty much always been a secure private residence and according to historian Henry Summerson it's one of the best-preserved medieval fortified manor houses in England. The property, which boasts an impressive timber-framed gatehouse, has changed hands a number of times over the years, and when its last owners fell into financial difficulties it passed into the guardianship of English Heritage. Stokesay Castle continues to be operated as a tourist attraction, receiving around 40,000 visitors each year and, although it wasn't actually open at the hour of my visit, it was nice to be able to view it from the grounds in the morning sunshine without the hordes of tourists. With a long march ahead of me, though, I couldn't afford to hang around too long and set off along a quiet minor road towards Much Wenlock.

*"Let a man walk ten miles
Steadily on a hot summers
Day along a dusty English
Road. And he will soon
Discover why beer was
Invented."*

Gilbert K. Chesterton – author and poet (1874–1936)

It had seemed like a good idea to take a break from 'invisible paths' and potentially muddy tracks, but as the day wore on the appeal of a firm road under my feet began to diminish. The whole route followed just two fairly quiet and straight roads, and in the heat of the day it soon became rather mind-numbing. It wasn't helped by the fact that, with typically impeccable timing, each pub I happened upon was closed. I almost jumped for joy when the B4368 became the B4378 at the tiny settlement of Shipton. I'd bought lunch in a convenience store en route and, having removed my boots and socks, sat eating it on the well-manicured grass verge outside Shipton Hall, a large and imposing Elizabethan country house in the village.

My map showed a campsite right on the route at Bourton Westwood Farm, about a mile outside Much Wenlock and only 6 miles down the road, and after lunch I set off with renewed vigour, arriving at the extremely basic but friendly campsite around 3.30pm. Within 15 minutes, I'd met the site owner, Peter, who allowed me to pitch up for free, and Joyce, a caravan owner and regular visitor to the site. On hearing about my journey she immediately made a £5 donation to the charity, made me a very welcome cup of tea whilst I pitched camp, and offered to drive me into town later.

My arrival in Much Wenlock, not to be confused with nearby Little Wenlock, was cause for some excitement and anticipation. In two days it would be my 60th birthday and my son Mike would be meeting me in town the next day to transport me 140 miles north to Hebden Bridge for a family celebration and a couple of rest days.

Planning for this trek had been fairly thorough but

I'd definitely been a tad ambitious when it came to my schedule. The original plan had seen me reaching Hebden Bridge the day before my birthday and needing to arrange accommodation for a large group in a popular tourist town meant that bookings had to be made well in advance. Unfortunately, my schedule had drifted somewhat, but as accommodation had been booked and paid for, the family were committed. Accordingly, I would be picked up on the Friday, driven north for the family reunion and dropped back in Much Wenlock on Sunday night ready to resume my journey on the Monday morning.

That evening, I needed to reconnoitre the town in order to arrange a suitable meeting place for the next day and considered it my sworn duty to sample as many hostelries as possible. I kicked off my exploration in the George & Dragon, a traditional pub dating partly from the Elizabethan era, for a couple of pints of *Tribute*. Then it was on to the Talbot Inn where I enjoyed a pint or two of *Sambrook's Pumphouse Pale Ale* accompanied by a good portion of fish and chips. I also booked a room here for my return on Sunday night. I finished the evening in The Gaskell Arms Hotel with two very pleasant pints of *Golden Wander* from the Hop & Stagger Brewery, which delightfully describes itself as "a small independent brewery located in the rural heart of Central England, brewing a range of handcrafted ales that reflect the wonderful traditions of brewing in the UK".

I settled on The Gaskell Arms as the best meeting place for two reasons. Firstly, it was conveniently situated just on the outskirts of town, and secondly it had its own large car park. Recce complete, and by now being in a pleasantly inebriated state, I weaved my way the mile back up the road to the campsite.

Descent into Redbrook on the Offa's Dyke Path

Stokesay Castle, Craven Arms.

The next morning, after enjoying another cuppa courtesy of Joyce, I broke camp and had a leisurely stroll back into Much Wenlock. My son was due to arrive around lunchtime, so I had the morning to do a bit of tourist stuff, but first I visited the post office to get my journey verification sheet stamped.

There are a wealth of period buildings in this pretty market town and the most prominent are the Guildhall and Wenlock Priory. The Guildhall is an attractive, timber-framed building just off the marketplace. It was built in 1540 to provide a courthouse and the courtroom remained in use until 1985. A short stroll further down the road I discovered the 12th- and 13th-centuries ruins of Wenlock Priory, built on the site of the even more ancient 7th-century Milburga's Abbey. This site is thought to be the final resting place of Saxon abbess St Milburga, who during her life is said to have brought a dead boy back to life and ordered a flock of geese to stop eating her crops.

Late morning, I headed to The Gaskell Arms where I fell into conversation with Roy and Alistair, founder members of the Shropshire branch of CAMRA (Campaign for Real Ale). We discussed the relative merits of *Golden Wander* and *Butty Bach* (a Wye Valley Brewery favourite) and of course were obliged to sample a pint or two of each. Mike arrived at 1.30pm and after lunch we set off on what would be a long journey to Hebden Bridge, due to roadworks on the M6, with the rich aroma of my unwashed walking gear stinking up the car. *I* may have lost my sense of smell over the past few weeks, but my son clearly hadn't.

Chapter Nine

My wife had booked a large cottage on the outskirts of Hebden Bridge for the weekend, and it was wonderful to see her and all the family again after a month on the trail. It was also nice to be able to give all my gear a proper wash, rather than just a cursory rinse in a B&B or hotel room sink, for the first time since setting off from Land's End. We had a great couple of days, which included a celebratory birthday meal and a pleasant stroll along the serene and picturesque Hebden Water through the deep, wooded valley of Hebden Dale. This was thoughtfully organised by my brother who was obviously labouring under the impression that I hadn't done enough walking already and needed the exercise. The weekend passed all too quickly, though, and as we drove out of Hebden Bridge on the Sunday evening, I ruminated on the knowledge that, all being well, I'd be back here on foot in about 10 days.

Back in Much Wenlock, I checked in at The Talbot before heading off to the local convenience store to pick up lunch for the next day, a task I habitually performed the evening before in order to save time in the mornings. Then it was back to the pub for a couple of pints of *Doom Bar* to solemnise the fact that I was now almost an OAP.

Having had a couple of rest days, I was raring to go on Monday 22nd May (Day 34) and I set off after an excellent full English breakfast in ideal warm, slightly overcast weather. I had planned a leisurely 14-mile walk today, which initially followed the Shropshire Way through farmland and woodland. The trail then picked up a disused railway track and there nestled in a spectacular wooded gorge stands a monument to British industry – the world's first iron bridge. Crossing the River Severn in a single arch with a span of almost 100 feet, it was designed by architect Thomas Farnolls Pritchard and built by Abraham Darby III in 1779. Using a total of 378 tons of iron at a cost of around £6,000 – significantly more than the £3,200 first estimated – this radical new structure demonstrated that 'project overspend' is not just a modern phenomenon. It became a UNESCO World Heritage Site in 1986 and remains an iconic feature of Britain's industrial past.

The town of Ironbridge, just south of the urban sprawl of Telford, grew up around the bridge and I couldn't resist a visit to Eley's, for a cup of coffee and one of their world-famous, traditionally hand-raised pork pies, before heading on down the Severn Valley. The area was one of the most important of the Industrial Revolution and, in addition to iron smelting operations, there were pottery, tile and brick works. Although virtually all the heavy industry has gone now, it has left a valley full of interesting reminders of its industrial past. After passing The Boat Inn (regrettably not open at the time), I crossed the river and a canal and climbed a path beside one of these relics in the form of the Hay Inclined Plane. Operational from 1793 to 1894, this ingenious device is a steep railway line up the valley side, once used to transport boats down to the River Severn from a canal leading from coal mines. Boats were floated onto a wheeled cradle which was then winched out of the water and lowered down the rails. The height difference between canal and river was 207 feet, which would otherwise have needed 27 locks to connect them.

Three miles beyond the inclined plane, I arrived at Kemberton just in time for lunch and seized the opportunity of a couple of pints of *Dizzy Blonde* at The Masons Arms while I ate. From here, various tracks and paths led me quickly east under the M54 to the small hamlet of Tong Norton, where I planned to halt for the night. A glance at the map confirmed what I'd already gleaned from my guidebook. Namely, that accommodation options in this tiny community were limited to camping in the corner of a friendly farmer's field. Tong Norton straddles the A41 and consists of a dozen or so houses, a petrol station with a limited shop and The Bell Inn pub. I'd spotted a small patch of grass, just big enough for my one-man tent, at the rear of the pub beside the car park and the bar manager kindly agreed to let me use it. After a meal of steak and ale pie, chips and peas, washed down with two or three pints of *Banks's Mild*, I pitched camp. The location had everything you'd want in a camping spot if privacy and peace and quiet were not primary requirements and a combination of traffic noise from the pub car park, the busy A41 and the 24-hour petrol station next door, gave rise to a restless night.

As a consequence, I was breakfasted and on my way by

7.00 the next morning. Another 14-mile hike lay ahead to reach the town of Penkridge. It was another warm, sunny morning and I set off in shorts which soon proved to be a mistake. Four miles into the day, I crossed the county boundary from Shropshire into Staffordshire as I skirted the village of Bishops Wood and shortly after that I was confronted by a field of rapeseed. The strip map in my guidebook indicated a route directly across the field but added that if crops prevented this an alternative path around the field edge should be taken. I set off around the perimeter and was soon having to pick my way through some bristly undergrowth. At this point, common sense dictated that I should have zipped the bottoms back on my *Craghoppers Convertibles* but, having by now already suffered multiple stings and scrapes, I bravely plodded on. For the next hour or so I fought my way through all manner of vicious vegetation, eventually escaping the field by hopping across a drainage ditch and clambering over a barbed-wire fence. It was a good 24 hours before my poor legs stopped throbbing.

I was now back on a clear track which joined the Staffordshire Way beyond the ruler-straight Roman Road of Watling Street (nowadays more commonly known as the A5) and the Shropshire Union Canal. Around lunchtime, I diverted to the small village of Whiston where I enjoyed a pint of *Black Country Bitter* in The Swan while I ate my sandwiches and licked my wounds.

It was mid-afternoon when I arrived in the ancient market town of Penkridge and, given that I'd barely slept last night, I was already weary. I headed for the post office to get my journey sheet stamped and the helpful lady behind the counter mentioned that a local plumber did B&B on the side. She looked up his number and within the hour Paul arrived in his van, heaved my weighty backpack in amongst his various plumbing fittings and fixtures, and transported me back to his house. The B&B was in fact a small self-catering cottage in his garden, which I thought quite a bargain at £30 for the night. It had a compact kitchenette and Paul and his partner Lindy had thoughtfully provided some basic provisions. After a refreshing shower I dined on an All Day Breakfast ration pack on toast before settling down with a cuppa for a quiet night in.

It was another early start the next morning. Today I would be heading for Abbots Bromley, a 16-mile trek, all of which followed the Staffordshire Way. The route out of Penkridge initially took me along the towing path of the Staffordshire & Worcestershire Canal. Despite the traffic noise from the nearby M6 motorway, it was a very pleasant stroll, but all too soon I left the canal to head north-east around cultivated fields. Just beyond the village of Bednall, I entered the Cannock Chase Country Park, one of the largest country parks in England at 3,000 acres, and once the 'happy hunting ground' of Kings and Queens who came to enjoy a good day's sport with local Lords and Ladies. A myriad of footpaths in this popular area of natural beauty caused me some initial navigational issues but with the aid of my trusty GPS and inspired by a hardy-looking group of Duke of Edinburgh Award hopefuls, I was soon back on track enjoying the trek and views across this vast expanse of heath and woodland.

The route took me past a glacial boulder believed to have been transported here from the Scottish borders by glacial action during the ice age. This well-known local landmark is set on a pedestal of Triassic pebbles and concrete, the latter being a reminder of when this area was a large military camp during the First World War.

I stopped for elevenses at a picnic table by stepping stones fording the babbling Sher Brook. Whilst taking a breather, I chatted with a couple of dog walkers, handing out some of the cards explaining my walk, in anticipation of an online charity donation. Around lunchtime I reached the Trent and Mersey Canal and conveniently happened upon The Wolseley Arms where I couldn't resist a pint of *Wainwrights Ale* to wash down my sandwiches.

Shortly after lunch I met my first fellow 'end-to-ender'. The route left the canal by way of a bridge about a mile beyond the pub and as I stood on the crossing checking my map, I noticed a heavily laden walker coming up the towpath behind me. Jill was from Belgium and, like me, she was on a lone trek following a route based on Andy Robinson's trail guide. She'd set off from Land's End four days after me on 23rd April but being somewhat younger and travelling lighter as she wasn't camping, she'd been able to maintain a brisker pace. After exchanging pleasantries, we buddied up for the next couple of hours to Abbots Bromley where I intended to stop for the night. Jill had accommodation booked in Uttoxeter, some 6 miles or so further and though I was conscious of slowing her down, in the warm afternoon sunshine she seemed to appreciate the more leisurely pace.

In addition to being a quintessentially English village, Abbots Bromley's claim to fame is the annual 'Horn Dance'. Believed to have been performed as far back as 1226, it's one of the few ritual rural customs to have survived the passage of time. The event, which attracts visitors from all over the world, takes place on Wakes Monday, which, for the uninitiated, is the day following Wakes Sunday, which is the first Sunday after 4th September. Six local men, carrying antlers or horns, set off from St. Nicholas Church, where the horns are housed, and proceed to dance round the parish. They return to the village in the early afternoon, via all the pubs, before finally returning the horns to the church until the next year.

After visiting St. Nicholas Church to view the famous antlers, I bade farewell to Jill, wishing her luck on her journey, before dragging myself into The Crown – one of four pubs in this pretty village – for a pint of *Thatchers Gold* cider. I discovered from Nicki, the landlady, that accommodation options in Abbots Bromley are somewhat limited and the two B&Bs she directed me to were both fully booked. She was, however, prepared to let me pitch camp in a corner of the pub garden, thoughtfully pointing out that the lawn had been freshly mown. Over a pint I discovered that a group of guys working locally had a spare room in the B&B they'd booked out next door to the pub. Sue, the owner, did me a deal and my bed for the night was sorted. All that remained was to enjoy another pint or two of *Thatchers Gold* and a superb mixed grill, whilst reflecting on a day that had been one of the best of the trip so far.

Seizing the opportunity of yet another full breakfast, it

was past 8.00 before I set off the next morning on a 21-mile stretch to the village of Thorpe. The day began with a pleasant ramble through the rolling arable countryside of Staffordshire. It was another warm, sunny day and I swung into a café on the outskirts of Uttoxeter for a pint of iced Coke before heading off around the famous racecourse. The trail then took me across broad floodplain meadows to meet the River Dove and into Derbyshire for the first time. After a quick pit stop in the clubhouse of a busy shooting club, quiet farm tracks and riverside paths brought me to the ancient village of Rocester. JCB, one of the world's top three manufacturers of construction equipment, were very prominent in the village, and indeed their factory dominated the skyline on my approach.

The pub was closed but I called in at the village convenience store for some sandwiches and kicked off my boots in the cool shade of a shelter across the road. In the afternoon I enjoyed a bit of leisurely riverside walking along the River Dove, stopping to chat with an angler who'd just netted a small brown trout. After passing through Ellastone and Calwich Park, the trail led me up through some attractive woodland and along little-used field paths which made for tricky wayfinding. It was by now getting quite late in the day and, although a couple of miles shy of my intended destination, I decided to call a halt at the tiny hamlet of Swinscoe, where I knew there to be a pub and the chance of some accommodation. The Dog & Partridge wasn't exactly cheap, but after a long day a pint or two of cold cider, a refreshing shower, and a comfortable room were all very welcome.

With another substantial 19-mile day in prospect, I decided to forgo the pub breakfast next morning in order to get an early start. So, having settled my bill the night before, I opted instead for a bowl of muesli and an All Day Breakfast cooked up in my room before hitting the trail at around 6.00am. After dropping down across a field, wet with early morning dew, the trail rose to cross the River Dove at the Coldwall Bridge. At this point I simultaneously rejoined the Limestone Way, passed into Derbyshire once again and entered the Peak District National Park. By 7.30am I was in Thorpe, munching an apple on the village green.

For the next few days, I would be following a route known as the 'Alternative Pennine Way' and just beyond Thorpe the trail led me down the grassy slopes of Lin Dale to stepping stones across the sparkling River Dove. Here, in the shadow of an isolated limestone hill called Thorpe Cloud, I began my journey along a 3-mile section of paradise. Dovedale is a classic limestone valley, considered by many the most spectacular in the country. An Area of Outstanding Natural Beauty, it attracts a million visitors a year, but at 8.30 on this sunny Friday morning, I had it virtually all to myself. Trout were rising in the clear water and it was easy to see why Izaak Walton, famous for his book *The Compleat Angler* was so drawn to it in the 17th century. Dovedale's scenic charms were also ardently praised by eminent writers and poets Samuel Johnson, Lord Tennyson and Lord Byron.

The wonderful woodland trail took me past dramatic limestone formations with evocative names such as the Twelve Apostles, Tissington Spires, and Lions Head Rock, and mysterious caves, known to have been used as tombs by Neolithic farmers around 4,500 years ago.

I crossed the River Dove at the beautiful village of Milldale by way of Viators Bridge. This medieval packhorse crossing was so-named when Izaak Walton, who in his celebration of the art and spirit of fishing wrote under the assumed name of 'viator' or traveller, rather scathingly described it as a bridge only wide enough for a mouse or wheelbarrow to cross. After a mid-morning break with a cold Coke and a slice of Bakewell tart from the small village shop, I continued on along the riverside track through Mill Dale, the continuation of the Dove valley above Milldale village. At a fork in the trail, I regretfully left the river and headed up the dry side valley of Biggin Dale to the village of Biggin, where The Waterloo Inn was nicely placed for a lunch stop.

After a roast beef sandwich and two pints of iced Coke, I was sorely tempted to heed barmaid Jane's suggestion to call it a day and pitch camp on the site opposite the pub. But I'd set my sights on reaching the village of Youlgreave, and after recharging my water bottles, I headed off east along quiet lanes and field paths before dropping down into the deep, wooded limestone valley of Gratton Dale. I decided to take a minor diversion from the 'official' route, taking a more direct country lane for the last mile and a half into Youlgreave, on the way passing a field of llamas.

Late in the afternoon and before abandoning myself to the pleasure of a pint or two of *Marston's Pedigree* in The Bulls Head, I booked into the youth hostel conveniently placed right next door. Opposite the hostel stands a squat, circular construction which appears to be a stone monument but is, in fact, the original water supply to the village, known as The Fountain. For centuries, the villagers had struggled up the hill with water from the River Bradford, and many deaths, particularly amongst children, were caused by contaminated water, especially in the 'fever months' of July and August. A fund was set up to pay for the conveyance of water to the village from nearby Mawstone Spring and the installation of 1,106 yards of iron pipework to The Fountain was completed two years later in 1829. The reservoir, which holds 1,500 gallons, filled each night and at 6.00am a village 'Waterkeeper' unlocked the tap to allow the queue of waiting ladies to fill their pails, each household paying the princely sum of sixpence a year for its use.

Since being forced to lighten my load back on the South West Coast Path and re-evaluate my overall timetable, I'd slipped into what *The End to End Trail* guidebook referred to as the 'Alternative Three-month Schedule'. Accommodation options over the next few days were somewhat limited. It was necessary to have a short day in order to provide manageable walking days which finished near some accommodation. This wasn't as critical for me as I was carrying camping equipment, but I was keen to stick to the schedule as far as possible. As such, Saturday 27th May would be the shortest day of the trip so far and I set off at a leisurely pace after breakfast on an 8-mile ramble to the village of Baslow.

Although a short day, it wasn't without interest, the route crossing Lathkill Dale and taking in farmland, woodland, pastures and parkland. I paid a brief visit to Haddon Hall, a country house dating back to the 11th century and originally owned by William Peverel, the illegitimate son of William the Conqueror. The house, once described as "the most complete and most interesting house of its period", later became one of the seats of the Dukes of Rutland. Between the wars, the 9th Duke made a life's work of restoring the hall, the interior and grounds of which have been used in many film and TV productions over the years. The Hall, which is open to the public, hadn't opened for the day at the time I arrived, but I got an impromptu masterclass in archery from a local 're-enactment' group who were setting up for a bank holiday weekend display.

Dropping down across open pastureland, with the magnificent Chatsworth House visible in the distance, the graceful and prominent spire of the Church of St. Peter signalled that I was approaching the village of Edensor (pronounced 'Enza'). Specially commissioned by the 6th Duke of Devonshire, the custom-built village features a delightful mix of traditional house designs, from mock-Tudor to Swiss cottage – all different but with the woodwork painted in the same shade of Chatsworth blue. The 6th Duke decided to demolish the old estate village and rebuild it out of sight in the 19th century, because it spoiled his view of the estate from Chatsworth House. The village's former post office is now home to Edensor Tea Cottage where I enjoyed a cold Coke and buttered scone around midday.

Just beyond the village I crossed the River Derwent into Chatsworth Park. Chatsworth House is home to The Duke and Duchess of Devonshire and since 1549 has been passed down through 16 generations of the Cavendish family. This imposing stately home is set in expansive parkland, backed by wooded hills rising to heather moorland. It contains works of art and valuable artefacts that span 4,000 years including furniture, neoclassical sculptures, books, and one of Europe's most significant art collections, and has been selected as the UK's favourite country house several times.

A short walk through parkland alongside the River Derwent brought me to the village of Baslow. En route, I discovered an engineering oddity in the form of The Cannon Kissing Gate. A 'kissing gate' is a type of gate which allows people to pass through, but not livestock. They are generally designed to be used by people on foot, but this inventive device was conceived to give access to the park for visitors in wheelchairs. It's effectively a 'C'-shaped, caged cylinder which rotates on a central spigot at the top. The wheelchair user enters via the open section, rotates the device and then exits along the path the other side. Inspired by a Mrs Jill Cannon and made and donated by Derbyshire firm, Mathers Engineering, it was opened by The Duke of Devonshire in March 1999 and is, as far as I'm aware, unique.

It didn't take long to discover that Baslow was fully booked on this bank holiday weekend. I spent a few pleasant hours in the bar of The Wheatsheaf Hotel catching up on some admin and sampling the *Wainwrights Ale* and a very passable mixed grill, before pitching camp for the night in the corner of a field on the Chatsworth Estate.

After a windy night – nothing to do with the ale and mixed grill – I set off the next morning on day three in the Peak District National Park. The park is essentially divided into two areas, The White Peak and The Dark Peak, the names stemming not from some mystic connotation but from their geology. The White Peak, through which I'd been trekking over the last couple of days, is a collective name given to the area found in the central and southern Peak District whose geology is Carboniferous limestone. Exposed rocks and crags, stone-built properties, together with mile upon mile of drystone walls constructed of fossil-rich stone, give the area a general grey or 'white' appearance. The Dark Peak is the higher, wilder and mostly northern part of the Peak District. It gets its name because (in contrast to the White Peak), the underlying limestone is covered by a cap of Millstone Grit which means that in winter the soil is almost always saturated with water. The land is thus largely uninhabited moorland plateaux where almost any depression is filled with sphagnum bogs and black peat.

A stiff climb up from Baslow brought me to Baslow Edge, the first of a series of gritstone edges. These outcrops of hard, grey sandstone extend north for over 10 miles and I looked forward to the views westwards over the River Derwent. Needless to say, the mist came down and the marvellous vistas were shrouded from view. I couldn't resist a minor detour to Wellington's Monument which sits at the head of the 'edge' high above the village. It is dedicated to the Duke of Wellington and a celebration of his victory at the Battle of Waterloo in 1815. By all accounts, it was erected by a local, called Dr Wrench, who as an Army man felt the need to counterbalance the memorial dedicated to Admiral Nelson on nearby Birchen Edge.

My route continued past Eagle Stone, a huge chunk of gritstone with an interesting local custom associated with it. Tradition dictates that before they are allowed to marry, the young men of Baslow have to prove their manliness by climbing onto the top of this enormous stone. There's no easy way up because some of the higher parts of the stone overhang the lower parts. That said, I believe the village has had its fair share of weddings, so plenty must have managed it.

The weather improved as the morning wore on and so, thankfully, did the views. Beyond Curbar Edge and Froggatt Edge, I passed The Grouse Inn, a wonderful-looking hostelry billed as a walkers' haven and famed for their steak pie. Being only 10am, it was closed and I instantly regretted not pushing on a bit yesterday and pitching camp in the vicinity overnight.

Around mid-morning, having had little more than a cuppa before breaking camp, I enjoyed a couple of bacon and sausage baps at Longshaw Lodge. Longshaw Estate was once the Duke of Rutland's shooting land but now belongs to the National Trust and the café in the Lodge was doing a brisk trade on this Sunday morning with the many cyclists, ramblers and runners enjoying the great outdoors. The trail took me up through the gritstone moorland to the outcrop of Carl Wark and onto the higher point of Higger Tor. From there I climbed to follow the longest and most impressive of the gritstone edges, Stanage Edge, passing the 500-mile point of my journey along the way.

Viators Bridge, Milldale

Camp on Derwent Moor

The northernmost of an almost continuous line of cliffs, Stanage's naturally weathered Millstone Grit face is one of the most famous climbing venues in the UK. The clanking of metal on rock as climbers hauled themselves up from below me was a regular sound as I followed the well-trodden path along the ridge, enjoying fantastic views across the surrounding moors and countryside.

By the time I reached Derwent Moor at the far end of the Edge, it was 5.00pm so I decided to pitch camp for the night in the lee of a grouse butt on the moor. The weather had improved steadily throughout the day and I had a strip wash in the cool waters of a pool in a small stream, before settling down for the evening with a ham salad sandwich, a cup of tea, and the fine view across to Moscar Moor.

After overnight rain I awoke to a thick mist on Derwent Moor. My planned route today would have taken me up to Black Tor, at 1,765 feet the highest point on the trail since the Black Mountains near Hay-on-Wye. This would have afforded me wonderful views down onto the Derwent Reservoir, but with limited visibility I decided to take a lower path along the Derwent Valley to ensure I didn't miss this famous body of water. For it was here, during the Second World War that the Royal Air Force practised low-level flights in Lancaster bombers and tested an ingenious device in preparation for 'Operation Chastise', better known as the 'Dam Buster' raids.

A clever chap called Barnes Wallis had developed a 'bouncing bomb'. On the night of 16th May 1943, Wing Commander Guy Gibson led Lancasters from the specially formed 617 Squadron on an audacious bombing raid to destroy three dams in the Ruhr Valley, the industrial heartland of Germany. Two of the dams, the Möhne and the Eder, were successfully breached. Of the 19 Lancasters that took part in the attacks with 133 aircrew, 8 planes were lost with the loss of 56 men, 3 of whom survived to become prisoners of war. On the ground around 1,300 people were killed in the resulting flooding. Although opinion is divided on the impact on industrial production, there is no doubt that the raid gave a significant morale boost to the people of Britain and 617 Squadron were immortalised in World War Two folklore. The Derwent Reservoir later became the scene of filming of *The Dam Busters*. This epic movie depicting the raids, starring Michael Redgrave and Richard Todd, was the most popular film at British cinemas in 1955 and remains one of my all-time favourites.

There are three reservoirs snaking along the Upper Derwent Valley – Ladybower, Upper Derwent and Howden. At the far end of Howden Reservoir at a spot known as Slippery Stones, an old packhorse track climbed up out of the valley and brought me to open and soggy moorland. I followed the Mickleden Edge for the next few miles in the mist and drizzle, with visibility reduced to around 30 yards, before dropping down to Langsett where the guidebook suggested accommodation may be found at the Wagon & Horses. Langsett is a tiny hamlet situated on the A616 with Sheffield off to the east and Manchester only a few miles to the west. It reminded me how close I came to major conurbations on my trek without even realising it as I journeyed through some of the finest countryside in Britain.

I must have appeared a very dishevelled figure when I arrived at the pub around 3.00pm. A very sullen barman looked me up and down with disdain and announced that they had just stopped serving and would be closing early on this damp bank holiday Monday. Also, despite the prominent sign proclaiming B&B, they didn't actually offer accommodation anymore. Thankfully, the excellent Bank View Café opposite was more helpful. I was at least able to assuage my hunger with a huge cheese and bacon burger and pick up some takeaway sarnies for lunch the next day. As I left, the friendly and efficient waitress wished me well and slipped me a complimentary slice of fruit cake. She later made a generous donation to the charity and left a wonderful message on my *JustGiving* page.

Despite getting a bit of a soaking that day, I was prepared to wild-camp for a third night, given that accommodation options in the area were limited. Fortunately, though, The Dog & Partridge – a couple of miles away and slightly off-route – had a room available. The landlady was ex-forces so I even managed to negotiate a discount on the B&B rate before savouring a pint or two of *Barnsley Bitter* and *Farmers Blonde* and a soak in a hot bath before bed.

Hopes of better weather the next day proved optimistic. I set off en route to the town of Marsden in steady rainfall after breakfast, on what would be one of those annoying days where the waterproofs are frequently donned and doffed. Initially following field paths and crossing open moorland, I was soon travelling parallel to the River Don along a disused railway line, now part of the Trans Pennine Trail. This I followed up the valley for a couple of miles to the remote hamlet of Dunford Bridge, which has a rather unfortunate history of railway-related deaths.

Dunford Bridge is where the railway once disappeared into the three Woodhead Tunnels which ran for several miles under Thurlstone Moors until they closed in July 1981. The first opened in 1845, at a cost of 26 men killed. The second opened in 1852 with 28 more dead, many from cholera. The third tunnel opened in 1954 as part of electrification of the line and even this resulted in six more fatalities.

A sharp climb brought me to the top of the dam at the head of Winscar Reservoir. The reservoir looms over the hamlet akin to the storyline from a Hollywood disaster movie, and when a leak was discovered in the dam in 2001, it had to be drained for emergency maintenance work. It's a popular sailing and birdwatching site and I passed a large flock of noisy Canada geese as I negotiated its eastern shoreline, with the surface of the water rippling in the keen wind. Just beyond Winscar Reservoir, I crossed some old quarry workings and entered West Yorkshire, where the woodland and drystone wall hill country, so typical of the region, made for interesting walking. I arrived at the village of Holme around lunchtime and seized the opportunity to pay a visit to the Fleece Inn, relishing an iced Coke, a packet of salted peanuts, and the sandwiches bought in the café yesterday, whilst drying off in front of a cosy fire.

After lunch and having dragged myself out of the snug bar, I followed a ruler-straight farm track for a mile before heading up onto the moor. The highest point of the day, at 1,480 feet, was reached at Wessenden Head as I crossed the Saddleworth Moor road. Soon after, I had my first encounter with the Pennine Way, although it would be another three days before I made its acquaintance properly, just beyond Hebden Bridge.

From Wessenden Head, an easy path followed the hillside contours on Wessenden Moor. In the much-improved late-afternoon weather, I was able to enjoy some extensive views down into the valley, as I shadowed a line of three small reservoirs before dropping down into the town of Marsden. My guidebook mentioned a campsite behind a pub called The Carriage House and, although almost two miles off-route, I decided it was worth the trek. After a long uphill plod, I arrived to find that the pub and site was closed on Tuesdays – today in fact – and the place seemed deserted. Regardless, and although disappointed to be missing out on a pint, I pitched up in the small field behind the pub. A rather unsavoury-looking guy who was living in a battered old caravan on the site kindly gave me the lock code to the site toilet and shower block. The facility was clean with plenty of hot water and with the bonus of access to the boiler room I was even able to dry out my jacket and boots. That evening I dined on an All Day Breakfast ration pack and BLT sandwich whilst gazing appreciatively at the fiery red clouds as the sun set over the distant moors.

After the mist and rain of the last two days, it was a treat waking up to a beautiful morning. In celebration of the sunshine and the fact that I was due to collect my next resupply box, I treated myself to an extra sachet of muesli for breakfast before breaking camp and hitting the trail. My target today was Hebden Bridge, 15 miles to the north and the place where I'd met up with the family to celebrate my birthday 11 days earlier.

After backtracking on the couple of miles I'd had to travel off-route the day before – thankfully downhill on this occasion – I headed out of the attractive old town of Marsden by way of the Co-op, where I bought lunch for the day and got my journey verification sheet stamped. Today's route would be a roller coaster ride in and out of five valleys. The terrain was varied and the views excellent, taking in moorland as well as areas of pasture.

Around mid-morning I crossed the M62, via an underpass, at the point of a curious phenomenon – a farmhouse sandwiched between the westbound and eastbound lanes of the motorway. The owner of Stott Hall Farm refused to sell his land when plans for the M62 motorway were approved back in the 1960s. The iconic 18th century farmhouse was eventually saved from demolition, not by the owner's protestations but by a quirk in the geology of the land, which made it too steep to build all six lanes on. It is now set to become the 'farm of the future' as part of a local initiative, having been declared a classic upland farm with biodiversity interest and cultural and landscape value. Despite its precarious location, the farm is also a haven for certain birds, and the plan is to improve and conserve the habitat to support the population of key species including merlin, snipe and twite. It's certainly become a talking point for the millions of drivers who speed past it on this busy highway.

Immediately beyond what has become known as 'The Farm on the Motorway', I passed Booth Wood Reservoir, one of many scattered throughout the area feeding the surrounding towns and villages – I counted seven or eight visible from the route alone. I stopped for lunch on Manshead Hill, the highest point of the day, enjoying the marvellous view back down across Baitings Reservoir, along the wooded shoreline of which I had walked an hour or so earlier.

Dropping into the fourth valley of the day, I arrived at The Hinchliffe Arms where I'd been relishing the prospect of a pint of iced Coke and a packet of peanuts. I was gutted to find it closed but peering forlornly through the window I managed to attract the attention of a member of staff who kindly opened up to serve me. Rested and refreshed, I set off on the last leg of the day. This involved a sharp climb up onto Bell House Moor followed by a steep descent into the Calder Valley via Crow Nest Wood to arrive at Hebden Bridge and the end of section three of my journey.

In the 1960s, Hebden Bridge was a run-down area with properties which could barely be given away. Now it's a sizeable, thriving town attracting artists, a small 'New Age' community, and as of 2004 the highest number of lesbians per head of population in the UK. In 2005 *High Life*, the British Airways in-flight magazine, declared it to be the fourth most "funky" town in the world – funky being defined as "modern and stylish in an unconventional and stylish way". All very Bohemian!

My wife had booked me into a disgracefully expensive room in the White Lion where we'd gone for a birthday meal two weeks before. Tomorrow would be a rest day and at the price I was paying for my two-night stay I was determined to extract full value. So, on arrival, I washed out my soiled gear in the bath, strung it out across the spacious bathroom on my trusty travel washing line, and suspended my damp tent from the wardrobe to dry out. After taking a shower, I left the room looking like a Chinese laundry as I headed back to the bar for a pint of *Black Sheep* bitter.

I spent a pleasant evening in the company of Karen and Lesley – a librarian and teacher, respectively – who lived in the town. They plied me with the remains of their ample cheeseboard to accompany my beer and regaled me with tales of Yorkshire community spirit during the Boxing Day floods of 2015. In the early hours of 26th December, the alert siren had warned of impending flooding in Hebden Bridge. Storm Eva had battered the region, bringing weeks of regular heavy rainfall, and after 5 inches fell in a 24-hour period, the River Calder finally burst its banks, destroying homes, businesses and livelihoods. It was estimated that the cost of the flooding exceeded £50 million with the cost of the damage to roads, bridges and other infrastructure alone put at £25 million. With typical Yorkshire resilience and spirit, Hebden Bridge was soon back open for business, and seeing this thriving community now, it was hard to imagine that we were less than two years on from that devastating event. I headed back to my room around 11pm, a very late night for me, and as I lay in my comfortable bed I looked forward to a rest day and a chance to take a look around this characterful town.

The first job next morning was to pick up my resupply box. So, after a lazy breakfast I wandered along to the town's main post office only to discover that it hadn't arrived! The box would contain all the maps and guidebooks I'd need for the next section, so I'd be stuffed without it and I'm ashamed to say that I read the poor woman behind the counter the Riot Act in no uncertain terms. It was only as I trudged back towards my lodgings in a foul mood that I thought to ring my wife to find out exactly when she'd posted it. I'd asked her to dispatch it during the course of the previous week as delivery time was four working days. She had, of course, left it until the Saturday which meant that it was due to arrive at sometime today, hopefully. Needless to say, our telephone conversation was not the most harmonious!

I returned around lunchtime and, as luck would have it, my box had just arrived. After sorting and repacking with all the stuff I no longer needed, I revisited the post office to send it on its way home, and after digesting a large slice of humble pie, I apologised profusely to the post office staff and hurriedly left.

Panic over, I could now start to relax and enjoy what was left of my rest day, starting with a tuna salad sandwich, two slices of cake and a cuppa at a bijou riverside coffee shop. I also took the opportunity to bring my journal up to date and review the route for the days ahead. I'd settled comfortably into my revised schedule and I now calculated that assuming I didn't lose more than a day or so for bad weather or, God forbid, injury, I should reach John o' Groats around 16th July.

Late in the afternoon, I returned to my room to repack for the morning, before adjourning to the bar of the White

Lion. Dinner consisted of a steak and ale pie washed down with a couple of pints of *Wainwrights Ale*, from the Thwaites Brewery, and Timothy Taylor's *Boltmaker*. Tomorrow, the Pennine Way and the prospect of a challenging trek along the backbone of England to the Scottish Borders.

Chapter Ten

Friday 2nd June, Day 45 of my journey, would be significant. A few miles north of Hebden Bridge, I'd be meeting the Pennine Way – the stuff of legend. Britain's oldest, toughest and wildest National Trail, the Pennine Way officially opened in April 1965 after a 30-year campaign by journalist Tom Stephenson to create what he described as a 'long green trail' on a par with the US Appalachian Trail. This rugged long-distance path rises and falls along the crest of the Pennine Hills, commonly known as the 'Backbone of England' and involves a cumulative ascent of 36,829 feet. It runs for 270 miles from Edale in Derbyshire to Kirk Yetholm in the Scottish Borders – although my 'end-to-end' route meant I would miss out the beginning and end sections – and passes through 3 National Parks, 7 counties, 2 National Nature Reserves, and 20 Sites of Special Scientific Interest.

Such is its reputation that I was feeling rather nervous as I set off that morning. I'd wanted to get going by 8.00am so the chef at the White Lion had kindly provided me with a pack of bacon sarnies to sustain me. Leaving Hebden Bridge, the route took me through the attractive, deep, wooded valley of Hebden Dale, known locally and somewhat ambitiously as Hardcastle Crags. Rambling beside Hebden Water, I passed Gibson Mill, a 19th-century cotton mill. Built around 1800, it was one of the first-generation mills of the Industrial Revolution and produced cotton cloth up to 1890. It's now run as an educational and community centre, powered entirely by sustainable energy.

Beyond Hardcastle Crags things went downhill a bit as I struggled along the river path which was, as my guidebook warned, "rough and wet in places", not to mention indistinct. Eventually, and more by luck than judgement, I managed to scramble my way up the bank of Alcomden Water, at the confluence with Hebden Water, to reach Holme Ends, and the start of my Pennine Way adventure.

Leaving behind the green folds of the Calder Valley, I skirted around the banks of the Walshaw Dean Reservoir and within the hour arrived at one of the most important landmarks in British literary history. Thought to have been built in the second half of the 16th century, the ruined farmhouse of Top Withens is regarded as the inspiration for the Earnshaw family house, *Wuthering Heights*, in Emily Brontë's celebrated 1847 novel. The Brontë Society refute such beliefs, even installing a plaque on the building to that effect in response to the many enquiries they've received over the years. It's true that Top Withens looks nothing like *Wuthering Heights* as you might imagine it from the book, and never did, even when it was complete. But here in the heart of Brontë Country, it would be easy to imagine the *location* as being in Emily's mind when she wrote about the moorland setting of the Heights.

I left Top Withens on a well-worn track and flagstone

path and had my lunch on the hillside overlooking Ponden Reservoir. The last few miles of the day took me into North Yorkshire and up across the featureless mound of Ickornshaw Moor, before dropping down to Cowling where I'd be stopping for the night. I called into the first campsite I happened upon on the outskirts of the village. There were no other tents pitched on the small, uneven site and Tom, the owner, could see I wasn't keen. Instead, he offered me use of an old summer house in his garden. The site shower facility was basic, but the summer house had both lighting and power and at £6, for which he'd throw in breakfast the next morning, the deal was done.

Having dropped off my pack, I strolled into the village where I quickly contributed to the local economy, visiting the restaurant for a Friday 'special' fish and chips supper, the Bay Horse pub for a pint of *Doom Bar,* and the village shop to purchase tomorrow's lunch. Still feeling a bit peckish, I picked up a large "Meat Eater" from the pizza parlour to take back to the summer house.

Saturday dawned on another fine, sunny morning and while I packed up my gear, Tom's wife knocked me up some coffee and a bacon and egg bap. I set off at 8.00am on what I knew would be a hefty 17-mile stretch to Malham. Crossing Cowling Hill, the route took me through the charming village of Lothersdale, home to Dale End Mill. This Grade II listed building was originally a corn mill which was converted to textile manufacturing around 1795 and is thought to house the largest enclosed waterwheel in England, if not the world. The wheel is in need of extensive restoration work and The Friends of Lothersdale Mill hope that sufficient money can be raised to save this important artefact for future generations to see.

Leaving the village, I climbed up through fields and onto heather moorland to reach the trig point at Pinhaw Beacon. From here I had commanding views back to the bleak South Pennines and ahead to the verdant Yorkshire Dales. Dropping down across Thornton Moor, I got my first taste of the peatbogs which are such a feature on the Pennine Way. Fortunately, as now, slabs and duckboards have been laid across the worst areas.

I had a quick breather in the village of Thornton-in-Craven, just beyond which I joined a level path besides the 127-mile-long Leeds Liverpool Canal. Here, I discovered an unusual double-arched canal bridge, designated 'Bridge 161'. This stone bridge, which has two round arches one above the other, was designed by Robert Whitworth and is a Grade II English Heritage listed building. It carries the A59 over the canal where the waterway passes through a particularly deep gorge and was built around 1790 when the canal was extended from Gargrave to Burnley. As I'm sure any good bridge engineer will tell you, the bottom arch is a strainer arch and is required to help support the unusually high abutments.

Now, my trek had been going brilliantly to date. Apart from taking a tumble on the South West Coast Path on Day 4, and the recent bit of unpleasantness in the post office at Hebden Bridge, all had been well. However, disaster was soon to strike in the form of a fairly major kit malfunction. I'd stopped off at the Cross Keys pub in East Marton for a brief lunch break and I hadn't long got back on the trail when my route took me over a stile. As I stepped over, I heard a dull crack and the small, plastic buckle on my backpack, connecting the two halves of the left-hand shoulder strap, disintegrated, leaving the weighty pack hanging loose on that side. I managed to tie the two halves together with a length of para cord but it was clearly only going to be a very temporary repair.

I'd hardly seen a soul on the trail all day, but as I sat fiddling with my damaged pack, a group of walkers came over the hill behind me and I explained my plight. Ken, the group leader, invited me to join them on their final stretch to Gargrave, only a couple of miles further on, and kindly offered to drive me into Skipton where he knew there to be some outdoor retailers. We tried a couple of small outlets without success and then happened upon a newly opened Cotswold store. Salvation presented itself in the form of a wonderful device called, appropriately enough, a 'field repair buckle'. The removable metal pin meant it slipped easily into the stitched-in loop on my rucksack and for about £4 the problem was sorted. Unfortunately, they only had one on the shelf so I wasn't able to buy a spare.

Ken, a retired biomedical scientist no less, then drove me back to Gargrave where his wife had been waiting in the local tea shop. I could not have more grateful for his kind assistance and immediately ordered us all a pot of tea and some cakes as a thankyou. With typical Yorkshire hospitality, he then refused to let me pay for them!

After the excitement of the afternoon, I decided not to press on for the final seven miles to Malham, my intended destination. Instead, I ordered a pint in The Masons Arms, booked myself a table for dinner later, and headed off to the campsite my map indicated on the edge of the village. The owner very kindly allowed me to pitch for free, and having sorted my gear and sampled the site shower facilities, I returned to the pub for a steak & kidney pudding dinner, accompanied by fruit pie and custard and a couple of pints of *Wainwrights Ale*. As I relaxed in the bar that evening, I reflected on my good fortune that Ken and his walking group had come along when they did, the kindness of strangers, and how lucky I'd been that the strap buckle had not broken in a more remote area.

I awoke the next morning to a grey, overcast day and broke camp between light showers. I decided to have a short day and stop at Malham tonight, rather than attempting to make up the time lost yesterday with a 21-mile push to Horton in Ribblesdale. Although I'd lose a day, it would give me a chance to explore the village and its famous Cove.

Apart from the first couple of miles beyond Gargrave, my route today followed the River Aire Valley and took me into the Yorkshire Dales National Park. This stage involved very little climbing, just a couple of low, grassy hills and a gentle riverside walk. Around 9.30am, I had a sudden craving for a cup of proper Yorkshire tea and a bacon sandwich and stopped off in the village of Airton in the hope that the café mentioned in my guidebook was open. Being still quite early on a Sunday morning, of course it wasn't. Beyond Airton, the path moved away from the river for a while before passing through an attractive parkland area where sheep grazed between tall trees by the riverside below Hanlith Hall. After a stiff climb up an access road passing the Hall, the trail drifted downhill to meet the river at Aire Head giving a tempting preview of Malham Cove in the distance, and from there an easy gravel path led me into the village of Malham. Fording a stream, I browsed a classic Fiat car show before heading for the youth hostel to secure my accommodation for the night. Having confirmed availability, the staff kindly agreed to hold onto my backpack, leaving me free to explore unhindered.

I'd arrived in the village around midday, and with the weather now fine, dry and clear, I decided to take a four and a half mile circular walk described on a leaflet I'd picked up in the hostel. It was a warm and sunny afternoon and it felt wonderful to be at large without my backpack. I felt liberated, able to walk upright with a spring in my step instead of slightly hunched with my eyes fixed on the ground.

My route took in Malham Cove, Gordale Scar and Janet's Foss, the three big draws to the area in addition to the village itself. The 260ft high and almost 1,000ft wide, gently curving limestone cliff of Malham Cove has been amazing visitors for centuries and is a well-known beauty spot. It was formed by a waterfall carrying meltwater from glaciers at the end of the last ice age, over 12,000 years ago – the curved shape being created by the massive amount of water flowing over the lip which naturally eroded more heavily than the sides. Today, the watercourse goes underground through 'sinkholes' before reaching the top of the cove, following a complex network of caves and tunnels in the limestone cliff before re-emerging as

Malham Beck at the bottom. On 6th December 2015, after heavy rainfall courtesy of Storm Desmond, Malham Cove became a waterfall again for the first time in centuries and for a few hours it was the highest 'single-drop' waterfall above ground in England.

The top of the cliff is reached via about 400 irregular stone steps, and I was quite relieved to not be carrying 'The Beast', although as these form part of the route of the Pennine Way, I knew I'd be making the same journey in the morning fully laden. At the summit, I picked my way between the cracks of a large limestone pavement and drank in the fabulous views out across Malhamdale. Both cove and pavement have made notable media appearances, most recently in *Harry Potter and the Deathly Hallows (Part 1)* in 2009, and the 1992 film version of Emily Brontë's *Wuthering Heights*.

Dragging myself away from the stunning viewpoint, I continued along the track soon reaching Gordale Scar. This impressive limestone ravine has overhanging cliffs 328 feet high, making it popular with climbers, and includes two waterfalls, though with the recent dry weather I wasn't seeing the watercourse at its best. Gordale Beck, the stream flowing through the scar, leaves the gorge to flow over Janet's Foss, a small waterfall which carries the beck over a limestone outcrop and into a deep pool below. The name is believed to refer to a fairy queen who inhabited a cave at the back of the falls and the stroll through this beautiful sylvan glade made a wonderful end to my circular walk as I headed back to the village.

I'd worked up quite a thirst in the warm afternoon

sunshine, so I called in at The Buck Inn where I discovered culturally unique British humour and great beer combined in the form of *Monty Python's Holy Grail* cask ale, from the Black Sheep Brewery. I'd never come across this golden ale – originally created to commemorate the 30th anniversary of Monty Python and famously "tempered over burning witches" – but certainly enjoyed its fresh, zesty taste. Whilst at the bar, I fell into conversation with actor Julian Sands. He had been born and bred in Yorkshire and was in Malham for a weekend's walking. Interested in my journey though he was, I have to say I was more impressed with *his* walking prowess when he mentioned that he'd walked the Pennine Way in only 10 days, a journey most would take 16 days over. He wished me luck with my trek and I headed back to the youth hostel to get checked in.

After sorting out my gear and taking a shower, I joined a couple of early retired IT guys from Derbyshire for a chicken Tikka Masala dinner in the hostel. Vic and Martin were experienced walkers six days into their own Pennine Way adventure, and I expected to meet them often over the next few days. I had a pint of *Main Line* bitter in The Lister Arms as a nightcap, before settling down in the hostel dormitory for the night.

The weather forecast had been poor for Monday, and indeed as I set off at 8.45am, it was raining steadily. I called in at the village outdoor shop for replacement bootlaces – bizarrely, I hadn't thought to pack any spares – then it was back up the stone steps to the top of Malham Cove and across a wet limestone pavement. It looked very different in the damp and misty conditions and I was so glad I'd been able to appreciate the views in the fine weather the day before. Skirting around Malham Tarn, Yorkshire's largest and highest natural lake, the track headed through woodland passing a field centre at Malham Tarn House before heading up onto the bleak moorland of Fountains Fell at a height of 2,133 feet.

I stopped for a short break at a point midway between two tall cairns and tucked into a Scotch egg in the shelter of a drystone wall. Suddenly, Vic and Martin came out of the mist behind me and we teamed up for the rest of the day. Our destination was the village of Horton in Ribblesdale, but first we had to negotiate Pen-y-ghent, a slumbering, monstrous giant which dominates the landscape with its distinctive profile. At 2,277 feet, Pen-y-ghent is actually the lowest of the famous Three Peaks of Yorkshire – the other two being Ingleborough and Whernside – but geographically the highest point we would reach today. Approaching along duckboards spanning boggy moorland, I was somewhat awestruck by its brooding eminence, the summit shrouded in low cloud and mist. We climbed in squally rain up a rugged stone path. The upper reaches were a bit of a scramble, no great obstacle to Vic and Martin who were travelling light but a considerable challenge to me with the weight of my backpack. Sadly, there were no views to be had from the summit in the heavy mist, so after posing for hazy photos, we started our descent and the last couple of miles into Horton in Ribblesdale.

Given the wet weather, I'd rung ahead and booked myself a room at The Golden Lion Hotel where my walking companions were staying. We arrived at around 4.30pm passing the celebrated Pen-y-ghent Café en route. The café, which is also a shop stocking all those last-minute and easily forgotten items such as batteries, first aid supplies, clothing and maps, is a popular place to start the Yorkshire Three Peaks Challenge, and something of an institution in the area's walking history. It wasn't open as we passed and at the time of writing I believe the café is closed until further notice due to family illness. I wish them well and hope they're back up and running soon.

The first job on arrival at The Golden Lion was to order a round of *Pen-y-ghent Bitter*, a popular ale from the Three Peaks Brewery. After a hot shower to drive out the chill, I had an excellent dinner of minted lamb suet pudding in a snug bar warmed by a roaring fire and a very pleasant evening in the company of other Pennine Wayfarers and several more pints of bitter. Before I headed off to my room, we checked on the weather. It had rained steadily throughout the evening and more was forecast for tomorrow.

After breakfast the next morning, I fed a couple of carrots to *Trotter* the hotel's pet pig before setting off with Martin and Vic. Today would be a relatively short 13 miles to Hawes, initially following an old cart track north out of the village and up the east side of Ribblesdale. A mile or so out, we stopped at Sell Gill Holes, where Sell Gill Beck, swollen by the recent rain, was pouring impressively into a hole in the ground to reappear who knows where. The limestone landscape in this part of the country is honeycombed with miles of caverns and underground passages making it very popular with cavers and potholers. In the Three Counties

Cave System, you could go underground in Yorkshire, move under Lancashire, and emerge in Cumbria. It's already the longest system in Britain and new entrances and passages are being discovered all the time – there are at least 40 different entrances and it's thought to be about 56 miles long.

Passing a number of potholes and areas of shakeholes – the latter being the hollows left when boulder clay is washed into fissures in the underlying limestone – we soon arrived at Old Ing Farm. This inconspicuous collection of buildings was a major milestone for me, as it marked the halfway point on my journey – 600 miles completed!

I posed for a photo to mark the occasion, then we headed across Ling Gill in the squally rain and followed the track on its steady rise to Cam Fell. We stopped briefly for lunch, crouched in the lea of a low wall with extensive views over a large area of woodland below, before the chilly wind forced us on along an old Roman Road, reaching a height of around 1,929 feet.

The descent into Hawes along the path above Widdale was testing. With wind gusting at 40–50 miles per hour, and my backpack acting like a sail, it was difficult to stand as we dropped down into the little village of Gayle. The wind gave way to heavier rain as we passed the Wensleydale Creamery en route to the youth hostel in Hawes and it brought to mind the recent death of actor Peter Sallis, known as the voice of Wallace in the Academy Award-winning *Wallace & Gromit* films, whose character so favoured the locally produced Wensleydale cheese.

It was a great relief to get checked in at the hostel and

deposit our wet gear in the spacious drying room. The weather cleared late in the afternoon and after a very passable chilli con carne dinner, I strolled down to The Crown, one of three pubs literally next door to one another, to sample a couple of pints of their *Theakston Old Peculier* before bedtime.

By morning, the weather had improved considerably and, although still breezy, the sun was working hard to force its way through the dark clouds scudding across the sky. At breakfast, I gratefully received a £5 donation for my charity from Chris, a Canadian guy staying at the hostel, before heading off for the day with Vic and Martin.

A mile or so beyond Hawes, we took the opportunity to detour through the bar of the historic Green Dragon Inn, paying a small entry fee to visit Hardraw Force waterfall. Situated in a wonderful wooded ravine in the grounds of this 13th-century hostelry, Hardraw Force comprises a single drop of 100 feet and is reputed to be England's highest unbroken waterfall *above* ground. Movie buffs might also recognise it as the location in the film *Robin Hood: Prince of Thieves,* where Maid Marian catches Kevin Costner bathing under a waterfall.

From Hardraw Force, a long, steady ascent brought us onto the vast area of high moorland known as Great Shunner Fell. Along the way, Vic impressed me with his knowledge of birds as he pointed out the curlews, lapwings, and black grouse we encountered along the trail. I was rather disappointed that I wasn't able to identify any of them myself, but as Vic was a volunteer Reserve Manager at Derbyshire Wildlife Trust, I was happy to have the benefit of his expertise.

Limestone pavement atop Malham Cove

Enjoying a pint at Britain's highest inn

We stopped for a bite to eat at a stone shelter on the summit, in the company of an elderly walker and his dog. At a height of 2,349 feet, this was the highest point reached on my journey so far and the extensive views were breathtaking. After lunch we started the lengthy descent into Thwaite, where we enjoyed a refreshing cuppa in the village tearoom. This tiny village, which boasts a permanent population of around two dozen people, was the birthplace of the Kearton brothers. Naturalists Richard and Cherry Kearton were among the world's earliest wildlife photographers, developing innovative methods to photograph animals in the wild. In 1895, they published the first natural history book to be entirely illustrated by wild photographs and were an inspiration to many of today's naturalists, including David Attenborough.

Our destination for the night was the iconic Tan Hill Inn and with around seven miles still to go on this 16-mile day, we were soon picking our way across the boulder scree on the slopes of Kisdon, high above Swaledale. Off to the right, I had great views across the river valley to the remains of the area's lead mining history, and the coast-to-coast path I'd walked in 2015.

Soon after 4.00pm, I crossed the River Swale just outside the tranquil little village of Keld and in so doing arrived at the literal crossroads of my whole length and breadth adventure. Keld used to be considered one of the most secluded villages in North Yorkshire but has become popular with walkers in recent decades as it sits where the Pennine Way and Alfred Wainwright's Coast to Coast route intersect. It brought back fond memories of my trip two years earlier when I'd arrived at this point, halfway across England, on my journey towards Robin Hood's Bay.

Four miles beyond Keld, high up on Stonesdale Moor in an extremely isolated and windy spot, stands the Tan Hill Inn, the perfect destination at the end of an excellent day's walking. This 17th-century inn claims the distinction of being the highest pub in Britain at 1,732 feet above sea level. There can't be many pubs that own their own snowplough, but up here it's a necessity. The inn has been snowed in more than 50 times since 2005 – on one occasion for 11 days – but the appeal of its isolated location and offbeat atmosphere is irresistible. The pub has played host to a number of TV adverts, most notably a legendary 1980s commercial for Everest windows in which the late Ted Moult used a simple white feather dropped next to a casement window to demonstrate the draught-proofing properties of the company's double glazing. The Tan Hill Inn has also been a lively music venue over the years. Visiting bands have included Arctic Monkeys, whose impromptu gig in 2008 apparently led to a line of roadside tents stretching 5 miles. I wouldn't have wanted to be queuing for a pint that night!

Fortunately, on this particular Wednesday evening, there was a more sedate atmosphere in the bar. We arrived around 6.00pm and promptly ordered a well-earned round of *Tan Hill Ale*. After checking into the bunk room and showering, I rejoined Martin and Vic in the bar, meeting up again with walkers Phil and Lisa, a couple of police officers from Liverpool, whom I'd first met two days before in Horton in Ribblesdale. Dinner comprised a giant

Yorkshire pudding, filled with steak, mash and carrots, followed by a wonderful home-made sticky toffee pudding. And, of course, a couple more pints of Tan Hill Ale.

At this point, I feel the need to go slightly 'off-piste' to extol the virtues of the 'Great British Pub' because as Dr Samuel Johnson once observed, "There is nothing which has yet been contrived by man, by which so much happiness is produced as by a good tavern or inn". Renowned the world over, the British pub is often the focal point of many and varied activities, quite apart from the actual consumption of alcoholic beverages. It's a unique social centre, an important part of our national culture, and a valuable community asset. One of the many pleasures on my trek was having the opportunity to visit all the wonderful pubs and sampling local ales on my route from one end of the country to the other. As a walker, I think there is something deeply gratifying about reaching a welcoming hostelry at the end of a satisfying day's ramble and relaxing in convivial surroundings with a decent pint. But sadly, the traditional pub is under threat. One in four pubs in Britain has closed in the past ten years, according to official data from the Office for National Statistics. Nationally, more than 11,000 pubs have closed since 2008. Over a longer period, the total number of pubs has fallen to around 39,000 down from 52,000 in 2001. Recent statistics from the Campaign for Real Ale suggest that 378 pubs shut down permanently between July and December in 2019 in England, Scotland and Wales, representing more than fourteen closures a week – that's a rate of one closure every twelve hours! I appreciate that business is business and certainly the big chains and 'gastropubs' serve a particular market, but I sincerely hope that there will always be people around prepared to invest in and run the traditional pub to ensure we keep what diarist Samuel Pepys once described as 'the heart of England' beating.

Chapter Eleven

The next morning, we breakfasted, collected our preordered packed lunches, and set off in a cheerless drizzle, bound for the quiet town of Middleton-in-Teesdale. On today's 17-mile stretch, it would be farewell to the Yorkshire Dales as we entered Durham, and essentially moorland walking all day. Sleightholme Moor is bleak, remote and famously boggy and we cheated slightly by following the parallel minor road for the first couple of miles.

Six miles into the day and just upstream from the village of Bowes, we crossed the River Greta by way of God's Bridge, a Site of Special Scientific Interest. Over 10 feet wide and several feet thick, this natural limestone structure was formed by the river gradually eroding the rock below to continue its progress downstream. There are at least three natural limestone bridges called God's Bridge in and around the Yorkshire Dales but, according to Natural England, this is the best example in Britain of a natural bridge formed in this way.

We stopped for lunch in a small timber shelter, thoughtfully provided for walkers by the landowner, at one end of a grouse hut. Then it was across the soggy moors again before gradually dropping down into the slightly off-route town of Middleton. I'd rung ahead during the day to secure a bed at the Brunswick House B&B where Vic and Martin were booked and once we'd got settled in the owner kindly agreed to wash a stack of my near-toxic walking gear, while we headed to a local hostelry for a pre-dinner pint of *Black Sheep* bitter. An excellent dinner of lamb cutlets and home-made raspberry cheesecake at the B&B was followed by a relaxing couple of hours in the comfortable lounge.

Day 52 would be a short day of only 9 miles to YHA Langdon Beck, a small, rural hostel located in the heart of Upper Teesdale and which, at 1,263 feet above sea level, is one of the highest in the UK. For the next couple of days I'd actually be walking in the wrong direction, but in the guidebook, Andy Robinson insisted it was one of the best sections on the whole trail and well worth it.

Back in March, I considered getting a new pair of boots for the journey, given that my Scarpas had already taken me across England and on a good many lengthy walks since. But, they had served me well, combining the requisite sturdiness with extreme comfort and I took the view that it would be quite something to say my boots had walked the length and breadth of the UK. However, the tread was now wearing a bit thin and the leather uppers were showing signs of cracking and becoming decidedly leaky, something I could have done without on the notoriously wet Pennine Way and with over 500 miles of my journey still to go. Martin suggested an application of beeswax. It wouldn't necessarily stop the leaks but it might just keep the leather supple enough to halt any further deterioration. So, after a late breakfast, I paid a visit to the local ironmongers for a tub of beeswax and applied a generous amount to my boots. I also took the opportunity to visit the post office to get my journey verification sheet stamped and post back, to the Hawes Youth Hostel, the room key I'd walked off with.

Chores complete, the three of us headed off around mid-morning in bright, sunny weather and enjoyed a very pleasant ramble along the River Tees. We encountered waterfalls – High Force and Low Force – their names derived from the Nordic word "foss" meaning waterfall, and while not flowing with their full vigour, were nevertheless very impressive. We stopped for lunch overlooking High Force which, although sometimes described as England's largest waterfall, is not the *highest* – that distinction belongs to Hardraw Force. It does, however, have the largest volume of water, falling 70 feet in an uninterrupted drop, and consequently claims the title of England's most *powerful* waterfall. We even managed to grab 40 winks on a grassy hillside overlooking the scenic Upper Teesdale river valley.

Youth hostels generally close during the day, as guests leave for their various activities, so we had a short wait until 5.00pm before we could get checked in at Langdon Beck. After dumping our gear in the dormitory we took a leisurely stroll down the road to the Langdon Beck Hotel, meeting up again with fellow Pennine Wayfarers Phil and Lisa and enjoying a pint or two of *Wainwrights Ale* before dinner back at the hostel. I'd be back on my own the next day as Vic and Martin were having a rest day, so after my beef lasagne dinner I spent the evening sorting my map and checking the route. I also met up with Louise, another 'end-to-ender', and we swapped stories and experiences on our respective journeys. She was following the route taken by Mark Moxon in 2003, which he wrote about in his book *When I Walk, I Bounce: Walking from Land's End to John o'Groats*, but it pretty much mirrored my own.

I set off the next morning in a light rain heading west along the River Tees and after negotiating a difficult section of riverside boulder scree, I reached Cauldron Snout waterfall. Cascading furiously down a channel from the Cow Green Reservoir immediately above, it's more of a chute than a waterfall and, at 200 yards long, it's reckoned to be the longest waterfall in England. I scrambled cautiously up the slippery rock steps alongside, eventually reaching a flagstone path and a narrow road below the dam wall of the reservoir.

Crossing the river above the waterfall, the trail left Durham and entered Cumbria. From here it was back up onto the moors where the many sikes and becks – small watercourses and brooks – often made the going very wet underfoot. As the trail steadily ascended, so the mist and cloud became heavier and by the time I reached High Cup Plain, at nearly 1,969 feet above sea level, visibility was down to about 10 yards. At this point, in clear weather, I would have had a fantastic view of a natural wonder known as High Cup Nick. This magnificent U-shaped glacial valley, nearly a thousand feet deep, and around 2 miles long, is often called 'the Grand Canyon of the Pennines'. It's considered one of the finest natural features in Northern England and in favourable conditions affords terrific views across the Vale of Eden to the Lake District. It would have been the highlight of the day, but alas in the heavy mist I saw nothing at all.

From High Cup Plain, a clear and easy path descended into the small, unspoilt village of Dufton. The rain hadn't really stopped all day on what had been a 12-mile trek, so I'd pushed on and in consequence arrived in Dufton around 2.30pm. It would be a couple of hours before I could check into the youth hostel, so I called at The Stag Inn for a few pints of *Guzzler*, passing a group of gypsies on the green outside.

Now, you can call me a bigoted old snob if you like, but I don't have a lot of time for gypsies or travellers (call them what you will). I apologise unreservedly to any of their clan who don't recognise themselves here, but in my experience the purpose of their existence seems to be to illegally take possession of any available piece of land they can get their fleet of generally untaxed vehicles onto, conduct whatever dodgy dealings they can get away with, and in the evenings cause as much trouble in the local hostelries as possible. Then, when the law finally grinds into action and evicts them, they move on, leaving a shit-tip of a site, the clean-up of which has to be funded by the hard-pressed local taxpayer.

Needless to say, I wasn't too chuffed when I learned that the small group on the village green was merely the advance guard, and that more were expected to arrive in the village, attracted by the Appleby Horse Fair. This annual event held in early June in the nearby town of Appleby is billed as the biggest traditional gypsy fair in

Europe. It attracts about 10,000 gypsies and travellers, 1,000 caravans, several hundred horse-drawn vehicles, and around 30,000 visitors. Clearly, they wouldn't *all* be staying in Dufton, but the staff in the pub were preparing for a busy and potentially raucous Saturday night and had already started serving pints in plastic beakers, which in itself is criminal!

I popped into the small village shop for the next day's lunch before checking in at the youth hostel. Phil and Lisa were also staying there and I met up with them back at The Stag Inn for a pre-dinner pint. Given that the pub would be heaving later, I decided on an early night and after some sweet and sour chicken, I repaired to the hostel lounge to contemplate the day. I was disappointed to have missed High Cup Nick and made a note to return at some future date. The weather had somewhat spoiled an otherwise brilliant day's walk and I hoped for some improvement as tomorrow would be a big day in both mileage and elevation.

My destination next day was the youth hostel at Alston, a fairly hefty 19 miles distant. Standing between me and it was Cross Fell, which at 2,930 feet is the highest point on the Pennine Way as well as my whole 'end-to-end' route, and the highest mountain in England outside the Lake District. Cross Fell is big and remote and holds the English record for bad weather. It is also home to the only named wind in the British Isles, a phenomenon known as the Helm Wind. This fierce north-easterly wind periodically blows down the slopes of the Cross Fell escarpment and is believed to take its name from the helmet or cap of cloud which forms above Cross Fell, known as the Helm Bar.

If that wasn't enough, unlike most of the Pennine Way, there isn't a clear path all the way, so I set off soon after 8.00 that morning with some apprehension. The weather, though, had improved marginally, and whilst breezy and overcast it was at least dry, and on the plus side I would be walking north in the right direction again. Phil and Lisa were heading off around the same time and as Phil had walked this section before and seemed very handy with his map and GPS, I seized the opportunity to tag along.

We followed a steadily rising track up to Green Fell at 2,624 feet and on to Great Dun Fell (2,782 feet), the dominating feature of which is the radar station operated by National Air Traffic Services, a key part of the air traffic control system for Northern England and Scotland. After dropping down slightly and crossing an expanse of bleak moorland, we climbed to Little Dun Fell (2,762 feet). Crossing the boulder-strewn plateau, we were exposed to the most incredible wind and proceeded with painstaking caution. Backpacks can often leave you with no recognisable centre of gravity and with my large rucksack acting like a sail, I had to lean sideways into it with all my strength just to stay on my feet. At one point we were forced to take cover behind a small stone shelter for fear of being blown over. It was extremely unnerving.

A heavy mist had settled by the time we reached the summit of Cross Fell and for the second time in two days I was deprived of any views. After a brief stop at the cross-shaped dry stone shelter on the summit, we headed on across the broad plateau, before dropping down to a remote bothy called Greg's Hut where we broke for lunch.

A former blacksmith's shop and miners' refuge dating from the early 1800s, Greg's Hut was named in memory of John Gregory who was killed in a climbing accident in the Alps in 1968. A group of his climbing club friends adopted the structure, rebuilt it from a ruin and maintained it for many years. As most of those people are now well past retirement age, the building is now maintained jointly by the Mountain Bothies Association and members of the Greg's Hut Association. The hut is the only bothy on the Pennine Way and has two rooms, one containing a sleeping platform and a small stove, which another walker had thoughtfully fired up. Given its strategic position on this lengthy section of the Pennine Way, I imagine that, over the years, there must have been hundreds of tired, cold and wet walkers who have appreciated this cosy facility, as indeed we did that day.

Leaving Greg's Hut, a clear and easy track descended gradually into Garrigill and it was just beyond this little village that I suffered a second kit failure. In exactly the same circumstances as the mishap near Gargrave, I stepped over a stile, putting additional pressure on my hard-pressed backpack, and heard the sickening crack as the small, plastic buckle, this time on the right-hand side, disintegrated and the shoulder strap assembly separated. With the kind assistance of Phil and Lisa, I nursed the backpack the 3 miles into Alston where I had an amazing piece of luck.

We arrived in England's highest market town just before 5.00 on a Sunday afternoon, and quite frankly I didn't hold out a lot of hope of finding anywhere open which might conceivably stock a replacement buckle. But we happened upon a small craft and outdoor shop preparing to close up for the day, and on the shelf they had just one of the field repair buckles I needed. Lady Luck was certainly smiling down on me that afternoon and I could have kissed her! Having now had to replace both buckles I made a mental note to take the issue up with Osprey and immediately messaged my wife to get a spare added to my next resupply box.

Chuffed with my good fortune, I swung into the Angel Inn, a very friendly hostelry, and enjoyed a pint or two of *Black Sheep* bitter before checking in at the Alston Youth Hostel. Later that evening, I met up again with Lisa and Phil in the Cumberland Hotel, where after an excellent game pie dinner, I rather overindulged in the local ales, sampling a pint each of *Yates Bitter*, a distinctive golden beer, *Dark Horse*, a classic Scottish dark ale, *Maori*, a New Zealand-style pale ale, and a strong, easy drinking northern ale called *Radgie Gadgie*, which is apparently Geordie for "mad man".

On paper, the next day's 16-mile walk to Greenhead looked pretty easy but it would follow tricky field paths and involve a fair bit of awkward route-finding. I left the hostel after breakfast, having failed to spot any of the red squirrels which, I was assured, regularly take food from the feeders outside the dining room window. For most of today, I'd be following the River South Tyne northwards on the hills along the west side of the valley. Just beyond Alston, I passed out of Cumbria and into Northumberland, which like many border counties has been shaped by generations of conflict. Field paths and woodland tracks led me through the village of Slaggyford after which the Pennine Way shifts onto the course of the Maiden Way Roman Road. This somewhat boggy old track soon brought me to an even boggier area of featureless moorland known as Blenkinsop Common, by far the wettest section I'd yet encountered on the Pennine Way. As I was planning to spend the night in Greenhead, which is not on the actual route, I detoured off the PW for the last mile to follow an invisible path across fields and over the A69 – the busy trunk road connecting Carlisle and Newcastle – before dropping down into the small village.

I made straight for the Greenhead Hotel and relaxed with a pint of *Theakston Best Bitter* before heading over the road to the hostel. This was once owned by the YHA but is now run by the Greenhead Hotel and, frankly, left a bit to be desired. There was no soap in the dispensers, the radiator in my dorm wasn't working, and the drying room was insufficiently heated so my boots were still wet the next morning. Having said that, the shower was good and it was fairly cheap. Phil and Lisa had arrived soon after me. They were very sensibly staying in the hotel itself and we met up for dinner in the bar, discussing tomorrow's walk with enthusiasm. Our route would take us into the Northumberland National Park, and along a section of the famous Hadrian's Wall.

Accommodation opportunities the next day were limited and, although I was equipped to wild-camp if necessary, I preferred at least the minimal facilities offered by a basic campsite. My options were a lengthy 21-mile haul to

Bellingham or to split the section with a short, 7-mile day to a campsite at the tiny hamlet of Twice Brewed and then a 14-mile trek the day after. I opted for the latter which would give me ample opportunity to savour the spectacular views from one of Britain's most awe-inspiring historic landmarks. After a leisurely breakfast in the hotel, I picked up some lunch from the tearoom opposite and set off soon after 10.00.

Just beyond Greenhead on the bank above the Tipalt Burn, sit the remains of Thirlwall Castle. The original simple motte and bailey castle was built here in the 12th century – motte and bailey being a form of castle situated on a raised earthwork and surrounded by a ditch and protective fence. As the area endured many years of fighting between the English and the Scots in these 'Debatable Lands', the castle was replaced by a fortified structure in the 14th century. The stone for this was plundered from nearby Hadrian's Wall, and unfortunately in the years since it has itself been further robbed to the point where there is now very little left of this Grade I listed building.

I stopped for lunch beside Hadrian's Wall to ponder the fascinating history of the structure and take in the spectacular views of this dramatic and rugged landscape. Stretching 73 miles from the Solway Firth to the River Tyne, the wall was a defensive fortification and the north-west frontier of the Roman Empire for nearly 300 years. Contrary to popular belief, Hadrian's Wall does *not* mark the border between England and Scotland, which, in places, lies some 68 miles further north. It was built by the Roman army on the orders of the emperor Hadrian following his visit to Britain in AD 122, taking a force of 15,000 men over six years to construct. The most famous of all the frontiers of the Roman Empire, Hadrian's Wall became a UNESCO World Heritage Site in 1987 and it's as astounding today for its sheer vision as it is for its engineering with the remains of barracks, ramparts and forts punctuating the landscape.

I continued along the roller coaster path until I reached Winshields Crag, the highest point on Hadrian's Wall, from where I had a spectacular view across the Northumberland National Park and the distant Kielder Forest, with the humps of the Cheviot Hills rising beyond. A footpath on the southern slope brought me down to the campsite at Winshields Farm, my destination for the night, and after pitching camp on a well-manicured field I strolled down the road to reconnoitre the Twice Brewed Inn. The pub is situated in the best named pair of tiny hamlets I would ever sink a pint in: Once Brewed, and Twice Brewed. There are several stories to explain the name of the inn. The most popular of which has it that, on the eve of the Battle of Hexham in 1464, Yorkist soldiers demanded their beer be brewed again because it lacked sufficient fighting strength. Apparently, the strategy was successful, as the Lancastrian army fled after an early morning raid. True or not, it's certainly a romantic theory and one I mused upon as I enjoyed a pint each of *Twice Brewed Bitter* and *Golden Plover*.

Although overcast it was a fine evening, so I boiled up a couple of All Day Breakfast ration packs and ate my dinner at a campsite picnic table while checking out the guidebook and map for the next day. Then, as the light faded, I turned in with a Sherlock Holmes novel.

I was awoken very early next morning by a flock of rooks who were cawing lustily in a stand of trees on the fringe of the camping field. Actually, I think the collective term for rooks is a 'building' or 'parliament', but whatever it is, the little blighters were making a hell of a racket. The site also catered for school field study groups and Duke of Edinburgh Award expeditions and in consequence had an onsite café. So, after breaking camp and picking up a bacon butty, I retraced my route up to Winshields Crag and headed east along Hadrian's Wall. Within a mile or so, I passed the ruins of a milecastle and turret. A milecastle was a small fortification built at intervals of, unsurprisingly, one Roman mile (around 1,617 yards), and which had a garrison of perhaps 20–30 soldiers. On either side of a milecastle was a stone turret, located about one-third of a Roman mile (540 yards) away. Thus, along the entire length of Hadrian's Wall, there would once have been 80 milecastles and 158 turrets, with the respective garrisons controlling the movement of people, goods and livestock across the frontier.

The Pennine Way left the Hadrian's Wall Path soon after and headed north. For the next few miles, the route took me across tussocky moorland and along some very boggy paths through conifer plantations on the fringes of Wark Forest, part of the vast Kielder Forest Park.

Early in the afternoon, the trail passed by the farm of Horneystead, where a sign announced a welcome 'Pit Stop' with an honesty box. I was very grateful of it and the opportunity to sit a while with some chocolate biscuits, Haribo sweets and a cold Pepsi. Passing the rather unfortunately named farm of Shitlington Hall, and the gritstone edge of Shitlington Crags beyond, the trail peaked at the mast of a relay station before dropping down to the small town of Bellingham. I called in at The Rose & Crown for a pint or two of *Exhibition Ale* before continuing on to the bunk house at Demesne Farm. There, I met up again with fellow 'end-to-enders' Louise and Vic and Martin, who arrived late in the day looking very weary having just completed the 21-mile trek from Greenhead which I'd split with an overnight stay in Twice Brewed. After a wash and brush up, I spent the evening in The Cheviot Hotel in the company of a couple of *Tyneside Blondes* (from the Hadrian Border Brewery) and a fish and chips supper, gratefully accepting two cash donations for the charity as well.

I wasn't particularly enthusiastic about the next day's walk. I'd read in one of my guidebooks that, although the views were extensive, foul weather had the potential to make it feel like typical Pennine Way purgatory and that it would be a day of bleak, featureless, boggy moorland followed by a trudge along forestry tracks. Needless to say, I went off to bed praying for fine weather.

Fortunately, it was warm and dry, if a little cloudy, as I set off at 7.00 next morning on the 15-mile stretch to the tiny hamlet of Byrness. Soon after leaving Bellingham, and having crossed an enormous field where marker posts indicated the route, I entered an area of open moorland and promptly wandered off the indistinct path. I spent the next half an hour floundering around in the boggy, tufty grass, until I managed to get back on track with the aid of my GPS.

The trail followed a number of vague paths across broad heather moorland but marker posts set at intervals across the terrain generally kept me moving in the right direction. It started to rain but mercifully never got beyond a light persistent drizzle. After a particularly boggy section along the edge of the Kielder Forest, the path joined a solid forestry road where I took a short break to eat the lunch I'd bought in the Co-op the night before.

The region's beauty is not confined to the landscape. In this, the most northerly English county, the sky itself is a natural wonder. The Northumberland International Dark Sky Park was unveiled in 2013, and covering an area of 572 square miles it's one of the largest expanses of protected night sky in Europe. Whereas those living in densely populated and light-polluted areas view only a handful of stars through an orange glow, up here you can feast your eyes on up to 2,000 at any one time. On a clear night, meteor showers, 'shooting stars' and the Milky Way itself are clearly visible.

For the next few miles my views were of pine trees in the 250 square miles of Kielder Forest, the largest man-made woodland in England. I'd hoped to catch sight of a red squirrel, given that it's estimated the forest is home to up to 75% of this herbivorous rodent's population on the English mainland. But regrettably I didn't spot a single one. It was at least dry underfoot on the seemingly endless forestry road, the march occasionally interrupted by a passing timber lorry, moving some of the 621,000 cubic yards of timber which is harvested annually. The road terminated at a small picnic area and information hut, and there I stopped for a short break in the company of Michael, a Pennine Wayfarer whose yellow backpack cover had been a beacon in the distance for the last couple of miles.

High Force on the River Tees

Remnants of a Roman fort along Hadrians Wall

I arrived in Byrness around 2.30pm. The settlement is little more than a handful of buildings and a church and I quickly found my way to the Spruce Cottage Bunkhouse. Joyce and Colin appeared to have cornered the market in Pennine Way accommodation in Byrness, running both the bunk house and a 'licensed house' opposite called the Forest View Inn. The bunk house wasn't officially open until 4.00pm but Colin let me in early and it gave me the chance to get cleaned up and settled before any other guests arrived. As it turned out the only other person staying in the bunk house that night was fellow 'end-to-ender' Louise who arrived an hour later. That evening, we joined Vic and Martin, and Lisa and Phil, for a farewell dinner at the Forest View Inn. Tomorrow, they would be heading over the Cheviot Hills and on to Kirk Yetholm at the end of their journey a couple of days away. I would be travelling north and on into Scotland.

Chapter Twelve

Friday 16th June, my 59th day on the trail, was a noteworthy day. I would be parting company with the Pennine Way, having followed it for 14 days and around 190 miles and within the next three hours I would leave England and enter Scotland. It would also be a long day at 19 miles so I had an extra sachet of muesli before setting off.

The route out of Byrness began with a steep and muddy climb through some forestry before a scramble up a low, boulder-strewn gritstone edge brought me to the top of Byrness Hill. Right on cue the mist and rain rolled in, somewhat obscuring my views east across the Northumberland National Park and the Catcleugh Reservoir, as I picked my way along the squelchy moorland crest.

It was around 9.30am when I crossed the border into Scotland. No fanfare or neon sign: in fact up here on the moors there was no sign at all, just an old, wooden gate through a fence. The track actually crosses back into Northumberland very soon after at Chew Green as it passes the remains of an ancient Roman encampment and it's a further couple of miles before, like a quarrelsome couple, the trail finally makes up its mind to split from the Pennine Way and heads north into the Scottish borderland.

For the rest of the day, I would be following the Roman Road of Dere Street. This ancient route originally ran from York to the Forth near Edinburgh. It was built by Agricola, who governed Roman Britain from AD 79 to 81, predating Hadrian's Wall by some 40 years. The road served to allow the legion garrisoned in York quick access to the eastern borderlands and, later, the eastern posts on Hadrian's Wall. It also found use in 1298, when King Edward I of England marched his forces north along Dere Street to the Battle of Falkirk. These days, it's considerably more peaceful along the route which is now part footpath, part tarmac road, part farm and woodland track. Wayfinding was straightforward, so as I walked, I found myself mentally reviewing my trek along the Pennine Way. I've heard it described as a 16-day trudge from the wild, peaty uplands of the Peak District to the wild, peaty uplands of Northumberland National Park, and I confess I agree with Alfred Wainwright who at times found it something of an endurance rather than an enjoyment. That said, I met some great people and delighted in the fantastic scenery. Along the way I passed England's highest single-drop waterfall, drank in Britain's highest pub, hopped between the cracks on Malham's limestone pavement, and yomped along the remains of the Roman Empire's north-west frontier. Although disappointed to have missed out on views of High Cup, I was blown away by the unspoiled beauty of the terrain, particularly the bleak, vast moorland, which I found both alluring and forbidding in equal measure. It's fair to say I reached the Scottish Borders with some relief, but overall it was a life-affirming experience.

My destination today was Jedburgh, my first Scottish

town and the end of Section 4 of my journey, which meant another rest day. It wasn't directly on my 'end-to-end' route so a short detour along a minor road was called for. I arrived around 5.00pm, and as the main post office was still open, I called in to collect the resupply box which, after the unpleasantness in Hebden Bridge, I was relieved to find waiting for me. Then it was into The Railway Tavern for a couple of pints of Scotland's bestselling ale, *Belhaven Best* bitter, before seeking out my accommodation. My arrival in town coincided with a major music event that weekend and my wife had had difficulty finding accommodation for me. She'd eventually managed to book me a room in the smart but rather expensive The Capon Tree Town House B&B. I even had my own balcony.

Before completing the formalities, I eased myself onto a stool at the bar and ordered a *Belhaven Best*. I was joined by Dave, and we struck up a conversation which inevitably centred around my epic journey. He glanced at the enormous backpack leaning against the wall and then eyed me cautiously before uttering, "I take it you're ex-special forces, then." I laughed, explaining that I wasn't but that I *was* walking in aid of SSAFA – the Armed Forces charity. He was very quiet and thoughtful for a while, then the furtive conversation continued thus:

"You are, you're ex-special forces."

"Honestly, I'm not. I'm just a long-distance walker on a charity walk."

"I know you blokes aren't allowed to talk about it."

"No, really I'm not. I've never even served in the forces myself."

"I'm sorry, I know you're not allowed to discuss it and now I've embarrassed you."

"Look, I'm just an ordinary bloke on a charity walk!"

The conversation bounced around like this for another five minutes and I'm not sure whether I ever really convinced him. But just as I was about to take the easy option and admit to being Bear Grylls in disguise, he got up to go, wishing me luck and leaving me with a £20 donation for the charity and a £30 ticket for the weekends Riverside Rock music event.

The coming Sunday was Father's Day and I was chuffed to find some cards from the family waiting for me at the B&B reception as I checked in. After unloading my gear, I sorted through my resupply box before heading out for some fish and chips. I'd covered over 200 miles since my last rest day and I was very much looking forward to exploring Jedburgh tomorrow.

Next morning, I drew back the curtains to unveil another fine, sunny day and enjoyed a cup of coffee on the balcony. The handrail provided an excellent means of airing my tent whilst I sat lovingly applying leather conditioner to my overworked boots. The first order of the day was a good breakfast, during which I turned on the charm and got one of the staff to agree to do a pile of washing for me. Then it was into the post office to dispatch my return box containing maps, guidebooks and miscellaneous items I no longer needed. Finally, I called at the local pharmacy for some cheap reading glasses. I'd left home with two pairs but had lost one somewhere along Hadrian's Wall and one arm of the other was hanging on precariously with the aid of a plaster. Jobs complete, I swung into a little tearoom for a coffee and cherry scone to plan my exploration of this bonnie town.

The Royal Burgh of Jedburgh is an attractive town just 10 miles from the border with England and very proud of its status as the historic gateway to Scotland. Up to the 17th century Jedburgh's position as a frontier town placed it in the midst of national battles and cross-border raids. It was a tempting target which was frequently fought over during the Wars of Independence (1296–1356) and again in the 1400s and 1500s. The town is dominated by the substantial ruins of Jedburgh Abbey which bear testament to its violent past and it was there that I now headed.

Jedburgh Abbey, built overlooking Jed Water, was one of four great abbeys established in the Scottish Borders in the 1100s. David the 1st founded an Augustinian priory here in 1138 and raised it to abbey status in 1154. It took around 70 years to complete, during which time architectural fashions changed, accounting for the unusual mix of Romanesque and Gothic features. It appears that English Earls were almost queuing up to inflict suffering and destruction on the place. The abbey was pillaged and wrecked by the Earl of Surrey in 1297 as retribution for his defeat at Stirling by William Wallace. It faced more destruction in 1464 by the Earl of Warwick. In 1523 the abbey was set ablaze by a later Earl of Surrey, and it suffered more indignity in 1544 at the hands of the Earl of Hereford. The end came for the great Abbey of St. Mary of Jedburgh in 1560 at the time of the Scottish Reformation.

Leaving the abbey, I took a backstreet route via the main bridge over the whiskey-coloured Jed Water, a tributary of the River Teviot into which it flows a couple of miles beyond the town. I happened upon another of Jedburgh's notable buildings, known as Mary Queen of Scots House. The visitor centre within this 16th-century tower house tells the story of Scotland's tragic queen at a turning point in her life. She is reputed to have spent a month in the fortified house in 1566, gravely ill after riding 30 miles and back in one day to visit her adviser and future husband, the Earl of Bothwell. She was forced to abdicate in 1567 and was executed by Queen Elizabeth I in 1587 aged 44. There is some doubt as to whether she was cared for here or at nearby Ferniehirst Castle, but whatever the truth, it's a picturesque old house, set in attractive gardens, and it was a pleasant place to while away an hour or so in the warm afternoon sunshine.

Having spent so much time on my own in peaceful open countryside over the past couple of months, I decided that even with a free ticket and the lure of Showaddywaddy, Pilot, and The Beatles Revolution, I couldn't face the crowds of the Riverside Rock music festival. So, after spending the afternoon wandering around the town, I headed back to the Capon Tree B&B, named, I discovered, after the Capon Oak Tree known as "King of the Woods", one of the last surviving trees of the ancient Jedforest, and reputed to be 2,000 years old.

I had a pint at the bar in the company of a couple on holiday from Grantham in Lincolnshire and recovered my washing which the waitress had even taken home to dry. I headed out to get some dinner around 7.00pm, but finding most restaurants and pubs heaving, presumably from the additional numbers of people attending the festival, I settled for another fish and chips supper from a chippy opposite the Abbey before heading back to my digs for a nightcap. As I prepared to start the next section of my journey, I reflected on the fact that I'd now been on the trail for 8 weeks and covered 757 miles with around 5 weeks and 411 miles still to go.

I was up with the lark next morning with an 18-mile trek to Melrose ahead of me. Father's Day was gloriously sunny and the walking, on my first full day in the Scottish Borders, would be among the best of the trip so far, traversing varied and interesting terrain and some beautiful countryside. I left Jedburgh via a quiet road, part of the Borders Abbeys Way, to rejoin the Roman Road of Dere Street. This soon morphed into St Cuthbert's Way as it crossed the River Teviot via a suspension bridge, then skirted the grounds of Monteviot House, the 18th-century home of the Marquess of Lothian – the politician better known as Michael Ancram – before running ruler-straight along a wood-fringed path for the next three and a half miles.

Around lunchtime, I arrived in the small village of Maxton where I stopped for a break in the shade of a bus shelter-cum-information point. From here I had a good view across the gently rolling countryside to the shapely triple peaks of the Eildon Hills, perhaps the best-known landmark in the Borders region and one I would be crossing within the next few hours. Reaching heights of up to 1,385 feet, they present a prominent feature on the landscape and have been the subject of much folklore. It is said that the wizard Michael Scot – an uninspiring name for a wizard in an age where we've come to expect them to be called things like Gandalf the Grey or Dumbledore! – split the one hill into three using his mysterious powers, giving the Eildon Hills their distinctive profile.

Just beyond Maxton, the trail brought me to the banks of the River Tweed which, at 97 miles in length, is Scotland's fourth-longest river after the Tay, the Spey, and the Clyde. The Tweed is considered one of the great salmon rivers of Britain and for the next couple of miles I enjoyed a classic river walk amongst the delightful wild flowers, trees and meadows. All too soon, the St Cuthbert's Way left the river and headed inland up the side valley of Bowden Burn before passing through the pretty little village of Bowden which lies at the foot of the Eildon Hills. From there the route took me through a plantation of woodland before the long, steady climb along the col between the two highest hills, Eildon Mid Hill and Eildon Hill North. The physical effort was rewarded with fantastic views from the heather-clad peak and I took a short break to enjoy the vista before heading on down the well-worn path to the town of Melrose.

After quenching my thirst with a couple of pints of *Belhaven Best*, I sought out the Melrose Gibson Campsite. My neighbours on the site were a couple of guys from Holland on a cycling holiday and we shared a chat and a cup of coffee before I headed back into town for some dinner. Melrose is the birthplace of Rugby Sevens, home to the striking ruins of an Abbey said to be the burial place of a casket containing the heart of King Robert the

Bruce and is overlooked by the Eildon Hills where King Arthur is supposedly buried. In fairness, though, if I had a pound for every town claiming to be either the birthplace or burial site of King Arthur, I'd have been retired long ago and would be spending my days tramping the countryside like my Pennine Wayfarer companions Vic and Martin.

There was no denying the imposing ruins of Melrose Abbey where I now headed. The Abbey was closed for the day, but not wishing to be denied a look around the grounds, I brought my new slimline, healthy physique to bear and hopped over a wall. One of the most famous ruins in Scotland, the Abbey was founded by David I in 1136 for the Cistercian Order. It was largely destroyed by Richard II's English Army in 1385 and most of the ruins that remain are 15th- and 16th-century. It was abandoned in 1545, but the surviving remains of the church are thought by many to be of an elegance unsurpassed in Scotland. Enhanced by the evening sunshine and without the tourist throngs, the Abbey cut a photogenic and atmospheric sight. Having worked up an appetite I headed to Burt's Hotel for a burger meal followed by a selection of cheeses, all of course, washed down with a couple more pints of *Belhaven Best*.

I left Melrose the next morning via the old Abbey, joining the Southern Upland Way which I would follow for the rest of the day. The weather was again warm and sunny and I had an enjoyable early ramble along the banks of the River Tweed. After a rather dull trudge alongside a newly opened railway line and a small industrial area, the trail started to climb across fields and along forestry tracks to reach open moorland which culminated in the summit of the 'Three Brethren'. At 1,522 feet, this low hill just north of Selkirk is topped with three impressive stone cairns built in the 16th century to mark the boundary of the Yair, Philiphaugh and Selkirk lands, and in the fine weather the views were extensive.

From the summit, the path continued across open moorland and between forestry in the Elibank and Traquair Forest, never dropping below 1,312 feet until I reached the shoulder of Minch Moor. This section of the track is known as the Minchmoor Road, a route once travelled by medieval monks, Highland drovers and, in 1296, by Edward I as his English armies headed towards Peebles on their rampage through Scotland. In the warm conditions with 'The Beast' strapped to my back, I'd got through a lot of water throughout the day. I was running desperately low and it was with some relief that I heard the tinkling of running water at The Cheese Well. This natural spring at the side of the Minchmoor Road is associated with the fairies. Tradition asserts that travellers left pieces of food – cheese was common, hence the name – as superstitious offerings to the 'little people' to ensure a trouble-free passage across the moor. These days most people leave coins, and I gratefully added one of mine to the small collection on a flat stone on the grassy bank before quenching my thirst in the wonderfully cool, clear water.

I'd planned to spend the night in the Minch Moor bothy, which according to my guidebook, was situated just beyond the spring. Unfortunately, I could find no sign of it – later discovering that since the publication of my *End to End Trail* guide, the bothy had been demolished –

and instead descended rather dolefully into Traquair. This ancient and tiny hamlet consists of a scattering of cottages and a phone box. Accommodation options were strictly limited so I headed for a campsite indicated on my map a mile or so off route on the outskirts of Innerleithen. En route to the campsite, I passed alongside the grounds of the area's prominent feature. Traquair House is believed to be Scotland's oldest continually inhabited house. Dating back to 1107, it's been visited by 27 Scottish Kings and Queens, including Mary, Queen of Scots and has been lived in by the Stuart family since 1491. It is home to the world-famous Traquair House Brewery which lies in the wing of the house directly underneath the chapel, though I was a little late in the day to sample their wares.

I arrived at the Tweedside Caravan Park late in the afternoon at the end of a 19-mile day and made straight for the sites niftily named "Tow Bar" for a *Belhaven Best* or two. Lynda, on reception, very kindly gave me a discount on my night's stay, charging only £5 instead of the usual £9 and I headed off to pitch camp in the tent area in the furthest corner of the site.

I awoke the next morning to another fine, sunny day and became faintly aware that I was now in 'midge season', as I swatted them away whilst breaking camp. Today would be a short walk of only 9 miles to Peebles. Of course, with wild camping being legal almost everywhere in Scotland, I had the flexibility to either go on or stop as the mood took me, but chose to follow my guidebook schedule. I felt it made forward planning a lot simpler and having the odd short day was no bad thing as it often, as today, allowed for a bit of sightseeing. After retracing my steps to Traquair, I opted for the easier walking route and followed the minor B7062, soon passing the famous Bear Gates of Traquair House. This is actually the main gateway to the house but the gates have been locked since 1745 under strict instruction they remain closed until the Stuart Dynasty returns to the throne, meaning that all entrants to Traquair House have to use the side entrance. The last direct male descendant of the Stuart Kings died in 1807, so it looks like the gates will remain locked for the foreseeable future.

The road route wasn't perhaps the most scenic of my options but it was quiet and never wandered far from the River Tweed, giving tantalising glimpses of the river through the trees and across the fields.

I arrived in the town of Peebles around midday, having now walked just over 800 miles since setting off from Land's End, and after a swift coffee break and a visit to the post office to get my verification sheet stamped, I headed for the rather grandly named Rosetta Holiday Park on the outskirts of town. After handing over my £10 and pitching camp I took a stroll back into the centre of Peebles, calling into an outdoor shop for some all-in-one detergent, a spare gas cylinder for my Jetboil stove and a new mug, as the handle had fallen off my old one sometime ago.

After taking in the views along the River Tweed from the road bridge, I felt in need of some liquid refreshment and popped into The Bridge Inn. This single-roomed town centre hostelry was voted the best in Scotland by CAMRA in 2017 and I sampled pints of *Latitude* and *Jarl* from the Orkney and Fyne Ales Scotland breweries, respectively, whilst getting a lesson in local history from the bar staff. In 2014 Creative Scotland awarded Peebles the somewhat obscure title of the most creative place of its size in Scotland. One of its most famous denizens was John Buchan, author of one of my favourite stories, the 1915 adventure novel *The Thirty-Nine Steps*. Before hitting the big time, simultaneously maintaining writing, political and diplomatic careers, he had briefly practised law in the town.

I'd noticed that many buildings, including private houses, were decked out in red and white bunting and wondered what it was all in aid of. It seems I'd arrived in the middle of the Beltane Festival which has been celebrated here since 1897. It was originally a day where the people of Peebles would take to the streets, marking the return of summer by burning their winter bedding. 120 years on, this annual festival maintains its traditional ceremonies which includes the crowning of the Beltane Queen and encompasses a wide range of activities, although these days people tend not to incinerate their bedsheets!

I spent the rest of the afternoon sightseeing. Having worked up a good appetite, I treated myself to a fish and chips supper before calling into Sainsbury's for tomorrow's lunch and heading back to camp for an early night.

Despite the next day being another relatively short trek of 12 miles to West Linton, I was on the road before 7.00am in anticipation of route-finding issues and possible bad weather. There had been some light rain in the early hours and more was forecast.

My route out of Peebles initially took me along the Tweed by way of a riverside path as far as Neidpath

Castle, a 13th-century 'rubble-built' tower house which occupies a commanding position overlooking the River Tweed. In common with most ancient fortifications in this part of Scotland, it has a dramatic history. During Oliver Cromwell's invasion of Scotland in 1650, Neidpath was attacked by General Lambert and suffered extensive damage to the tower on the riverside. Some sources say that the castle was surrendered without a fight but others suggest that it required the longest assault on any stronghold south of the River Forth to force its surrender. Today, it's a popular tourist and wedding venue but I only had time to have a brief look at the exterior before leaving the River Tweed for the last time and heading up into the hills.

The main route, by way of very indistinct paths, included a stiff climb to the summit of White Meldon. I opted to avoid this and in so doing managed to lose my bearings, wandering aimlessly around the moor before my trusty compass got me back on track. Entering a plantation, I followed a forestry track which, after a mile or so, brought me to the remote settlement at Harehope. Emerging from another area of forestry, a vague path led me across the moor and down into the valley of Flemington Burn, from where I picked up the path of the Cross Borders Drove Road. I paused for lunch on a grass bank taking in the view back along the valley, under a lead grey sky, relieved that I would now be on clear paths for the rest of the day.

After lunch, I dropped down into another valley alongside Fingland Burn before passing along a very wet path through a narrow band of forestry. From here just over 3 miles of minor road-walking brought me to the outskirts of the ancient village of West Linton. I stopped at a tearoom for a welcome cuppa and a slice of carrot cake before calling in at the village post office to get my sheet stamped. Then I headed on up to the Gordon Arms Hotel for a pint or two of *Belhaven Best*, and to enquire about accommodation. I'd arrived during the week of the Royal Highland Show, held annually just outside Edinburgh. This is one of Scotland's most iconic events, showcasing the best of farming, food and rural life and, predictably, the hotel was fully booked. It also set alarm bells ringing on the chances of getting a comfortable bed anywhere for the next few nights. The barmaid kindly made a few fruitless telephone calls to check the availability of accommodation, but I eventually settled for another night under canvas, this time on a small area of parkland on the banks of Lyne Water, a tributary of the River Tweed.

I awoke at 5.00 next morning. Heavy rain overnight had cleared the air after a hot and humid evening and I wandered into a stand of trees, set back from the river, to carry out my morning ablutions. I can't say I relish heeding the call of nature in the great outdoors. It always seems such an ordeal bracing against trees in damp undergrowth whilst trying to avoid stinging nettles and brambles. But there is also something wonderfully serene about al fresco toileting and you get a heightened sense of your surroundings, which probably comes with the vulnerability of squatting in the wilds with your kecks down. My campsite was clearly on a route popular with runners and dog walkers, and I was pulling up my trousers when I heard voices. I hastily washed in the cool waters of the river, then breakfasted on muesli and coffee before breaking camp.

By 6.45am I was back on the Cross Borders Drove Road, initially on a long, steady climb out of the village. The gradient became easier beyond Baddinsgill Farm and Reservoir as it continued across wild and bleak moorland and over the Pentland Hills. On this peaceful stretch of countryside, the silence was only broken by my own footfall and the occasional cries of the birds of prey hunting over the open moorland. But this ancient drove road once echoed with the noise of up to 150,000 cattle a year being herded on their way to the markets of Northern England on what was possibly the busiest drove road in Scotland. It is also known, as many drove roads are, as the 'Thieves Road' and one may suppose that it must have been used by a fair number of cattle rustlers as well as legitimate traders.

At a pass with the curious name of Cauldstane Slap, the trail left the Borders region of Scotland and entered West Lothian. I marked the occasion by losing the path and floundering around in the boggy heather moorland for a while. Once I'd recovered my bearings, it was up over Corston Hill which, despite its relatively diminutive height of 1,142 feet, afforded extensive views north-east to the sea between the Forth Bridges and Edinburgh. I took a short break to savour the view as this would be the last hill on the route for a while.

Descending Corston Hill on an invisible path towards the boundary of the moor, I spooked a large flock of sheep, sending them into a frenzied stampede. A field gate gave access to a minor road which I followed to an area of woodland just outside Mid Calder. For the next couple of days, I'd be trekking through the Scottish industrial heartland which would have a different feel to the walking I'd experienced over the last few weeks. It was, however, surprisingly rural and on this peaceful section along the Linhouse Water valley I was barely conscious of the sizeable housing estate less than a quarter of a mile away.

One of the really great things about stepping out of the 'rat race' on a long-distance trek is that you can clear your mind of the often complicated problems and issues which face you in everyday life. The myriad relationship, commuting or work-related problems seem to melt away. Stephen Graham, in his classic *The Gentle Art of Tramping*, urges us to escape the constraints of jobs we hate, 'to cease to be identified by one's salary or by one's golf handicap'. Although published nearly one hundred years ago, this is perhaps even more relevant in these busy times. On the trail you have no engagements, commitments, obligations or duties; no special ambitions and only the smallest, least complicated of wants – the need for food, water, and somewhere warm and dry to lay your head at night. Late in the afternoon that day my thoughts were turning to the last of these. I'd not booked any accommodation and there were no campsites showing on my map anywhere in the vicinity, so I'd resolved to find a likely-looking spot to wild-camp for the night. Needing to replenish my water supply, I approached a couple of houses set just off the path. I was greeted by a huge, barking dog at the first and though I had become accustomed to this familiar reaction, having been yapped at, growled at and snarled at by just about every canine between East Calder and Land's End, I thought discretion to be the better part of valour and beat a hasty retreat. At the second house I met owners Ann and Phil. They were enormously interested in my journey and Ann kindly offered to give me a lift to a nearby B&B.

As anticipated, the Royal Highland Show meant they were fully booked along with, we were reliably informed, just about every hotel, guest house and B&B for twenty miles around. The proprietor was, however, able to point us in the direction of a local campsite and off we sped. The Linwater Caravan Park turned out to be quite a find with a good toilet and shower block and a small shop in reception. For £11, I managed to bag what appeared to be the last pitch and set up camp. The site had no bar and the nearest pub was a fair way off, but I was pretty weary from the day's 16-mile trek and with the prospect of a 19-mile stretch tomorrow, I settled on a quiet night in with a Pot Noodle and an All Day Breakfast.

I set off the next morning at 7.00, overnight wind and rain having given way to a light breeze and overcast conditions. A surprisingly short walk, along a field path and hedgerow, brought me back to the valley path pretty much at the point I'd left it yesterday and I followed it alongside a feeder channel beneath a leafy canopy. Within about 3 miles, this flowed into the Union Canal as it crossed the River Almond valley 75 feet up via the impressive Lin's Mill Aqueduct.

The Edinburgh and Glasgow Union Canal, to give it its full name, runs from Edinburgh to Falkirk. It opened in 1822 and was initially successful, bringing coal to the capital. The construction of railways, however, diminished its value as a transport route. It was closed to commercial traffic in 1933 and officially closed in 1965. Having benefited from the general revival of interest in canals, it reopened in 2001 through the £84.5m Millennium Link Project, which was the largest canal restoration in the UK at the time and was reconnected to the Forth and Clyde Canal just beyond Falkirk. Today it enjoys renewed popularity for leisure purposes, including walking, and I would be following its towpath for the best part of 20 miles to my destination at Falkirk.

Beyond the aqueduct the walking along the canal towpath became less inspiring as it passed through the housing estates of Broxburn. Once out of the town, though, the scene became more rural, meandering through fields and passing Niddry Castle. Built in 1490, this compact tower house is situated opposite the village of Winchburgh adjacent to an oil shale waste heap. This aspect entirely belies its past splendour as the seat of the princely Setons of East Lothian, and as a residence grand enough to host Mary, Queen of Scots, who stayed here in May 1568 after her escape from captivity in Loch Leven Castle.

The towpath continued on through a wooded area for three or four miles and here I met Barbara from Newcastle. She was on a lone 'end-to-end' journey in the opposite direction (JOGLE as opposed to LEJOG) and had set off from John o' Groats four weeks earlier. I had to admire her spirit, given that she'd had rain every day for the first three weeks. It's at times like that that you need to dig deep into your bag of resolve. An unsupported long-distance walk is as much a mental challenge as a physical one. It's difficult for most people to stay positive and single-minded for such a long time, particularly in the face of adversity such as bad weather or injury. The enormity of the endeavour can be rather daunting and often leads to people giving up. Desmond Tutu once wisely observed that there is only one way to eat an elephant: one bite at a time. In other words, the best way to tackle something big is to break it down into smaller pieces, taking on just a little at a time. For me, the day's walk of between 15 and 20 miles was the target rather than the whole 1,200 miles.

Around lunchtime, I arrived in Linlithgow, a town I'd never heard of until two years ago, when my last employer arranged for me to attend a course here just before my hip operation. I decided to break off and grab a bite to eat in town, taking the opportunity to revisit Linlithgow's two most prominent landmarks, the Palace and the Loch. The Palace, on which construction began in 1424, is the town's chief historic attraction and the birthplace of James V and the ubiquitous Mary, Queen of Scots. The loch, despite having an average depth of only seven and a half feet, is the largest natural freshwater loch in Lothian. It was once famed for its wild brown trout, but the sport for the many boat anglers out on the water today was coming from stocked rainbow trout.

As I'd spent the last five nights under canvas, I decided to treat myself to a proper bed that night, so whilst I lunched on a substantial burger in the Old Post Office Bar, I went online and booked myself a room in a reasonably priced hotel in Falkirk.

Back on the towpath after lunch I was again in pleasant rural surroundings which soon included the spectacular Avon Aqueduct which crosses the River Avon. This twelve-arched structure, built between 1819 and 1821, shares its design with the aqueduct at Lin's Mill. At just over 810 feet long and 86 feet high, it's the longest and tallest aqueduct in Scotland, the second-longest in Britain, after the Pontcysyllte Aqueduct in Wales, and as if that weren't enough, a category 'A' listed building. Just beyond the aqueduct, the trail merges with the John Muir Way, named after the influential Scottish-American naturalist and author who was born in 1838 not a million miles away in Dunbar, East Lothian. His tireless work for the preservation of wilderness areas in America earned him the nickname "Father of the National Parks".

Late in the afternoon, as I reached Falkirk, the Union Canal disappeared into a 2,067-foot-long tunnel through Prospect Hill. It was built between 1818 and 1822 solely to appease William Forbes, the wealthy owner of nearby Callander House, who would not allow the canal to pass within sight of his property. A handrail prevented me from wandering off the flagstone walkway kept damp by water spilling through the roof at various points. The atmospheric tunnel was made more eerie by the knowledge that navvies-turned-murderers Burke and Hare, who murdered 16 people to provide their bodies for medical experimentation, had apparently worked on its construction.

Falkirk is the biggest town on the entire 'end-to-end' trail, if you ignore Bristol where the route only really passes around the outskirts. I can't say that Falkirk has much to commend itself to tourists, though it is home to The Kelpies, an impressive 98-foot-high horse-head sculpture opened in October 2013 as a monument to Scotland's horse-powered heritage. In a 2011 poll conducted by STV, Falkirk was voted as Scotland's most beautiful town, ahead of Perth and Stirling in second and third places, respectively, and it walked away with the title of Britain's Best Walking Neighbourhood in 2019.

At the end of the Falkirk Tunnel, a path led me up towards the town centre and after a swift pint or two in a local hostelry, I eagerly sought out the Hotel Cladhan. After dinner, I was quite content to spend the evening in the hotel bar, contemplating my route for tomorrow and chatting to a couple of Irish Guardsmen – in town for a parade of some sort – who had spotted the SSAFA shirt I habitually wore in the evenings and were keen to hear about my walk.

When plans were being prepared to reconnect the Union Canal with the Forth and Clyde Canal, the problem of how to overcome a massive height difference between the two waterways presented itself. Until 1933, they had been linked by a staircase of 11 locks – long since demolished and replaced by housing – which took nearly a day to transit. The solution, using 21st-century, state-of-the-art engineering, was the mechanical marvel known as the Falkirk Wheel, and as I set off next morning I was looking forward to checking out this iconic landmark right on my route just west of the town.

The 115-foot-high steel structure, which is the only rotating boat lift of its kind in the world, opened in 2002.

Jedburgh Abbey in the Scottish Borders

The Falkirk Wheel – a mechanical marvel

It has two gondolas each containing 300 tons of water and up to eight boats can be carried at any one time. Once the boats have entered, watertight gates seal off the gondolas from the water in the canals and the wheel starts to turn, taking around four minutes to move boats up and down the height of eight double-decker buses to and from the Union Canal, 82 feet above. Archimedes' principle, in relation to floating objects always displacing their own weight in water, ensures the balance and stability which contributes to the wheel's remarkable energy efficiency – it uses only 1.5 kwh of energy to complete one-half turn, the equivalent to boiling 8 electric kettles. Fascinated as I was, I only had time to watch one revolution of the Wheel before I headed off along the towpath now on the Forth and Clyde Canal.

The Forth and Clyde opened in 1790 and at 35 miles long, it provided a route for seagoing vessels of the day between the Firth of Forth and the Firth of Clyde, avoiding the long and dangerous route around the north coast. At the same time it provided a transport link for goods and passengers between the towns, industries, Lowland farms and Glasgow suburbs along the way. As seagoing vessels became larger and could no longer pass through, it fell into decline. The railways added a further nail to its coffin, and by the early 1930s the canal had ceased to be a viable commercial waterway. The Forth and Clyde was closed in 1963, but fortunately, like its sister canal, more recent ideas have revived it for leisure use.

My route today would take me 19 miles to Lennoxtown at the foot of the Campsie Fells, a range of gently rolling, volcanic hills just north of Glasgow. A large slice of the trail would be along the canal towpath and all of it on the John Muir Way. As much as I enjoyed having a firm, flat and dry path under my feet all day, the novelty does tend to wear off and I found myself yearning for the hills once more. That said, the Forth and Clyde seemed more picturesque to me than the Union Canal and ran through a predominantly more rural environment. I stopped for lunch at Auchinstarry Bridge, within sight of an attractive marina. By mid-afternoon I was skirting the northern edge of the sizeable town of Kirkintilloch, where I parted company with the canal as my route joined the Strathblane Railway Walkway to my night's destination at Lennoxtown.

I dined in the smart Glazert Country House Hotel that evening, on steak pie and chocolate fudge cake, washed down with cloudy Strongbow cider. The hotel was a popular wedding venue and on this busy Saturday they were fully booked, so a bed for the night was clearly out of the question. A brief search online produced no results on available accommodation, so I trudged off to pitch camp on the edge of a playing field I'd passed just off the trail. I shall say nothing more about Lennoxtown other than I wasn't keen on the place. In fairness, though, this opinion was probably clouded by my poor choice of campsite. I'd tucked myself away by a small, wooded area on the banks of Glazert Water, a minor river which flows past the town along its southern edge. Lennoxtown appears to be on the main flight path to Glasgow and what with almost constant aircraft noise and traffic till the early hours on a previously unnoticed main road, I got precious little sleep.

The icing on the cake came early next morning when, no doubt due to my proximity to water, trees and mild air, I was besieged by a swarm of midges. I hurriedly broke camp and set off at 7.15 vowing never to return!

Chapter Thirteen

Having not bothered with breakfast, I was feeling rather peckish by the time I arrived in Strathblane, around 5 miles into the day. I stopped off at the Kirkhouse Inn Hotel for a coffee and bacon sarnie before nipping into the local Co-op for some supplies. Around midday, I reached Dumgoyach Bridge, the point at which my trail joined the West Highland Way, Scotland's first long-distance route and by far the most popular. Stretching for 95 miles from Milngavie, just north of Glasgow, to Fort William at the foot of Ben Nevis, the route offers a fabulous introduction to the Scottish Highlands and tremendous variety. Beginning here in the rural landscapes beneath the Campsie Fells, it passes Loch Lomond and continues on into the increasingly rugged and majestic Highlands. The Way then crosses the vast, awe-inspiring expanse of Rannoch Moor, before crossing the hills to Loch Leven, finally reaching Fort William via Glen Nevis. Most people complete the walk over six to eight days.

I immediately became aware of the increased volume of pedestrian traffic and with around 50,000 people walking the West Highland Way each year, I realised this would be a sociable trail. Late in the afternoon, I pitched camp at Easter

Drumquhassle Farm just outside Drymen. The facilities were basic but adequate and at £5 for the night it was certainly cheap. There, I met Emily, a radio journalist from Alaska, two German couples, and Matthew, a beekeeper from a small town just outside Sydney, Australia, who was doing the walk to escape his wife's father! It was certainly a very cosmopolitan group and for most, their first long-distance hike. I found myself answering questions on such things as how best to deal with blisters, what midge repellent I used, and the relative merits of merino wool trekking socks. For the first time since setting off from Land's End, I realised with satisfaction that I had become something of a trail master.

I had a better night's sleep and was consequently in a much-improved frame of mind as I set off the next morning on my first full day on the West Highland Way. Yesterday had been a gentle introduction to the trail. I suspected that today would involve a bit more hard work. After making a short detour to Drymen village to pick up some supplies, I headed up into the Garadhban Forest and the Trossachs National Park. Covering 720 square miles, the park is home to 21 mountains, 22 lochs, 2 forest parks, and more than 50 designated nature conservation areas, and a pleasant walk followed with occasional glimpses through the trees to what is probably the park's best-known feature – Loch Lomond. The loch covers 27.5 square miles, making it the largest lake in Britain if measured by surface area, and I would be closely following its eastern shore for the best part of the next two days. Beyond the forest the trail crossed the Burn of Mar and climbed the steep-sided and aptly named Conic Hill which rises to a height of 1,184 feet. The path itself doesn't actually go all the way to the summit, which can be reached by another route, but the views from the wide shoulder of the hill across Loch Lomond with its myriad of islands, were stunning and I didn't feel the need to clamber the last few metres to the peak.

Following a steep descent, the trail took me through a small forest plantation, and another swarm of midges, to my lunch stop at Balmaha. This attractive little village sits on the shore of Loch Lomond and is a popular tourist destination. I lunched at Weir's Rest by Balmaha Bay, a garden area dedicated to Tom Weir. Dubbed "Scotland's most-loved mountain man", this climber, author and broadcaster became a pioneering campaigner for the protection of the Scottish environment and was best known north of the border for his long-running television series *Weir's Way*. He died in 2006 and the bronze statue of him on the shore of the loch was unveiled in 2014 to mark 100 years on from his birth. Just as I was setting off again after lunch, I ran into Emily and Matthew from the campsite and we enjoyed a pleasant ramble for the rest of the afternoon, primarily along forestry tracks skirting the banks of the loch.

I'd managed to book a bed for the night at the popular Rowardennan Lodge Youth Hostel, a former hunting lodge which sits in an idyllic location right on the banks of the loch at the foot of Ben Lomond. Arriving around 5.00pm, I bade farewell to Emily and Matt who had planned to spend the night in a bothy some five miles further on and after settling in had a relaxing evening in the hostel's spacious lounge, enjoying wonderful views of the loch whilst supping *Loch Lomond Craft Lager.*

Heavy rain overnight and into the early hours had fortunately dwindled to a light drizzle by the time I set off at 8.30 the next morning on a 13-mile trek to Inverarnan. Initially on a good path, the route took me along the very edge of the loch, although often in thick woodland and in the mist of a damp morning the views were not extensive. The trail passed a crag known as Rob Roy's Prison, where, according to tradition, he incarcerated prisoners and hostages in the late-17th century. Whether there's any truth in that is another matter but it reminded me that I was now entering the territory of Rob Roy MacGregor, a figure who still looms large in Scottish history.

On long-distance trails walkers generally travel along at much the same pace following similar itineraries. You therefore tend to become part of an informal group, from different age groups and walks of life but all experiencing the same weather, same discomforts, same landscapes, same peculiar impulse to hike from, in this case, Milngavie to Fort William. About seven miles along the loch at the Inversnaid Hotel I happened upon Emily and Matthew in company with Michael from Frankfurt. They had all spent an uncomfortable night in a nearby bothy and had stopped off at the hotel for some breakfast. After a coffee break we all headed off together – the Englishman, the American, the Australian, and the German – and if that's not a cue for a joke, I don't know what is! With us all coming from such varied backgrounds and far-flung places, conversation was interesting and plentiful and having spent so much time on my own over the last ten weeks I found it quite pleasant.

The trail continued to trace the shoreline of Loch Lomond, although at times it was slow-going clambering through rocky areas on steep slopes along the 'bonny, bonny banks'. Another milestone was reached just beyond Inversnaid, at which point I'd covered around 900 miles and completed three-quarters of my journey!

Around 2.00pm, we stopped for a brief lunch break on a grassy area at the water's edge. The light rain, which had persisted for most of the day, had now stopped and a weak sun was forcing its way through thick cloud. From the end of the loch the trail became easier, crossing rough pasture and woodland, eventually reaching Beinglas Farm Campsite where the others were pitching camp for the night. After a swift pint in the site bar I pushed on, across the River Falloch, the short distance to The Drovers Inn where I'd been fortunate to have secured a late booking. As I left the campsite, I couldn't help noticing how 'midgy' it was and thanked my lucky stars I'd be indoors tonight.

Opened in 1705, The Drovers Inn is one of the oldest licensed premises in Scotland and was traditionally frequented by the Highland drovers who used to move their cattle down the side of Loch Lomond to the markets. From the moment you enter the atmospheric reception hall you realise you're in a unique hostelry, with its suit of armour and collection of stuffed birds and animals, which includes a full-grown grizzly bear. It is also rumoured to be one of the most haunted hotels in Britain, though I can't say I personally experienced any spectral activity that night. To be fair, after a couple of pints of *Caledonian Best* with my steak and Guinness pie dinner, I was dead to the world myself.

There are 35 species of midge in Scotland and, although only 5 of those will actually bite, it doesn't stop the other 30 being a bloody nuisance. These vicious wee beasties were once described by 'literary pedestrian' John Taylor, on his travels in the Highlands in the early 17th century, as "a creature that hath six legs and lives like a monster altogether upon man's flesh" and it is indeed a very apt description. There are a number of products on the market which claim varying degrees of success in deterring the little blighters. *Smidge* is the nation's favourite midge repellent, but *Avon Skin So Soft body oil* is a proven winner. It's a secret weapon worn by many workers in Scotland and the Royal Marines swear by it. To combat the worst swarms, the head net I carried was possibly the best fiver I'd ever spent. Midges tend to be at their worst from the end of May until September and prefer cool, damp and still conditions which, of course, was precisely what I set off in the next morning.

My planned route today would take me 12 miles to Tyndrum where I'd booked myself a bed at the Dalkell Cottage Guest House B&B. Initially, the path shadowed the banks of the River Falloch, passing impressive waterfalls along the way. For the most part, the route followed a good track on an old military road. This is part of a network of over 250 miles of road built by General George Wade in the first half of the 18th century to pacify and control the Highlanders, and the West Highland Way follows Wade's roads in a number of places.

Just before Crianlarich, the trail converges on a railway line and the A82. To pass under the former, it goes through a low tunnel called a 'sheep creep', the negotiation of which proved quite an inelegant and strenuous experience with "The Beast" strapped to my back. At Crianlarich junction, I arrived at the halfway point on the West Highland Way and once again met up with Emily and Matthew. As we crossed the stile at the head of Bogle Glen, so we stepped for the first of four times across the British watershed. This is an almost imaginary line running the length of Britain, on one side of which waters eventually flow into the North Sea and on the other side into the Irish Sea. After a very pleasant ramble through a couple of miles of forestry and woodland, we stopped for lunch by the River Fillan at which point Matthew announced that he thought he'd left his cooker back at the Beinglas Campsite. Later in the day he took a bus all the way back before realising it had been in the bottom of his pack all the time.

Beyond the remains of St Fillan's Priory, a 12th-century monastic site dedicated to the memory of an Irish monk, we passed an enchanting pool of water known as the Lochan of The Lost Sword. The story goes that in 1306, Robert the Bruce was facing defeat by the Clan MacDougall aided by the English, at nearby Dalrigh. Forced to flee, he ordered his troops to lighten their loads by throwing their heavy weapons into a small lochan on their route. Amongst these weapons was Robert the Bruce's legendary, metre-long Claymore which, it is said, still lies beneath the surface of the water, guarded by the 'lady of the lake'. Shortly afterwards and only a mile from the loch, Bruce's pursuers caught up with him but despite now being only lightly armed they fought them off and lived to fight another day. Another version of the same tale suggests it was William Wallace and not Robert the Bruce. To be honest, there's not a lot of historic evidence to support either tale but it's a great story nevertheless.

A short riverside stroll brought us to Tyndrum, a small village at the southern tip of Rannoch Moor. I made straight for the Tyndrum Inn for a post-ramble pint of *Edinburgh Castle*. I was joined by Emily, and later Matthew once he'd returned from his unnecessary journey back to Inverarnan, and we spent the evening reviewing what had been a very enjoyable day's walking.

I was the only guest at the Dalkell Cottage B&B that night, so was well looked after by owner Chris, and he sent me on my way next morning with a substantial breakfast inside me. Today would be a long, 18-mile trek to Kingshouse and with heavy rain forecast for later, I set off smartly at 8.00am to get a few miles under my belt ahead of it. The WHW climbed steadily out of Tyndrum along a good track beside a burn, once more crossing the British watershed. The wind picked up as the well-signposted path contoured around the slopes of Beinn Odhar. Around mid-morning, I arrived at the tiny hamlet of Bridge of Orchy which is little more than a smattering of dwellings with a station and the Bridge of Orchy Hotel where I stopped for a coffee break. Shortly after resuming the trek, I was caught up by Emily and Matt and together we followed a clear, though sometimes rough path by way of forest tracks and an old military road around the western tip of Loch Tulla.

Beyond that, an excellent cart track led us north across remote moorland. The forecast rain arrived around midday and we lunched beneath a stone bridge beside a small stream, steeling ourselves for the crossing of Rannoch Moor. The main watershed was crossed again and from here to John o' Groats the trail would be entirely in the Highland region of Scotland.

One of the last remaining wildernesses in Europe, Rannoch Moor is a stunning area occupying roughly 50 square miles of uninhabited peatbogs, lochs and heather hillocks. It can be bleak and beautiful at the same time depending on the conditions and in bad weather it has the potential to be one of the most inhospitable places in Scotland. Halfway across the moor, I arrived at Ba Bridge which carries the West Highland Way over the River Ba. It seemed the perfect spot from which to admire the fantastic scenery, so my companions plodded on while I took a break. The heavy rainfall that had been threatening for most of the day finally arrived mid-afternoon and I pushed on for the last five miles or so in driving rain. Now I'm certainly not just a fair-weather walker, but I do not particularly relish hiking in waterproofs. There is something disheartening about the stiff rustle of overgarments and the incessant patter of rain on synthetic material. Worst of all, you don't even stay dry. Even the best waterproofs eventually make you sweat so much you become clammily sodden.

I hadn't booked any accommodation for the night and already knew that the Kings House Hotel, sited in an isolated position on the edge of the moor, was closed for major refurbishment. Rannoch Moor is actually 82% water or bog, making it the largest area of blanket bog in Britain and I was beginning to wonder where I might be able to pitch camp for the night. Salvation came courtesy of the Glencoe Mountain Resort, located just off the track beyond a small area of woodland. Emily and Matt had already arrived and with none us relishing the prospect of putting up a tent in the wind and rain, the three of us shared the cost of a 'Hobbit House'. These green, cylindrical huts had power, lighting and a small, portable heater with mattresses and sleeping space for four people. Add a sleeping bag, and for £17 each we had a snug dwelling for the night and access to showers and a drying room. The resort also had a good-sized lounge with a limited food menu and I was able to enjoy a fish and chips supper whilst appreciating wonderful views of the surrounding mountains in the evening light before turning in.

After yesterday's route march in the wind and rain, the prospect of a short day was very appealing. Today's walk to Kinlochleven, on my penultimate day on the West Highland Way, was only 9 miles, although it would include a fairly hefty ascent. I had a couple of sachets of muesli for breakfast then set off with Emily around 8.30am. Matthew had decided to have a lie-in and a full breakfast in the resort café but as a fit guy in his twenties, he would undoubtedly catch us up during the course of the morning. The weather had improved considerably and, although rather cloudy it was dry and the views were good. Off to the left, Glen Coe, forged in the heat of a supervolcano and shaped into an eye-catching trench by a glacier. Standing guard at the entrance to Glen Coe and Glen Etive is the impressive mountain of Buachaille Etive Mor, possibly the most photographed triangle in Britain (when you can actually see the peak).

Just west of the Kingshouse, the trail once again joins General Wade's old military road and heads up a steep col between two peaks on a zigzagging route known as the Devil's Staircase. Reaching a height of 1,798 feet, this is the highest point on the West Highland Way. Despite its rather fearsome reputation, the section is not overly strenuous and the rewards are great. At the summit, we discovered an honesty 'tuck shop' selling drinks and snacks from under a couple of small tents and which some very enterprising person was obviously keeping well stocked. This gave us the opportunity to take a break with a soft drink and a bag of sweets whilst enjoying the breathtaking scenery. The retrospective view across to Buachaille Etive Mor was unforgettable. Ahead, although the conditions were not ideal, we got our first glimpse of Carn Mor Dearg, the Mamores, and the highest peak in the UK – Ben Nevis.

From the top of the Devil's Staircase, the rocky trail descended as it crossed the hillside before joining a well-metalled vehicle track servicing the nearby Blackwater Reservoir. On the descent I met Vera, an Israeli lady on her own 'end-to-end' journey. She was a very experienced walker whom I'd heard about along the trail. I was chuffed to learn that she'd heard about me as well – it seemed we were both mildly legendary.

The track wound its way down through an area of forestry before eventually following a section of pipeline into the village of Kinlochleven. Surrounded on three sides by steep mountains, the village was formed from two previously separate settlements following the construction of an aluminium plant in 1909. The plant was powered by a hydroelectric scheme using water from Blackwater Reservoir, and Kinlochleven became the first village in the world to have every house connected to electricity (famously before even Buckingham Palace). Although the plant produced some of the highest-grade aluminium, its small size in comparison to modern US smelters led to its closure in 1996. This was a massive blow to the economy of Kinlochleven as the plant had at one time employed up to 700 people.

The village is, however, an important tourism destination with the West Highland Way and other walking, biking and climbing activities attracting over 85,000 people each year. It's reckoned that mountaineering alone is worth around £164m a year to the Highlands and Kinlochleven is home to the National Ice-Climbing Centre, which boasts the biggest indoor ice climbing wall in the world.

I arrived in the village around lunchtime, and immediately contributed to the local economy with a couple of pints of *Caledonian Coast to Coast Pale Ale* and a packet of peanuts, before heading off to find the B&B I'd booked. I'd not slept particularly well in the 'Hobbit House' the night before so I took the opportunity to grab a couple of hours, shut-eye before a fish and chips supper in the village chippy. The owners had moved to Kinlochleven from Essex seventeen years previously and certainly found that trade from the West Highland Way helped to keep them going.

Loch Lomond on the West Highland Way

Buachaille Etiv Mor from the Devil's Staircase

Saturday 1st July would be my last day on the West Highland Way with a 14-mile trek to Fort William. I wished my hosts Danny and Marian well for their wedding anniversary later in the month – they had married on the day England won the World Cup in 1966 – and set off for the local Co-op where I'd arranged to meet Emily. After collecting Matthew from the local campsite, we commenced the climb out of Kinlochleven, getting some great retrospective views back down the glen to the village. The old military road followed a deep trench between Beinn na Caillich on the left and the peaks of the Mamores on the right. After about five miles, the trail swung north on a good track through a cleared forestry area where we stopped briefly for lunch.

The route then began its final rush to Glen Nevis and the long, steady descent at the foot of Ben Nevis. At 4,411 feet above sea level, this mighty peak is the highest mountain in Britain and one I climbed a couple of years earlier. The conditions then seemed to be about the same today, with the peak shrouded in mist and a persistent rain starting to fall. The forest track joined the road leading to the outskirts of Fort William at Nevis Bridge and the sign declaring the 'Original End of The West Highland Way'. In recent years, the 'official' end of the trail has become the statue of a seated figure a mile further on down Fort William High Street, but frankly, in the squally rain we were prepared to call it 'job done' at the bridge. After a team photo, we repaired to the Edinburgh Woollen Mill outlet for a cuppa and complimentary West Highland Way completion certificate.

Fort William is a key tourist centre and the second-largest settlement in the Scottish Highlands behind Inverness. It was also the end of section five of my journey which meant another rest day. There's plenty of accommodation to be had in Fort William but it gets booked up quickly in the summer and it didn't help that I'd timed my arrival to coincide with a major walking event in Glencoe. As a consequence, the only place I'd been able to book for the next two nights was campus accommodation designed for students. My first job, however, was to collect my last resupply box from the main post office, open surprisingly late on this damp Saturday afternoon. Having done that I ambled off to find my lodging which turned out to be a small, functional room in a soulless, modern building and I immediately hated it. Its only saving grace was its location just a few minutes from the town centre.

I washed out a few of the more necessary items of clothing then headed into town for the evening. The Grog & Gruel is a traditional Scottish alehouse located along Fort William's pedestrianised High Street, and a very popular venue. It was rather too busy and noisy for my liking, though, so I wandered along to the Ben Nevis, whose Jacobite lounge was virtually empty. I enjoyed a quiet pint or two of *Deuchars IPA* whilst chatting to a group of local youngsters. They spotted my *End to End Trail* guidebook and were keen to hear about my trek, kindly donating £40 to the charity between them.

My first night in the 'hotel' was the worst ever. The whole building was oppressively warm with no obvious means of regulating the temperature. I dared not open the window too wide for fear of inviting in swarms of midges and in any case, I wouldn't have been able to sleep as the drainpipe outside my window was dripping all night producing a rhythmic and constant tapping. To cap it all, the occupants of the room above returned around 3.00am and proceeded to do a passable impression of a herd of elephants. There was no onsite staff but I had been given the mobile number of the duty facilities manager. Needless to say he wasn't available so early on a Sunday morning. I wouldn't have minded so much if it had been cheap – but it wasn't!

It was still raining at 7.15am as I strolled, bleary-eyed, down to the Brewers Fayre to take advantage of their £8.99 'all you can eat' breakfast. After a visit to the local supermarket and outdoor shop for some supplies and a spare gas cylinder, I whiled away an hour or so in a coffee shop waiting for the post office to open at midday, so I could send my supply box home for the final time. I once again ran into Emily and Matthew. Emily would shortly be heading to Edinburgh before flying back to Alaska, and Matthew had decided to continue his trek with a few days on the Cape Wrath Trail, before returning to his honey farm outside Sydney. The weather hadn't really shown any sign of improvement, so I wandered back to my unspeakable lodgings and spent the rest of the day catching up on my sleep, preparing my backpack for the next morning and reviewing my route for the final stage of the trek. It amuses me that, two years on, I was still getting emails announcing accommodation deals at Lennoxtown and Fort William. They didn't have any availability at the time. Did they think I'd been lost there without a roof over my head ever since, still in need of a bed for the night?

Chapter Fourteen

From Land's End to Fort William, I'd been following Andy Robinson's *End to End Trail* guidebook. From here, though, that route struck northwards into wild and largely uninhabited terrain. Given that my navigation and survival skills had never really been tested in anger and that I had a hankering to see Loch Ness, I decided to follow the Great Glen to Inverness and from there take a route closer to the east coast to John o' Groats.

So, for the next six days I would be travelling the Great Glen Way. This ruler-straight trail stretches for 79 miles from coast to coast across the Highlands, linking the main centres of Fort William and the regional capital of Inverness. Following a 400 million-year-old major fault line, the Glen is laced by the scenic Caledonian Canal, and links Loch Lochy and Loch Oich with the massive expanse of Loch Ness.

After a marginally better night, I set off at 7.00am and headed back to the Brewers Fayre for breakfast, seizing the opportunity to grab a bacon sarnie and some additional pastries for lunch. The trail starts, or finishes, depending on which direction you're travelling, from the remains of the old fort which lies at the confluence of Loch Linnhe and Loch Eil. The original wooden fort was built in 1654 by General George Monck (Cromwell's Commander-in-Chief in Scotland). It was replaced with a stone fort in 1690, gained notoriety for its role in the infamous Glencoe Massacre of 1692, and was later fortified by General Wade in 1725. The fort was named Fort William after King William III with the town itself later taking the same name.

Leaving the old fort, I set off at 8.15am in drizzly rain, on the 11-mile walk to Gairlochy. I anticipated a comfortable day's walking, being mostly along a canalside track in the shadow of Britain's highest mountain, although in the mist and low cloud, not much of that would be visible. Initially, the well-marked path followed a tarmac track then crossed a meadow to pass Inverlochy Castle. Originally dating back to the 13th century, Inverlochy was the backdrop for major historical events during the Civil Wars of the 1640s, notably the first and second Battles of Inverlochy. The castle was abandoned in 1654 in favour of the larger timber fortification at nearby Fort William.

Just beyond the castle ruins, I fell in behind a woman wearing a sizeable backpack and striding so confidently along that I took my eye off the waymarkers. We had both reached a road junction when I asked her whether she was walking the Great Glen Way. "No," she replied, "I'm going to work." And with that, she gave me a very funny look, scuttled across the road and disappeared onto a small industrial estate. Somewhat embarrassed I hurried on, fortunately still on track.

A hike along the shore of Loch Linnhe brought me to

a point just outside the village of Corpach. Not being in need of any supplies, I turned east and headed off along the embankment of the Caledonian Canal. This 60-mile-long waterway connects the east coast at Inverness with the west coast here at Corpach. Only around 22 miles of it is man-made, though, the rest being formed by Lochs Lochy, Oich, and Ness. The canal was constructed by legendary Scottish engineer Thomas Telford between 1803 and 1822, primarily to allow safe passage for naval and trading vessels during the Napoleonic Wars. Today, although large commercial vessels do still use the canal, most are among the 53,000 leisure craft a year out to enjoy the fantastic scenery.

The small village of Banavie, four miles north of Fort William, is home to the impressive Neptune's Staircase. This tightly packed series of eight locks – on which more than a hundred masons laboured for nearly four years – raises the canal by 62 feet over a quarter of a mile and takes around 90 minutes for a boat to travel up or down. The sun had by now decided to put in an appearance, so I took a seat on the patio of a lock-side café and enjoyed a cup of coffee and a buttered scone whilst contemplating the leisurely pace of life on the canal.

Continuing along the canalside track, I arrived at the attractive Moy Swing Bridge which seemed the perfect spot for a brief lunch break. It's the only surviving original bridge on the Caledonian Canal and quite possibly one of the oldest moveable bridges of any kind in Britain. It still has to be operated manually to allow the farmer from Moy to drive farm equipment down to his riverside meadows on the banks of the River Lochy. The river runs parallel to the canal as far as Gairlochy and effectively creates a long, narrow 'island'. Because each half of the bridge has to be swung separately, until recently, the keeper had to row across the canal each time the bridge was operated.

A mile or so beyond Moy Bridge, I reached the scattering of houses forming the tiny hamlet of Gairlochy. I headed off-route down a minor road in search of the Gairlochy Holiday Park where I planned to camp for the night. It was still only early afternoon when I arrived and having paid my £7.50 and pitched camp, I decided to take a stroll, unburdened by 'The Beast', a mile or two further down the road to visit the Commando Memorial just outside Spean Bridge.

Unveiled in 1952, the monument is dedicated to the officers and men of the British Commando forces who died in the Second World War. It consists of a cast bronze sculpture of three Commandos facing south towards Ben Nevis and overlooking the training area of the wartime Commando Training Depot. I found the experience quite moving and took a seat on a bench to soak up the atmosphere whilst a succession of coaches came and went with their cargo of tourists.

I returned to camp around 5.00pm and dined on a tuna bean pasta ration pack and trail mix, washed down with a cup of coffee. The weather had improved steadily throughout the day and I spent the evening sitting outside my tent on a plastic garden chair sunning myself and chatting to some neighbouring campers, one of whom was recovering from cancer and was walking the Great Glen Way as a personal challenge. When the midges became too unbearable I zipped myself into my tent and read until lights out.

Day two of the main route indicated a 12-mile walk to Laggan Locks where facilities are very limited. Instead I opted for what's known as the 'Invergarry Link'. Although 5 miles longer, this route would bring me to the village of Invergarry and a range of facilities including the Saddle Mountain Hostel where I'd booked myself a bed for the night. I broke camp early, setting off at 7.00 on a dry and slightly overcast morning. After retracing my steps to the point where the Caledonian Canal joins Loch Lochy, I followed the loch along its wooded northern shoreline, by path and minor road. Along the way, I discovered a variety of information boards detailing different aspects of the Commando training which took place in the countryside around the wartime Commando Basic Training Centre at nearby Achnacarry Castle. Home to the Chief of Clan Cameron, the building and estate were used between 1942 and 1945 to put around 25,000 Commandos and US Army Rangers through some of the toughest military training in the world. I came across the remains of a concrete base in the shape of a landing craft, which had been used for beach storming training. Another information board was sited by an old boathouse which had once been used by the Commandos to store their canoes and boats.

At the far end of Loch Lochy, the trail descended to Laggan where I broke for lunch and watched a couple of naval patrol vessels negotiate the locks. Back on the richly wooded track, I had occasional glimpses of Loch Oich, the smallest of the three lochs linked by the Caledonian Canal, before arriving at the Saddle Mountain Hostel. It was still a little early to check in so I continued on to the village of Invergarry to sample the *Belhaven Best* in the bar of the Invergarry Hotel. It was to here I returned later in the evening for an excellent fish and chips and *Scottish Lager* supper.

I woke next morning with a thick head – note to self, not to mix *Belhaven Best Bitter* and *Saltire Scottish Lager* – so it took a bit longer to get motivated and it was 9.30am before I hit the trail. I wasn't unduly concerned as the sun was shining and today would be a very leisurely 8-mile ramble to Fort Augustus.

From the woodland above Invergarry, the route descended to meet the A82 as it crossed the swing-bridge at Aberchalder, and I got a sharp rebuke from the bridge operator for crossing on the road, rather than using the pedestrian walkway alongside. The River Oich empties into the loch at this point and just a few yards from the modern road bridge stands the now redundant Bridge of Oich, an innovative suspension bridge built in 1854 by James Dredge. This replaced the old stone bridge which was swept away by flood water in 1849 and incorporated a unique double cantilever chain support system anchored by huge granite pylons on either shore. The bridge fell out of use in 1932 due to increased traffic loads, but its unique construction prompted Historic Scotland to take it into state care as a historic monument.

From Aberchalder a level canalside track led me into Fort Augustus, the halfway point on the Great Glen Way, just in time for an expensive lunchtime pint at the Lock Inn. Situated on the shore at the far south-west end of

Loch Ness, Fort Augustus is a picturesque village which at this time of year bustles with tourist activity. The village is effectively cut in two by the Caledonian Canal, and a flight of five locks moves the water traffic from one level to another. It is also believed to have been the birthplace of Ordnance Survey – whose maps and guides are so favoured throughout the world – on 21st June 1791.

I'd booked a bed at Morag's Lodge Hostel but as I couldn't check in until 4.00pm I had some time to kill. So, after posing for a lochside photo, I enjoyed a soft drink in a café while a piper in full Scottish dress entertained a group of enthralled Far Eastern tourists. Then it was into the local supermarket to stock up on lunch items for the next couple of days before seeking out my accommodation for the night.

Thursday 6th July, day 79, would be another short day with a 10-mile walk to Alltsigh. I left the hostel at around 8.30am under a leaden-grey sky in mist and drizzle – what's known in the Highlands as a 'mizzle'. I had two options today: a low-level route through woodland along the shoreline of Loch Ness, or a high-level route which climbs above the thickly forested northern slopes and affords more expansive views of the largest body of fresh water in the British Isles. As I approached the point where the trail divides, a couple of young guys emerged through the trees from the other direction. They were travelling very light and had set out to walk John o' Groats to Land's End in only 31 days! I wished them well and they sped off along the track behind me.

I decided to take the 'high road' and after a steady climb the track rose from the forest onto a moorland slope. Even in the mist and low cloud, the views of Loch Ness and back across Fort Augustus towards Loch Oich were breathtaking. I stopped briefly at a low stone shelter and there met up with Dick and Chris, a father and son from Australia who were on an extended visit to the UK and had decided to walk the Great Glen. Dick was a railway enthusiast and was able to provide an answer to something that had been puzzling me for a couple of days. Almost from the start of the walk from Fort William, I'd been coming across sections of what looked like miniature plastic track either in lengthy runs or little heaps. It seemed that a week or so earlier, a TV production company had been filming a groundbreaking programme for Channel 4, called *The Biggest Little Railway in the World*. This had involved a team of 56 model railway enthusiasts and engineers, led by presenter Dick Strawbridge, attempting to do what our Victorian ancestors couldn't – build a railway connecting Fort William with Inverness. The Victorians gave up because the terrain was simply too challenging and inhospitable for railway building but the team succeeded, the only difference being, they did it in miniature, in the process building the longest model railway in the world at 71 miles. All they had to do now was go back and pick up all the track.

I joined forces with Dick and Chris for the rest of the morning as far as Invermoriston, just outside of which we broke off to view a picturesque humpback bridge. The stone structure was believed to have been built in 1813 by Thomas Telford, the prolific early-19th century civil engineer, without whom we would be devoid of many of our bridges, roads and canals, not to mention aqueducts, harbours and tunnels. It crosses the spectacular River Moriston Falls and originally carried the main road between Inverness and Fort Augustus until it was replaced with the new adjacent bridge in 1933. It was around lunchtime when we arrived at the village of Invermoriston. The Glenmoriston Arms Hotel was a welcome location for a pint and a cheese and ham sandwich while my walking companions went off to explore the local craft shop.

I set off, after lunch, on the last couple of miles of the day. The trail followed a steep, narrow road which zigzagged its way out of the village through heavy woodland. Once again picking up the 'high-level' route, I eventually reached an area of forest which had been partly felled. Here, I stumbled upon 'The View Catcher', an interesting circular sculpture constructed from interwoven branches of Caledonian pine mounted on a plinth of local stone. The effect is to create an 'eye in the sky' to highlight the stunning view. It was also something of a milestone, being the point at which, I calculated, I'd now walked 1,000 miles!

Just beyond the sculpture, I left the main route to follow the river Allt Saigh down through the forest to Alltsigh, where I'd managed to secure a bed for the night at The Lochside Hostel. As the name suggests, this independent hostel is in a wonderful location right on the shores of Loch Ness with direct access to the water's edge. I spent a pleasant evening admiring the views from the terrace before dining on a couple of packs of 'All Day Breakfast' prepared in the self-catering kitchen. I turned in around

10.30pm and drifted off to the soothing sound of water lapping the stony shore.

As I sat eating my muesli the next morning, I had a message from Jill, the Belgian lady on her own 'end-to-end' trek, who I'd met just outside Abbots Bromley six weeks before. Sadly, her father had passed away soon after we first met and she'd had to go home. The good news was that she was now back on the trail and planned to reach John o' Groats at around the same time as me. I wished her well and agreed to meet up towards the end of our respective journeys.

The day had started reasonably clear and dry but within an hour or so of my waking and preparing to set off, it was raining and a light mist had settled across the loch. Today, I would be heading 12 miles north along Loch Ness to the village of Drumnadrochit, initially following a steadily rising track along the contours of the Creag-nan-Eun Forest. Around mid-morning I reached the Loch Ness Clay Works Pottery tearoom where, once they discovered I was on a long-distance charity walk, I was treated to a free pot of tea and a plate of delicious fruit cake. I left 45 minutes later, fully refreshed and £10 richer, having received a generous donation to SSAFA from a young lady staying there.

From the pottery, the terrain became more pastoral, the forest tracks replaced by a minor road. The heavens opened as I plodded along but, fortunately, I was by now within an hour or so of my destination. I descended into Lewiston, just outside Drumnadrochit, and had a pint in the Loch Ness Inn before heading across the road to the

Loch Ness Backpackers hostel where I'd be staying that night. They didn't have a drying room as such but kindly put all my wet gear in their tumble dryer while I had a hot shower, a cuppa and a doze.

One of the major tourist attractions in the area is Urquhart Castle, which sits about a mile and a half from Lewiston beside the busy A82. The weather had improved considerably and after a fish and chips supper in the pub, I decided to take a stroll down to view it in the early evening sunshine. The gate from the car park was unlocked and I wandered down the path to the castle, spooking a deer which had been grazing on the well-manicured lawn outside the castle walls. Urquhart Castle is one of Historic Scotland's most visited sites and one of the most photographed places in Scotland, with its picture adorning many a chocolate box and biscuit tin. It's easy to see why, in its dramatic and picturesque location perched on the headland of Strone Point overlooking Loch Ness. It was a treat to have it all to myself, and even in this peaceful setting I could really get a sense of the site's turbulent history. Following its capture by Edward I of England in 1296, Urquhart Castle played a key role in the Wars of Scottish Independence which went on intermittently throughout the first half of the 14th century. The MacDonalds launched raids on the castle during the 15th century before it was granted to the Clan Grant in 1509. The castle was garrisoned for the last time in 1689, following the exile of King James VII, with the bulk of the damage to the structure being done with explosives in 1692, to prevent it becoming a Jacobite stronghold.

Although the present ruins date from the 13th century, Urquhart Castle is known to have been built on the site of a much earlier fortification. St. Columba apparently visited the site around AD 580, spawning the mystery of the Loch Ness Monster when he was said to have saved a man from being attacked by a 'water beast' in the River Ness. The modern legend was born when a sighting made local news on 2nd May 1933. *The Inverness Courier* related an account of a local couple who claimed to have seen "an enormous animal rolling and plunging on the surface". But it was the "Surgeon's Photograph", supposedly taken by Dr Robert Wilson in April 1934, of a long-necked monster in the loch that sealed Nessie's fame. Thousands of people now visit intent on spying this elusive, mythical creature and with Loch Ness containing more fresh water than all the lakes in England and Wales combined, Nessie has plenty of places to hide. Coincidentally, there were more 'official' sightings in the year of my journey than any other this century. Admittedly, the number of official sightings logged was only eight, but that's a lot for a mythical beastie. Whatever the truth, it remains the UK's greatest unexplained riddle.

As the light started to fade, I gave up scanning the calm waters for a chance sighting of Nessie and strolled back to the Loch Ness Inn for a *Belhaven Best* nightcap. Tomorrow would be the last day on the Great Glen Way and with a long 19-mile stretch to Inverness in prospect, I needed an early night.

I was up at 6.00 the next morning, much, I'm sure, to the

annoyance of the other six people in the small dormitory. Breakfast was booked for 7.30am and with a long day ahead of me, I planned to be on the road by 8.00am. In contrast to yesterday, the weather was dry and pleasantly sunny.

At the outset, the route today followed the A82 through the village of Drumnadrochit and on past "Nessieland", a themed tourist attraction, before skirting the banks of Loch Ness at Urquhart Bay. It was here on 29th September 1952, that John Cobb, the famous Brooklands racing hero and holder of many speed records, was killed when his craft 'Crusader' disintegrated after hitting an unexplained wake whilst attempting a world water speed record. He became the fastest man on water, with a speed of 206.89mph, but didn't achieve the record as the accident occurred before he could complete a second run over the measured mile. John Cobb's body, which had been thrown 50 yards beyond the wreckage, was swiftly recovered by his support team, but with debris sinking to depths of over 650 feet, the jet engine of his boat wasn't recovered for 50 years.

Beyond the bay the trail headed away from the loch, climbing through woodland and providing a last view back to Urquhart Castle. For the next few miles the track meandered through forestry, rising to a high point of around 1,247 feet before entering the community-run Abriachan Forest. I'd come across a community-run pub in Cumbria on my coast-to-coast journey across England in 2015, but I'd never heard of a forest being run by a community and I was keen to learn more. It seems that in 1998 the scattered rural community of nearby Abriachan, which numbers about 130 people, raised around £150,000 to purchase a large chunk of forest and open hill ground from Forest Enterprise. They formed the Abriachan Forest Trust and since then have managed the land to create local employment, improve the environment, and encourage public enjoyment of the great outdoors through a network of wonderful paths, mountain bike trails, and education opportunities. Funding comes from organisations such as Scottish Natural Heritage and Forestry Commission Scotland, as well as businesses and lotteries, and if the online reviews are anything to go by, it's been a great success.

As I plodded along, I spotted a rather odd-looking chap coming towards me wearing a Scout Necker and a pith helmet. It turned out to be Sammy Dawkins, a 19-year-old from East Sussex who was 12 days into his own journey from John o' Groats to Land's End. We exchanged brief pleasantries, then like ships passing in the night, continued on our respective ways.

Halfway to Inverness and a mile or two beyond the forest, numerous colourful signs pointed to the Abriachan Eco-Campsite Café. This extraordinary place, which also claims to be the highest inhabited croft in Scotland, has been open every day, all year round since 1999, offering refreshments and friendly service to weary travellers. I sat at a rickety wooden table in a woodland clearing enjoying a pot of 'proper' tea and two bacon baps, while fighting off the attentions of several chickens and a large black pig. Dick and Chris, the father and son from Australia, arrived shortly after me and we walked together for the next few hours, stopping for a brief lunch break on a log in a woodland clearing.

Monuments and monsters. Urquart Castle on the banks of Loch Ness

Abriachan Eco Café – The 'coolest café on the Great Glen Way'

Around mid-afternoon, I glimpsed the waters of the Beauly Firth away to the north – the term Firth being used to signify coastal waters, particularly an inlet or strait in Scotland. This was the first indication that Inverness, the capital of the Highlands, wasn't far off. The route wound its way through the outskirts of the city, then crossed the Caledonian Canal and followed the banks of the River Ness to the finish point at Inverness Castle. This impressive red sandstone structure, which sits on a cliff overlooking the River Ness, was only built in 1836 but there has been a defensive fortification on the site from as far back as the 11th century. Only a small part of it is open to the public as it's a working building housing the Inverness Sheriff Court.

I'd booked a bed for the night at the student hostel which I knew to be somewhere in the vicinity. My immediate requirement, though, was for a celebratory pint and the Castle Tavern, across the way from Inverness Castle, beckoned. This was clearly popular with people finishing the Great Glen Way, as they issued a complimentary personalised completion certificate. I fell into conversation with Mike and Tricia, a lovely Scottish couple on a short break in the city. We had a few drinks and I left with another £20 for the SSAFA charity fund. As luck would have it, the hostel was only a few doors up from the tavern so after checking in and cleaning up, it was back to the pub for a steak and ale pie dinner and a couple more pints of *Belhaven Best*. Tomorrow I would set off along the east coast of Northern Scotland with my final destination only 128 miles and less than two weeks away.

I'd been keen to complete my journey along the John o'

Groats Trail, a coastal walking route under development along the eastern shores of the Moray Firth from Inverness to John o' Groats. However, work was still ongoing to bring the route up to usual walking trail standards and in a few places the path required crossing of barbed-wire fences, river fording, boulder scrambling, and strenuous walking through summer vegetation. Such were the differing opinions regarding its current walkability that I decided to keep it simple and stick to the A9/A99, using minor roads, cycle tracks and footpaths where possible. I now had a finish date to aim for and, although this wouldn't necessarily be the most inspiring route, it was direct and predictable.

Chapter Fifteen

After a basic breakfast at the hostel, I set off early next morning, the weather cloudy but dry. The quiet Sunday morning suburbs of Inverness quickly led me over the Kessock Bridge to the Black Isle. Despite its name, this is not an island but a peninsula, famous for its rich farmland and surrounded on three sides by water – the Cromarty Firth to the north, the Beauly Firth to the south, and the Moray Firth to the east. My destination today was the small village of Evanton, some 17 miles north of Inverness. After picking up lunch supplies in North Kessock, the first settlement beyond the bridge, I headed off along the grass verge beside the notorious A9. Arguably the most dangerous road in Scotland, I would follow this for the rest of the day apart from a brief respite along a cycle route via the village of Tore. Around 2.00pm, as I approached the bridge carrying the main road over the Cromarty Firth and away from the Black Isle, a glorious sight met my eyes – a road sign proclaiming that John o' Groats was now only 109 miles away. In that moment, after being on the trail for 82 days, I knew that the prize was within my grasp and I celebrated with a cup of tea and a jam scone in the Storehouse of Foulis, a farm produce and gift shop sited on the banks of the Cromarty Firth just beyond the bridge.

My map showed a campsite on the outskirts of Evanton, but on arriving in the village around 5.00pm my first thoughts were for a beer. I called into the Novar Arms and soon fell into conversation with a group of guys who were working on power lines in the area. And what a great bunch they were. Within half an hour they'd had a whip-round and collected £85 for my charity and over a substantial carvery roast dinner and another four pints of *Caledonian Best* bitter, offered me the use of a spare luxury caravan for the night. Absolutely priceless!

I had a comfortable night in the caravan and after a muesli breakfast left the campsite at 9.00am bound for Tain, Scotland's oldest Royal Burgh. The skyline on the route out of Evanton is dominated by Fyrish Hill, and atop of this sits the Fyrish Monument. This impressive structure of three central arches and four flanking towers was built in 1783 by Sir Hector Munro, the local Laird. Sir Hector had been serving as a general in India when we defeated the Dutch at the Battle of Negapatam in 1781, and the monument is a replica of the gates of that town. It was built at a time when the local population were being dispossessed during the controversial period in Scotland's history now known as the Highland Clearances. Beginning in the mid-to-late 18th century this involved the forced eviction of inhabitants primarily to allow for the introduction of sheep farming. After the fashion of the time, famine relief was provided only in return for work, so, in addition to enhancing Sir Hector's glory, it kept the locals in employment.

Four miles north of Evanton lies Alness. This attractive little town regularly entered and won flower competitions in the 1990s and early 2000s, and in 2018 was crowned Scottish Champion at the Great British High Street Awards. I stopped off to buy lunch and a sweet treat for elevenses. It was then I discovered that sugar-coated jam doughnuts and facial hair are not an ideal combination.

I'd planned a route along quiet minor roads and a cycle track, so apart from a couple of miles at the tail-end, I'd been able to avoid the dreaded A9 all day. The weather had improved steadily as the day wore on and by the time I reached the outskirts of Tain around 4.30pm, the sun was shining. My destination was a campsite just before the bridge over the Dornoch Firth and about four miles beyond the town and the Glenmorangie Distillery, whose product has been the bestselling single malt in Scotland almost continuously since 1983. After today's 20-mile trek, I was somewhat disappointed to discover that the site's bar had closed down and the washing machine wasn't working. But the shower facilities were good and I made do with a cuppa and accepted that my clothes would smell for a bit longer. Dinner was an 'All Day Breakfast' and a Cornish pasty, after which I settled down to plan my route for the next day.

The Dornoch Bridge carries the A9 over the Dornoch Firth, which itself forms the boundary between Ross & Cromarty to the south and Sutherland to the north. The bridge was opened in August 1991 and at almost 2,953 feet in length was, at the time, one of the longest bridges of its kind in Europe. It wasn't a crossing I'd want to make in poor weather but fortunately, after light rain overnight, the day had started dry and calm. The Dornoch Firth is designated as a national scenic area, one of 40 in Scotland, and the bridge crossing at low tide afforded extensive views across the mudflats and sandbanks to the enclosure of heather moor clad hills beyond. As I stood admiring the vista, an Australian cyclist stopped for a chat. He'd set off from the Orkney Islands a few days before and was heading south to Land's End from where he planned to cycle across Europe and back to his home in Melbourne!

Beyond the bridge, I followed a minor road to the pretty village of Dornoch, the name derived from the Gaelic for 'pebbly place'. In addition to being home to a world-class golf course, Dornoch is notable for being the last place a witch was burnt in Scotland. The unfortunate lady's name was reported as Janet (or Jenny) Horne, and it is believed she was tried and condemned to death in 1722. I had a fair march ahead of me to the coastal village of Golspie, so around 11.30 I stopped off at a small café for a decent brunch of scrambled egg on toast with bacon and smoked salmon, followed by a large slice of apple pie.

From Dornoch, my route took me around Loch Fleet, a sea loch renowned for its wildlife, including ospreys, otters and common seals. On its southern shore lies the ruins of Skelbo Castle which is thought to have been built during the reign of David I (1124–53). Attacked by Robert the Bruce in 1308, the castle was later rebuilt in stone and remained a residence into the 18th century. Loch

Fleet is effectively a large tidal basin open to the Moray Firth via the narrow gap at Littleferry. It was reduced in size by over a mile in 1816 when The Mound was built to carry what is now the A9 over it. This half-mile-long causeway acts as a tidal barrier which stops the sea short of its former limit, with sluice gates allowing salmon and sea trout to migrate up the River Fleet to their spawning grounds. The build-up of silt in the shallow fresh water upstream of the bridge created the ideal conditions for alder and willow trees. The Mound Alderwoods is now one of the largest of its type in Britain and is a designated nature reserve.

The sky had been steadily darkening as the afternoon wore on and the inevitable rain began to fall just as I reached The Mound. I quickly donned my waterproofs and watched a large fish leaping from the water in an effort to avoid becoming dinner for a seal diving in pursuit.

The grass verge disappeared along this section of the main road which, like so much of the A9/A99, has not evolved to favour the pedestrian. In the poor light and rain it was, at times, a bit hairy as the Friday early-evening traffic sped past showing little consideration for a weary walker. Fortunately, the attractive little seaside resort of Golspie lay only four miles beyond and I arrived safely late in the afternoon. After getting my journey verification sheet stamped at the post office, I popped into the Cabarfeidh Hotel for a pint and to enquire about a bed for the night. Louise, the landlady, let me have a room at a discounted £35, and on hearing about my journey, a local gent bought me the pint. After a fish and chips supper in the local chippy, I had a very pleasant evening in the bar in the company of some of the regulars. Among them was Brian, a retired cameraman, who'd moved to Golspie from Stoneleigh in Surrey, only a couple of miles down the road from my own home, 15 years before. He regaled us with amusing tales from his time with Thames TV in the 70s but, with an eye to discretion and the protection of the innocent, I decline to name any names here!

The weather next morning was fine and sunny and clear enough to appreciate the view of Ben Bhraggie which, at an elevation of 1,303 feet above sea level, dominates the skyline above the village. The summit itself is crowned by the 100-foot-tall statue of the first Duke of Sutherland who became notorious through the part he played in the Highland Clearances. My destination today was a campsite just beyond the village of Brora, and as the total distance was only around 6 miles, I took my time over the substantial full English breakfast provided by my hosts Louise and David. I had covered just under 1,100 miles in 84 days. It was a sobering thought that on this day, 12th July, in 1809, Captain Robert Barclay Allardice completed the astonishing feat of walking 1,000 miles in 1,000 hours (42 days) for the prize of 1,000 guineas. He became known as the 'Celebrated Pedestrian' and, although he did all his miles in Newmarket, Suffolk, he was, perhaps, a founding father of the 'end-to-end' journey.

I set off at 10.30am and soon reached Dunrobin Castle. Sitting in pleasant grounds overlooking the Moray Firth, this impressive building, with towering conical spires, resembles a French château. Home to the Earls and, later, the Dukes of Sutherland, it's the most northerly of Scotland's stately homes, and with 189 rooms it's certainly one of the largest. Dating back to the early 1300s, Dunrobin is also one of the oldest continually inhabited houses in Britain. I didn't feel particularly disposed to paying the entrance fee to tour the house, but I did manage to persuade a very dour concierge to allow me to take a brief look at the attractive gardens before moving on.

A mile or so beyond the castle, on the seaward side of the A9, lies Carn Liath, the remains of a circular Iron Age dry stone structure known as a broch. It was thought to have been built in the last century BC or 1st century AD and, although opinions differ on what it would have been used for, the common belief is that it was a defensive structure providing protection to the native farmers and their livestock from marauding neighbours.

I reached the small village of Brora around lunchtime and headed for the Sutherland Inn for a packet of peanuts and a pint or two of *Latitude* from the Orkney Brewery, to celebrate the fact that I was now only 70 miles from John o' Groats. The name Brora is derived from the ancient Norse meaning 'river with a bridge' and having got another stamp on my journey sheet and picked up some supplies, I crossed the bridge over the River Brora and headed for the coast path. I'd never really associated Scotland with fine beaches but the walk along the dunes to Brora Campsite was a delight. The two-mile stretch of sandy beach here is stunning and one of many along the east coast.

The campsite was primarily a caravan park but they had a small number of pitches for tents and on discovering the nature of my journey the proprietor allowed me to pitch up for free. The washing facilities were good and a couple of ladies gave me a quick tutorial on the use of the washing machine so I could get my malodorous walking gear laundered. Neil, the guy in a neighbouring tent, was having a couple of days sea trout fishing in the River Brora and before he set off for the night, he kindly donated £10 for my charity, a couple of bottles of Budweiser, and loan of his camping chair so I could sit in comfort to enjoy them. As the sun set I enjoyed an 'All Day Breakfast' dinner and midge-free views across the dunes.

The sun was shining as I broke camp and set off for Helmsdale the next morning on an uneventful trudge along the A9. My children would probably find it incomprehensible that I don't listen to music when walking in the countryside, and I hadn't even bothered to pack my *iPod*. I much prefer the more harmonious natural soundtrack of the landscape. Birdsong, the lowing of cattle, the bleat of sheep, the burble of a river, or the gentle lapping of water against the shoreline is the only audio-stimulation I generally need. I confess, though, on this particular morning, a few tracks from my varied collection would have been a welcome distraction. I lunched on the beach just outside the village watching a seal bask in the sunshine offshore and a dolphin arch through the water in the distance.

Overlooking the village of Helmsdale and its harbour is 'The Emigrants Statue'. Unveiled in July 2007 by Alex

Salmond, then First Minister of Scotland, it provides a focus for the commemoration of the huge numbers of people evicted from their homes during the Highland Clearances. Many of these found their way to new homes abroad such as the 100 people who set sail for Canada in the summer of 1813 and helped establish the city of Winnipeg.

On my way through the village, I struck up a conversation with Alison, the proprietor of the Bannockburn Inn. The evocatively-named hostelry conjured up mental images of Highland skirmishes of old and the famous 1314 battle which was such a landmark in Scottish history. There were no campsites in or around Helmsdale, and options for wild camping looked fairly limited, so I booked myself in for the night. After shedding 'The Beast', I wandered down to the village post office to get their stamp on my verification sheet then enjoyed a pint or two in the Belgrave Arms before returning to my room for a couple of hours' sleep. Suitably rested and refreshed, I headed out to La Mirage. This local eatery boldly proclaimed itself to be 'The North's Premier Restaurant' and had been recommended by the manager at the Brora Campsite. There, amongst the pink walls, and unusual statues and lamps – one of which was a model of the bottom half of a lady, the lampshade formed from her basque – I had the biggest fish and chips supper I'd ever eaten and still found room for an ice cream sorbet served in a scooped-out lemon.

The next day started fine and dry after a little overnight rain. Whilst I wasn't walking the clifftop route of the John o' Groats Trail, I had decided to follow the route itinerary. Dunbeath was 16-miles along the coast and a campsite was indicated on my map just beyond the village. I'd been told that the route out of Helmsdale involved a fairly hefty climb so I set off at 7.30am to take advantage of the cooler conditions and get a jump on the traffic. As it turned out, the walk wasn't nearly as strenuous as I'd anticipated and I had a pleasant stroll alongside the A9 before the road dropped steeply down to Berriedale.

Along the way, I took time out to visit the haunting ruins of a 'clearance village' at Badbea. Until as late as 1860, families were forced to eke out a meagre living in this beautiful though windswept and bleak spot, having been cleared from their fertile plots inland to make way for more lucrative sheep farming. This now abandoned clifftop settlement was so inhospitable that the residents had to tether their animals and even small children to avoid them being swept over the cliffs by high winds. A striking monument stands among the remains of scattered stone cottages and crumbling walls as a moving reminder of the hardships faced by the people of Badbea during this inglorious period in Scotland's history.

The small estate village of Berriedale sits on the coast in a deep, wooded valley at the confluence of Berriedale and Langwell Waters. On the hill above the settlement sit two towers in the shape of chess pieces. The purpose of these stone structures has been the subject of much debate, with some claiming that they were watchtowers when there was a castle in Berriedale. Others believe they were either lookout posts for fisherman or simply ornamental follies built by one of the Dukes of Portland. Another school of thought is that they were chess pieces left behind by giants, and personally I prefer that theory.

At Berriedale, the wee River Bothy Tearoom appeared like an oasis in the desert and I couldn't resist calling in for a coffee and a bacon sarnie – actually two. I struck up a conversation with a Scottish couple from Perth who were touring the Northern Highlands. They were very interested to hear about my trek and by way of a charity donation, and unbeknown to me, they paid my bill before they left. The tearoom had only recently reopened after being closed since the 60s. Their location just off the A9 and on the route of the John o' Groats Trail and the North Coast 500, a 516-mile scenic route around the north coast of Scotland, would stand them in good stead, and as I left I wished the new owner well with her new venture.

I arrived on the outskirts of Dunbeath around 2.00pm and enjoyed a couple of pints of *McEwan's* in the Bay Owl Inn before checking in at the campsite. The pub sits on the clifftop overlooking Dunbeath Bay and affords great views across to Dunbeath Castle, which, although dating back to the 15th century, is of mainly 17th century origin and clearly has more recent extensions.

The village of Dunbeath was in the news on 25th August 1942, when 14 people, including Prince George, Duke of Kent, were killed in an air crash nearby. They were en route to Iceland when the Short Sunderland Mk. III aircraft in which they were travelling crashed into a hillside in foggy weather. Prince George, who was on duty as an air commodore in the RAF, became the first member of the British Royal Family to die in active military service for over 450 years.

After finishing my beer and salted peanuts, I strolled the short distance up the road to the Inver Caravan Park, where I managed to get a pitch for a very reasonable £8. I dozed for a couple of hours before heading back to the Bay Owl for an early evening steak pie dinner.

Overnight rain had cleared by the time I came to break camp the next morning, but heavy cloud and a freshening breeze foretold of more rain to come. My destination today was Lybster and, although it was only a short, 9-mile stroll, I felt the need for a good breakfast to fortify myself. The Laidhay Café and Tearoom, which shares a site with a croft museum housed within a 250-year-old thatched Caithness longhouse, was conveniently located a half mile or so from the campsite and provided a very decent full English. By the time I was ready to set off again, the rain was falling and looked set for the day. At the tiny village of Latheron, I took my leave of the A9, which heads north to Thurso from here, and joined the A99 which would lead me to my ultimate goal in just a few days.

By the time I reached the village of Lybster around midday even my Gor-Tex waterproofs were beginning to surrender to the steady rainfall. There was hardly a soul about on this damp Saturday lunchtime and I made my way to the village shop and post office with a view to getting some information about B&Bs in the area. With my usual impeccable timing, I'd arrived during a major local event. On this occasion it was the annual Caithness County Show, and the helpful couple running the shop suspected that most places would be fully booked. They kindly put in a telephone call to a chap they knew just outside the village and my bed at the Antlers B&B was sorted. All I had to do was get there and quickly as the proprietor and his daughter would shortly be going out for the afternoon. The B&B was in Occumster, a scattering of houses about a mile and a half beyond Lybster, which had effectively been a station on the Wick and Lybster Light Railway until the line closed in April 1944. Antlers was located down a long minor lane off the main road, and I plodded resolutely along, arriving around half an hour later.

Sandy and his daughter Sandra could not have been more welcoming. After peeling off my wet waterproofs and being shown to a room with a four-poster bed, they sat me down in the lounge in front of the telly with a pot of tea and a selection of chocolate biscuits. They were heading out to the said County Show and asked if I would be good enough to keep an eye on things and see the other guests in if and when they arrived, thoughtfully indicating who would be in which room. Snug and warm, sitting with my feet up in the comfortable lounge whilst the rain lashed against the window outside, I was quite happy to oblige. Later, in return for my 'house-sitting' Sandra cooked me an excellent steak dinner. That evening Sandy regaled me with tales from a long and colourful life during which he and his family had been Caithness cheesemakers, sheepskin producers, salmon smokers and manufacturers of kilt socks, even including members of the aristocracy amongst their customers.

I awoke bright and early next morning and breakfasted

on a pair of Scottish kippers whilst pondering on the itinerary for the last few days of my epic journey. A few weeks ago, my son Chris had made it known he was planning to travel up to John o' Groats to meet me at the end of the trail. At that point, I'd had to give serious thought to an intended finish date. My niece was getting married on 22nd July, so I knew I needed to be home by then. Given my intended route and with a bit of forward planning and allowance for injury or mishap, I settled on Thursday 20th July as the day I'd arrive at John o' Groats. This was a particularly poignant date as it would be the 30th anniversary of my father's passing. The direct route I'd taken along the east coast from Inverness had put me a little ahead of schedule, and my 12-mile walk today would see me in the sizeable town of Wick with three days to spare. Being the last major settlement on the trail, I decided to have a few rest days there and then push on to the finish line on Thursday 20th.

Bidding farewell to my friendly hosts, I set off in glorious weather on what would be the penultimate day's walking. During the course of the morning, I took the opportunity to detour off the main road to visit a couple of Scottish Heritage sites. The Hill o' Many Stanes, near Mid Clyth, consists of about 200 small flagstone slabs arranged in a fan shape of 22 rows running down a low hill. Other stone row monuments have been linked to Bronze Age graves which suggests they could be 4,000 years old and this is considered to be the largest such monument in the British Isles.

A mile and a half south-west of Ulbster near a small loch

just off the A99, I discovered an impressive chambered burial cairn at a site known as Cairn o'Get. About 5,000 years ago, this would have been a sacred place for ancestral spirits where the living gathered to seek the help of their dead. Although much ruined, the central circular chamber would have originally stood around 10 feet high, but it is thought the stone was robbed to build a nearby dam in the 1800s.

A short distance from the Cairn o'Get on the seaward side of the main road lies another site of interest, the Whaligoe Steps. Here a man-made stairway of over 350 steps zigzags down the cliffside to a seemingly inaccessible natural harbour where fishing boats used to land their catch. The steps date from the early 18th century and were once used by fisherwomen to haul up the creels of herring, affectionately known by fishing communities as "silver darlings". After the fish had been gutted, the women, some quite elderly, would carry them up the steps in baskets and take them on foot to be sold in Wick, some 8 miles away. I didn't fancy making the descent carrying 'The Beast', and as the small café on the site was closed for a private function, I didn't have anywhere safe to leave it. So, I satisfied myself with the sea view and a short break on a bench at the top.

Around lunchtime, I arrived in the village of Thrumster and thought it rude not to swing into The Old Smiddy Inn for a pint and a packet of peanuts. I met up with a couple working with Action Challenge, a company I'd done several of my 24-hour endurance walks with. They were recceing for The Great Tesco Walk, a charity Land's End to John o' Groats trek via a bunch of Tesco stores due to take place the following year. They were very interested to hear about my own journey, particularly the health and safety implications of walking the A9.

I arrived in Wick around 4.00pm. With the influx of additional visitors attending the Caithness County Show I was unlikely to find any B&B vacancies, so I headed straight for the Wick Caravan & Camping Site on the outskirts of town. My plans for the next couple of days were a bit fluid so I paid for a two-night stay and pitched camp. I had a ration pack and rice for dinner at a picnic bench and only just managed to get cleared away before the gathering rain clouds burst over the campsite. It rained on and off for the rest of the evening but the forecast for the next day was more encouraging.

Heavy overnight rain had cleared by the morning, creating the moist, humid conditions so favoured by Scottish midges. In an effort to avoid becoming their breakfast, my mind turned to my own. En route to the campsite the day before, I'd passed The Corner Café, advertising their 'Big Breakfast' and that seemed like the perfect place to plan my exploration of Wick.

Straddling the River Wick, and wrapping itself around both sides of Wick Bay, this former Viking settlement is the principal town in the far north of the UK mainland. Steeped in history, the town's name is derived from the Norse word Vik, meaning bay. With the completion of harbour improvement work in 1813, Wick got into the fish business in a big way. By the mid-19th century it was the busiest herring port in Europe, boasting a

1,120-strong fishing fleet and employing some 12,000 people in the season. So much herring was landed there that it was said that your nose would pick up Wick many miles before reaching the Royal Burgh. Apart from a few old warehouse buildings there is little sign of that flourishing industry today, although an active and successful shellfish industry still operates from the port landing lobster, scallops, crab and prawns.

There were several places of interest I wanted to see over the next few days but first I needed to pay a visit to the office of the *Caithness Courier.* I'd been contacted by Phil, one half of the charming couple I'd met almost a month ago back in East Calder when I'd called at their house to top up my water bottles. He was a photographer and journalist and thought a colleague of his at the paper would be interested in my walk. I met with a reporter called Katrina and gave her the low-down on my journey. She thought it would make a great local story and we agreed to meet again the next morning for a photo in time to get the article into the issue due out two days later. She also gave me a tip about a local B&B she believed had a vacancy. They did, and I promptly booked for the last two nights of my stay in Wick.

I spent the afternoon exploring the harbour and marina before swinging into the Alexander Bain for a pint or two of Titanic Brewery's *Steerage,* described locally as a fruity, golden session ale. I took a slow stroll back to the campsite and after a wee nap in my tent, cooked up the last two ration packs for dinner. Reflecting on my journey, there had been many good days and one or two tough days, and

I was certainly looking forward to getting home to my wife and family. But sitting here at a picnic table in the early evening sunshine under a clear blue sky, I was also rather sad that it was all coming to an end.

In the wake of a cloudless night, a bright, clear and relatively midge-free sunrise gave promise of a warm and sunny day. After two nights on the campsite, I would be moving to a B&B and after energising myself with two cups of coffee, I broke camp and headed off soon after 9.00am. The first port of call was the *Caithness Courier* where I had a photocall arranged with Katrina. That done, I went in search of some breakfast.

Fed and watered, I now felt ready for the day and headed off towards the B&B to get checked in and offload my gear. The route took me past the main post office and I called in to get the penultimate stamp on my journey verification sheet. A very officious lady confronted me across the counter and flatly refused to stamp it, insisting that it would contravene some regulation or another. The fact that my sheet clearly showed that every other post office I'd called at between there and Land's End had *not* had a problem putting their stamp on it, didn't seem to sway her. After a further fruitless discussion, I pointed out that I was on my way to the local newspaper office where they were writing an article about my walk. I would be sure to tell them how unhelpful the local post office had been. She looked at me rather dubiously, as if trying to gauge my sincerity on the matter. Then, as the implications slowly dawned, and with a scowl and a mutter, she stamped my sheet.

Having dropped off my gear at the B&B, I headed back

into town to visit the interesting Heritage Centre which sits on the south side of the River Wick in what used to be known as Pulteneytown. Home to the famous Old Pulteney Distillery, this used to be a separate community but was merged into the burgh in 1902. I don't think I've ever come across so many fascinating artefacts on display in such a relatively small building as the museum and yet it didn't seem cluttered. The centre houses a number of furnished rooms and exhibitions portraying Wick's herring fishing heritage. There are displays highlighting working and social life in the 18th and early 19th centuries, as well as a famous photographic collection depicting over a century of Wick history. There is even a working lighthouse and a harbour setting.

Later in the day, I came across Mackays Hotel, a long, narrow building shaped like a finger. Their 'No. 1 Bistro' is the single address on Ebenezer Place, which at only 6 feet 9 inches wide is officially the shortest street in the world.

I'd been contacted by fellow 'end-to-enders' Jill and Louise, who both planned to arrive in Wick that day. They'd booked a local French restaurant and we spent a very enjoyable evening chatting about experiences on our respective journeys. Louise would be met by her parents at John o' Groats the next day. Jill would be moving on to Keiss about 8 miles up the coast. I would spend another day in Wick, and if all went according to plan, Jill and I would both complete our treks the day after.

I enjoyed a leisurely breakfast the next morning in the company of Russell, a small-animal vet from Australia. He was in the UK tracing his family history and over a full English we discussed a range of topics from politics to the Second World War.

It was another fine day, so I took a stroll along the coast path to the Trinkie Pool. Trinkie is the Scottish word for 'trench', and this sea pool was created about 70 years ago on the rocky shoreline together with several others along the east coast of Scotland. All but two have now gone, having been concreted over or allowed to crumble away, but the Trinkie Heritage Preservation Group is working hard to preserve this unique facility, in which many local people have learned to swim – presumably during the very short season in which you wouldn't suffer hypothermic shock getting in!

Just beyond the Trinkie, perched on a narrow promontory, lies the ruins of Wick Old Castle, one of Scotland's oldest fortifications. Thought to have been built around 1150, its history is somewhat obscure. At this time Caithness and Sutherland, as well as many of the islands along Scotland's northern and western coasts, were under the control of the King of Norway. The castle is believed to have been built by Earl Harald Maddadsson who, as the King's representative, may well have intended the castle to be his HQ on the mainland. It passed into various hands over the intervening years and ceased being used as a residence entirely in the 18th century.

Heading back into town for a spot of lunch, I passed the Black Stairs. This flight of flagstone steps built in the 1820s was the inspiration for a famous painting by L.S. Lowry. Better known for his matchstick figure art and industrial landscapes, Lowry was a regular visitor to Scotland in the 1930s. 'Steps at Wick' was painted in 1936 and in 2013 I believe it sold for £890,500.

After a substantial burger and a couple of pints of *Gone Fishing E.S.B.* for lunch, I felt in need of an afternoon nap, so I headed back to the B&B. On the way, I called in at the newsagent's to pick up a copy of the latest *Caithness Courier* and there, within the pages, was my article, my bearded face beaming out at me. I couldn't be bothered to walk back into town for dinner that evening, so I heated up the last of my dried pasta meals in my room. Later, as I was getting my gear sorted for the big day ahead, I was contacted by Frances, an SSAFA volunteer who'd seen the article in the local paper and was organising a small reception committee for my arrival at John o' Groats. She'd arranged for another volunteer to make contact with me along the route the next day to confirm my expected arrival time.

Considering the fine weather of the past few days, I was somewhat disappointed that the next morning started dull and overcast. Heavy rain was forecast and although it hadn't yet arrived, the sky was beginning to sag with the weight of it, like a soft grey pillow waiting to split apart. After a good breakfast, I thanked John and Phyllis for their hospitality and set off soon after 8.30. I stopped to pick up some lunch supplies at the Wick Tesco store then, finally ready for the last 19 miles of my journey, I hit the A99 with gusto.

Mid-morning, I passed the beautiful sandy beach of Sinclairs Bay, which, in order to fend off possible German invasion during World War II, had been one of the most heavily mined spots in the UK. I know this because at a subsequent Land's End-John o' Groats Association annual presentation weekend, I fell into conversation with Warren who had been inspired to undertake his own 'end-to-end' journey by his remarkable aunt. In 1949, she rode on horseback all the way from Land's End to John o' Groats *and* back and made particular reference in her diary to having enjoyed a canter along the beach at Sinclairs Bay. What she hadn't realised until later, was that at the time, it still hadn't been totally cleared of mines and she was lucky not to have been blown to smithereens.

At the far end of the wide sweep of Sinclairs Bay lies the small fishing village of Keiss where I was to meet locksmith and SSAFA volunteer Kevin. We had a coffee in the Sinclair Bay Hotel and I was able to let him know that my son's flight up from Gatwick had been delayed. By the time he'd collected the hire car from Inverness Airport and driven up, he didn't expect to arrive at John o' Groats much before 6.00pm. As we chatted, the rain that had been threatening all morning finally arrived. For the next 30 minutes it absolutely poured down, but thankfully the rain had eased off considerably by the time I resumed my plod along the tarmac.

About a mile north of the village, standing dramatically on the windswept cliffs overlooking Sinclairs Bay, sit the ruins of Keiss Castle. The exact year of its construction is not known but the castle is believed to have been built by George Sinclair, the 5th Earl of Caithness, in the late-16th or early 17th century. It was seized when the Earl defied King James VI, who was apparently annoyed by his consistently unruly behaviour, and by the 18th century it was considered ruinous. In 1755 then owner Sir William Sinclair commenced building a new mansion house and the castle suffered further decay. Recent collapses in the structure have left it in a dangerous state and the site is now fenced off.

The New Keiss Castle, as the mansion house has become known, changed hands several times and was extensively rebuilt in the Baronial style in 1860. It sits close to the old castle across a wide expanse of lawn. There didn't seem to be any obvious public access to either it or the old castle, but so determined was I to visit the site that I crept stealthily down the driveway, around the grounds of the mansion house and across the lawn. It had started raining again, so after a brief viewing, I retraced my steps to the main road, fortunately unchallenged, and continued on my way.

I'd always imagined the far north of Scotland to be mountainous and rugged, but beyond the Highlands, Caithness itself is actually generally flat, being a land of open, rolling farmland, moorland and scattered settlements. The road which now only led to one place, headed due north, slightly inland and across that open moorland. I crested a low rise in the road at a point on the map called Black Loch and suddenly there it was in the distant haze, a little muddle of houses on the edge of the sea – John o' Groats. I recalled the scene from *First and Last* when the walker, after several months on the trail, first sees 'the holy city' and weeps. My emotions were mixed. On the one hand, there was the elation of knowing I would soon be reunited with my family having completed a 30-year personal ambition, but on the other a tinge of sadness that my 'great adventure' was coming to an end.

I reached the outskirts of John o' Groats around 4.30pm but my actual target was the lighthouse at Duncansby Head two miles further on. This is geographically the furthest point from Land's End and the most north-easterly point on the UK mainland. The Head's main feature is the two prominent sea stacks just off the coast, impressive despite the cloud and drizzle. As I gazed out across the choppy waters, I was jolted from my musings by a message from my son announcing his arrival, and I set off around the coast on the last leg of the journey to John o' Groats. On the way, I scrambled down onto the beach to collect a sandstone pebble to accompany the small piece of stone I'd picked up from the clifftop at Land's End at the start of my journey.

I crossed the finish line at the landmark "Journey's End" signpost at 6.40pm on Thursday 20th July, after three months on the trail and having completed around 1,168 miles. Among the welcoming committee was the owner of the Seaview Hotel who proffered a very welcome glass or two of Old Pulteney single malt, and a contingent of volunteers from the Caithness Branch of the SSAFA. In the freshening breeze, they struggled valiantly with a charity banner and kindly presented me with a certificate in recognition of my trek. My son was there to greet me, and as a complete and very pleasant surprise, so was my wife Lynn. We were booked to stay in the Seaview Hotel that night and later met up with Jill, who had completed her trek earlier in the day. She joined us for dinner and we shared a bottle of champagne in celebration of the successful completion of our respective journeys which had taken us the entire length of mainland Britain.

SSAFA welcoming committee at John o' Groats

The weather next morning was glorious. Our flight from Inverness to Gatwick was booked for 5.30pm, giving us time for a bit of sightseeing. So, after breakfast and a visit to hotel reception to get the final stamp on my journey verification sheet, we set off to check out the village. Local legend has it that John o' Groats takes its name from one Jan de Groot, a Dutchman who operated a ferry service to Orkney in the 16th century, charging twopence a trip. The coin for this denomination became known as the 'groat'. A ferry service still runs from the harbour to the Orkneys, an archipelago of over 70 islands just 10 miles off the coast, although I suspect the price of a trip has risen considerably. Apart from its significant location as the start or finish point of countless 'end-to-end' journeys, the village is not wholly inspiring. In fact, in 2010 it won a Carbuncle Award as the most dismal town in Scotland. Perhaps unsurprisingly, John o' Groats refused to accept it and the award was passed to runners-up, the Stirlingshire town of Denny.

We took advantage of the sunshine for a photo shoot at the 'end-to-end' signpost by the harbour and rummaged around in the First and Last souvenir shop. Then we drove the short distance to Duncansby Head to view the two red sandstone pinnacles, the largest of which, the Great Stack, is nearly 200 feet high and rises above the summit of the adjacent cliff. After elevenses in the Old Schoolhouse Tearoom, we finally said goodbye to John o' Groats and set off for Inverness.

With Lynn at journeys end

Chapter Sixteen

The 120-mile journey by car to Inverness Airport took around three hours. It seemed rather odd travelling back so quickly over much of the same ground it had taken me 9 days to walk. Jill had booked an overnight stop in Inverness before flying to Edinburgh the next day, so we had dropped her off before making our way to the airport. We arrived at Gatwick soon after 7.00pm to be met by my granddaughters sporting a 'Welcome Home' banner, and a couple of hours later I was back home with the family enjoying a late supper of – what else? – fish and chips.

It was probably a good thing that, in the aftermath of my walk, I didn't have to go straight back to work. I think if I'd had to return to the mundane routine of a day job after three months of stress-free fresh air and wonderful country walking, I'd have descended into a deep depression. As it was, my return home coincided with a family gathering at my niece's wedding and the start of Lynn's long summer break from school. The garden needed some serious attention, as did my allotment and, of course, there was also the small matter of finding another job, though I decided that this could wait until after the big family holiday in Majorca that August – something I'd been particularly looking forward to.

Shortly after my return from John o' Groats, I had an email from Luke, the Community Fundraising Officer at SSAFA, inviting me to present one of those oversized charity cheques for publicity. They offered to come to the house for the 'ceremony' but I thought it would be nicer for Lynn and me to travel up to SSAFA HQ in the City, have a spot of lunch and make an afternoon of it. It was great meeting Luke and his colleague Jim and they seemed genuinely interested as I regaled them with tales of my epic trek. So much so that, shortly after, I was asked if I'd like to take part in a SSAFA fundraising video. They were looking to include some inspirational yarns to fire the imagination of other potential fundraisers and thought my story would fit the bill.

So, at 9.00 on a crisp, bright Sunday morning in late-November, Danielle, George and Simon, from Kartoffel Films, turned up on our doorstep laden with equipment and promptly turned the ground floor of the house into a film set. We shot some interview scenes which covered such matters as my motivation for undertaking the walk, challenges along the way, why I'd picked SSAFA, and how I'd gone about fundraising. Then I was persuaded to don my walking gear, complete with 'The Beast' – the 105-litre backpack that had been my constant companion on the trek – for some outdoor shots in Nonsuch Park. They finally left after a good feed of bacon and sausage sarnies, at around 4.00pm.

Initial fears that my job hunt would be a long, painful process were thankfully unfounded as, towards the end of

October, I was pleased and proud to be appointed as the Facilities Manager at Royal British Legion HQ in London. Being officially an old fart now, I was also able to apply for my 60+ London Oyster card which meant that travelling to and from work would be free!

Shortly after starting my new job, I met up with an old pal who happened to work nearby. Don, an ex-para and keen collector of military memorabilia, had lovingly restored a Mark lll, 1944 military prismatic compass, and presented it to me along with a certificate of authenticity in recognition of my journey. It was a marvellous gift and one I shall treasure.

As 2017 drew to a close, I was left to reflect on a year that had started with me rather nervously resigning from my job back in the winter, had seen me celebrate my 60th birthday and complete a 30-year personal ambition in the spring and summer, and secure a job with a remarkable and uniquely British institution in the autumn.

In January 2018, Lynn and I attended the annual Land's End–John o' Groats Association Presentation weekend in Torquay, accompanied by my brother and sister-in-law. In addition to collecting a certificate commemorating my journey, I was surprised and pleased to pick up the "Shanks Pony Trophy" for 2017, which is awarded to the person or persons who, at the discretion of the Committee, achieves the best performance on foot. I was honoured to receive this award and it reminded me that I was now part of a unique group of people who have had experiences which sometimes can't be adequately described, but which would always stay with them.

The one blot on the landscape was the passing of my Aunt Molly at the age of 87. An enthusiastic walker herself, having been an active member of the Surrey branch of the Long Distance Walkers Association into her early eighties, she had taken a keen interest in my journey. I feel sure I'd inherited the walking gene from the last of my late father's siblings and she will be sadly missed.

In the early summer, I was particularly honoured to be asked to give an 'inspirational' talk to the 6th-formers at Blenheim High School where Lynn had worked as a teaching assistant for many years. It was a bit nerve-racking, but I think the talk was well received. My '6 P's Principle' certainly struck a chord and I suspect that if I were to visit the school again, I would see emblazoned over the reception desk *"Proper Preparation Prevents Piss Poor Performance"*. To cap it all, we had the hottest summer since God was a boy – well, since 1976 anyway – and the England football team reached the semi-finals of the World Cup for the first time in 28 years, during the course of the tournament winning a penalty shoot-out for the first time ever! All in all, it had been a truly memorable year and I was reminded of the quote by Dr. Seuss, "Don't cry because it's over, smile because it happened" – wise words indeed!

So, did I achieve my objective and what did I learn along the way?

I'd set out to walk the length and breadth of the UK in lone, unsupported, essentially off-road, single trips, to experience the best of the British countryside. It was, of course, a long-standing personal ambition, but along the way I also wanted to raise some money for charity. Despite a rather lengthy bit of road-walking on the last stretch to John o' Groats, I would certainly say that in both regards I achieved what I set out to do.

I could never describe a landscape or location in the same vibrant prose as the great fell walker and author, Alfred Wainwright, or with the humorous and perceptive insight of American author Bill Bryson, but my journey through the UK confirmed my long-held belief that, though we may not be blessed with a wealth of record-breaking natural features, we live in a wonderful safe country bursting with spectacular countryside, awesome scenery, and with a rich and fascinating history. It occurs to me that the freedom and safety we enjoy and often take for granted have, to a great extent, been fought for and won by the men and women of our armed forces and it's for that reason I consider SSAFA – the Armed Forces charity – to be such a worthy cause.

It was, for me, a life-enhancing and unforgettable experience. Quite apart from the pleasure of walking through some of the most beautiful and dramatic scenery in Britain, my faith in human nature was restored by the kindness of strangers. There was Julia in Bucks Mills on the South West Coast Path, who offered me use of her summer house when I discovered that the campsite I was aiming for that night had closed down. She even threw in a couple of pillows and fresh milk for my morning tea. There was Ken, who drove me to Skipton and back to get a new buckle for my backpack shoulder strap when it failed just outside Gargrave on the Pennine Way. He even refused to let me pay for the tea and cake I'd ordered for him and his wife as a thankyou! Then there were the Scottish power line workers I met in the pub in Evanton, who donated £85 to my charity within half an hour of meeting me and offered the use of a luxury caravan on the local campsite. And of course, there were all the people I met along the way who let me camp for free or discounted the price of my room for the night or posted such wonderful messages of support on my *JustGiving* page as they kindly donated to the cause. It was quite amazing and humbling to discover that my journey had inspired others as I'd never considered myself particularly inspirational before.

I saw a lot and learned a lot but, as is often the nature of things, I'm sure I overlooked a lot as well. For a brief, proud period I was slim and fit, proving that you *can* enjoy a staple diet of fish and chips and beer and still lose twenty pounds. I learned to slow down, to look deeper, and by looking, to better appreciate nature and the wonderful countryside which surrounds us on this beautiful island. More importantly, I learned that there are far more good people in the world than bad, and I silently vowed to try to be kinder and more tolerant myself – and that's not a bad thing for us all to aspire to, particularly a grumpy old cynic like me.

"Be bold and courageous. When you look back on life, you'll regret the things you didn't do more than the ones you did."

H. Jackson Brown – American author